# The Illustrated Directory of
# Guitars

# NICK FREETH

**PEPPERBOX
PRESS**

Pepperbox Press Ltd.,
Cordwainers, Caring Lane,
Leeds, Maidstone, Kent ME17 1TJ
    United Kingdom.
© 2011 Pepperbox Press Ltd.,

ISBN: 9780681958517

Photography by Neil Sutherland
Printed and bound in China

# CONTENTS

# ALEMBIC ENTWISTLE BASS

ALEMBIC IS BASED in Santa Rosa, California, and its history is closely intertwined with that of the San Francisco Bay Area's rich rock music scene. The company, formed by electronics expert Ron Wickersham and his artist wife Susan in 1969, very quickly became involved in the

*Alembic comments that the Spyder's large upper body "makes a fine armrest for between songs!"*

development of custom-built gear for members of the Grateful Dead, and went on to supply equipment and technical expertise for the band's live shows and elaborate recording projects. In 1974, however, Alembic decided to devote itself solely to guitar making, and since then, its exquisitely designed, technically innovative instruments have become the choice of many leading performers, from Bay Area stalwarts like the Grateful Dead's Phil Lesh to jazzman Stanley Clarke and Mark King of Level 42. Another high-profile customer was the late John Entwistle of The Who. "The Ox" started using Alembic basses in the 1980s, and had been discussing the creation of a new custom instrument with the company shortly before his death in 2002. As a tribute to Entwistle, the Wickershams have gone on to produce a limited

*These sterling silver "web" inlays are a feature borrowed from earlier Alembic Entwistle basses.*

*Above:* Illuminated LEDs add a distinctive touch to the Spyder's ebony fingerboard.

*Above:* Alembic's logo, designed by Bob Thomas in 1969, incorporates a number of astrological and mystical symbols.

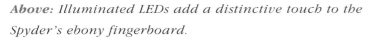

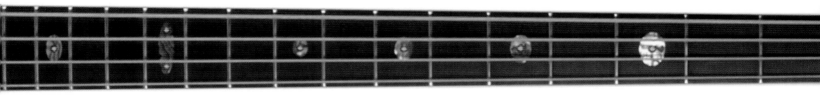

edition of "Spyder" basses, modeled on previous designs developed for him, and comprising 50 4-string basses (one of which is seen here) and 25 8-stringers.

Appropriately, the Spyder (the name is inspired by Entwistle's famous song "Boris the Spider") features silver "web" inlays on its maple top. Like most Alembics, its body is in three layers, glued together "sandwich-style": maple is also used for the bass's back, and it has a center section made from walnut.

# ALEMBIC DRAGON BASS

THE WHO'S JOHN ENTWISTLE also has a connection with the Alembic Dragon bass shown on these pages. It was inspired by a design originally conceived by Susan Wickersham for a custom Entwistle model with (as she puts it) "a dragon's wing for a body and a dragon's claw for a peghead."—and, like nearly all Alembics, it makes use of Ron Wickersham's unique pickup circuitry.

The bass's so-called "Signature"-type electronics include volume and pan knobs, and two filter controls, one associated with each pickup. These can be used in two alternative modes: either as a simple low-pass circuit that "rolls off" the treble; or in conjunction with

the instrument's "q" switches, which introduce an additional boost to the frequencies "swept" by adjusting the filters. A vast range of sonic colorings can be produced by this method, making Alembics among the most adaptable—as well as the most aesthetically attractive—of all electric guitars.

The provision of such "tailoring tools" is central to Alembic's philosophy, which its co-founder Ron Wickersham summed up to this author in *The Electric Guitar* (published by Courage Books in 1999): "Rather than handing a musician something and saying, 'We have this great inspiration, and if you take our instrument, you'll be famous just like somebody else,' we do the opposite; the musician is free to come to us, and we don't try to talk him out of his dream."

*Below: Flame maple is used for the Dragon's top and back.*

*This body shape, though unconventional, is perfectly balanced and extremely comfortable for the player.*

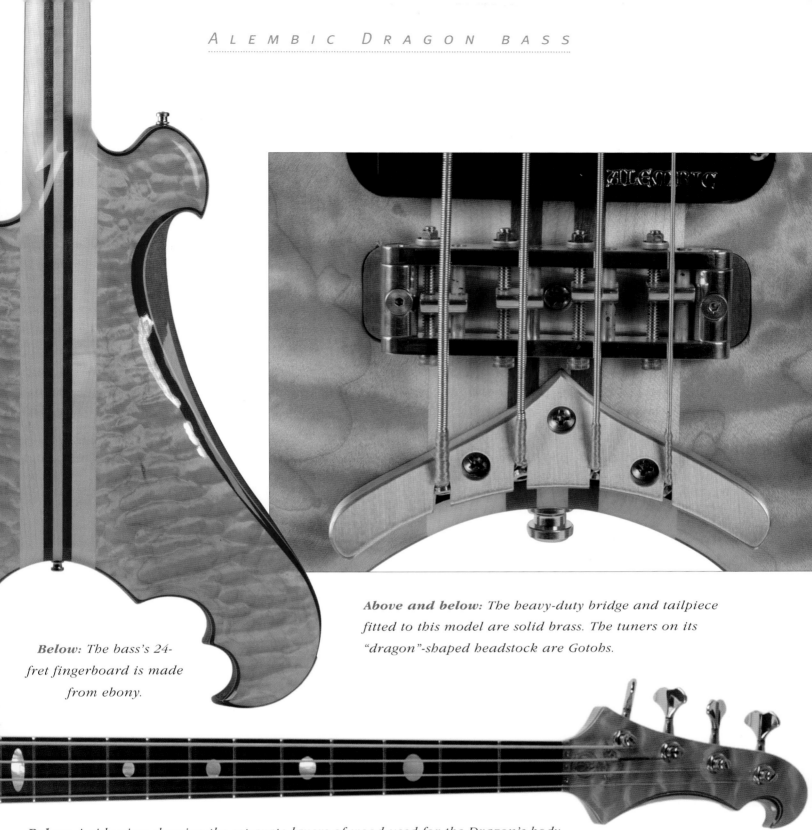

**Above and below:** *The heavy-duty bridge and tailpiece fitted to this model are solid brass. The tuners on its "dragon"-shaped headstock are Gotohs.*

**Below:** *The bass's 24-fret fingerboard is made from ebony.*

**Below:** *A side view showing the separate layers of wood used for the Dragon's body.*

# ALEMBIC TRIBUTE

JERRY GARCIA (1945-1995) the charismatic lead guitarist and frontman for the Grateful Dead, used a wide range of electric instruments during his extraordinary career. Like many impecunious young players, he started out with a Danelectro, and was subsequently seen with a Guild Starfire, Gibson SGs and Les Pauls, and a Fender Stratocaster, as well as some more unusual models, such as the aluminun-necked Travis Beans he sported in the 1970s. However, the luthier he was most closely associated with is Doug Irwin, a former Alembic staffer who went on to build no less than five custom electrics for him, including the famous Tiger model that he played from 1979 until the early 1990s. Recently, Alembic—which, in its early days, was responsible for customizing the electronics on several of Jerry's guitars—has produced a Garcia Tribute instrument with some similarities to Tiger, and it is featured here.

The Tribute shares Tiger's overall shape, as well as its multi-ply body—an exotic "sandwich" including layers of flame maple and padauk (a coco bolo/flame maple combination is also available). However, its electronics are unmistakably Alembic's: the three pickups have their own individual filters and on/off/bright switches, and there is a switchable effects loop. The guitar's neck is made from flame maple, purpleheart and cherry, and

*Below: The Tribute's pickups are Alembic-designed units: two HGs, plus an STR nearest to the neck.*

*These inlaid ovals are made from mother of pearl.*

*Right:* One interpretation offered by Alembic for its mystical logo reads: "Mankind takes everything available in the universe and in an infinite search for wisdom, focuses energy into the alembic resulting in the purest goal."

*Bottom:* A brass bridge contributes to the Jerry Garcia-inspired guitar's unique sound, as does the "sandwich" of high-grade timbers used for its body.

its ebony-faced headstock is graced with a sterling silver-inlaid version of Alembic's logo, decorated with abalone and mother of pearl. In a reference to the Grateful Dead's famous song "Truckin'," Alembic guarantees that the Tribute will remain "clean, clear and responsive" throughout any "long, strange [musical] trip."

9

# TOM ANDERSON HOLLOW DROP TOP

A KEEN GUITARIST from the age of eight, Tom Anderson spent several years as a professional musician before becoming involved in designing, maintaining and modifying instruments. Between 1977 and 1984 he worked at Schecter (see separate entry), going on to set up his own, California-based company in 1984. This initially focused only on pickup manufacturing, but, thanks to the success of the Anderson's ProAm electric in the late 1980s, its emphasis soon shifted to guitar production, to which

The one seen here is a "Hollow Drop Top," containing sealed chambers that add extra richness and character to the guitar's tone. There are three pickups, plus a Strat-like 5-way selector, a toggle "splitter" switch, and an additional control, built into the tone knob, giving further permutations of signals from the bridge humbucker and the neck and middle transducers. Like all the company's models, the Hollow Drop Top uses the Buzz Feiten Tuning System: this corrects some of the inaccuracies in intonation suffered by all fretted instruments by means of what Anderson's publicity describes as "visually undetectable structural neck change[s] in combination with slightly altered bridge intonation offsets."

the firm has been exclusively committed since 1990.

The Drop Top—whose name refers to the instrument's maple (or sometimes koa) upper surface, molded over a basswood or alder body—is one of Anderson's enduring classics; launched in 1991, it has subsequently appeared in a variety of different forms.

**Left:** *The rich purple of the Hollow Drop Top's surface is complemented by the instrument's chromed hardware, including an Anderson "vintage tremolo."*

**Right:** *Anderson's trademark: in its first-ever catalog, the firm described itself as "dedicated to creating the world's finest feeling, playing and sounding" guitars.*

# TOM ANFIELD "GARY BONER" GUITAR

THIS TOM ANFIELD ELECTRIC carries the Guitar Tree name on its headstock; the Guitar Tree Luthiery was Anfield's previous, London-based business, and for a while, he used its "brand" for some of his instruments. This model was built in 2004 for Gary Boner, guitarist and singer with British blues-rock combo Roadhouse, whom Anfield describes as "one of my great proponents." Its body is made from swamp ash, combined with layers of black sycamore and (on top) flamed alder, and it boasts three pickups: two single-coils, and a humbucker at the bridge. Its original electronics were slightly different, and when they were replaced, Anfield mounted the new transducers on the ebony plate beneath the strings.

*Below: Flamed alder and swamp ash provide an ideal combination of good looks and body density.*

PHOTOGRAPHS COURTESY OF TOM ANFIELD

*These loacking tuners are made by Gotoh.*

*Gary Boner's band Roadhouse was formed in 1991.*

**Above:** *Two black "trees" help ensure a straight path for the upper strings.*

**Bottom:** *A sideways view of the instrument's body, showing how the upper layers of wood are shaped to follow its contours.*

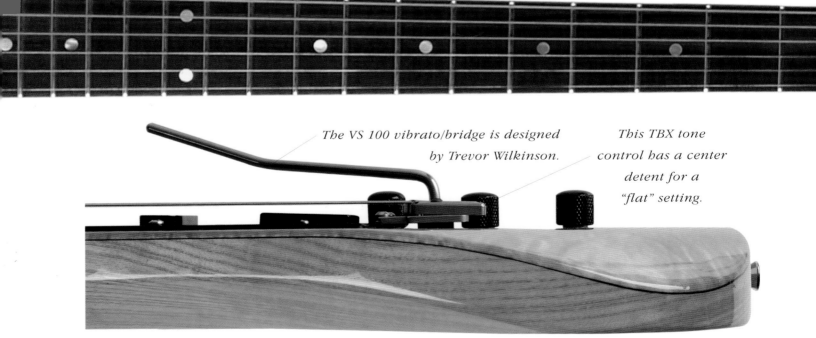

*The VS 100 vibrato/bridge is designed by Trevor Wilkinson.*

*This TBX tone control has a center detent for a "flat" setting.*

*Below:* A relatively straightforward pickup set-up is now used on this "workhorse" guitar.

The panel to the right of the pickups is a remnant of an earlier switching configuration.

# TOM ANFIELD BUBINGA GUITAR

**B**UILDING GUITARS for a living is hard work, and can occasionally take its toll on a luthier's health—as Tom Anfield discovered when, in 1985, he spent three months carving the model shown here out of a solid slab of bubinga. This timber, grown in Cameroon, Gabon and Zaire, is sometimes called African rosewood, and is described by Anfield as "one of the toughest, meanest, highest tensile-strength woods you can get." Unfortunately, it can also cause problems when its dust is breathed in, and, after completing the body for his bubinga guitar, Anfield suffered a severe and prolonged chest infection.

The guitar that emerged from this painful production process was, however, well worth the effort. The bubinga (combined with ebony, which can be seen on the fingerboard and headstock) provides exceptional sustain, and Anfield went on to use the completed instrument, which has had various different pickups and electronics fitted to it over the last decade, for a good many concerts—though, due to its heavy weight, it has now been "semi-retired."

*The tuners fitted to the guitar are built by Schaller.*

*The body is carved for maximum comfort—a crucial consideration for such a heavy guitar.*

**Above:** *A stylized "Anfield" logo graces the instrument's ebony and bubinga headstock.*

*The distinctive sound made by bubinga bodies is especially favored by some bass manufacturers.*

# ARIA FA70-BS

SHIRO ARAI, a keen classical guitarist, set up a company bearing his name in the Japanese city of Nagoya, some 200 miles southwest of Tokyo, in 1953. When it became involved in manufacturing and marketing guitars for export, it initially labeled them Diamond and Arai, but eventually settled on a trademark that was both an anagram of Mr. Arai's name and a suitable musical term: Aria. After some years of handling only acoustic instruments, Aria started to produce electrics in 1966, and was soon established as a major international brand. Most of its guitars are manufactured in Japan or Korea, with the exception of its "concert classical" nylon-strung models, which are made in Spain.

Aria has an especially high reputation for its archtop jazz guitars. These first appeared in the late '60s, and have, in the past, been used by major names such as Joe Pass and Ike Isaacs, and are now favored by leading musicians like Larry Coryell and top Scottish player Jim Mullen. The instrument shown here is part of the

*Below: Aria semi-acoustics have been favorably compared to far more expensive models.*

PHOTOGRAPHS COURTESY OF IVOR MAIRANTS MUSICENTRE, LONDON

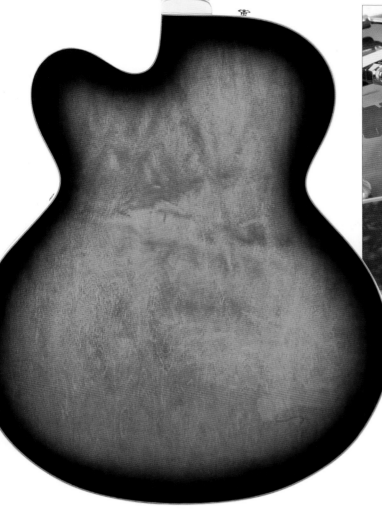

*Above:* This two-pickup Aria is complemented by other FAs with single and "floating" transducers.

*Left:* The instrument's generously proportioned body contributes to its mellow sound.

*Left:* The binding around the FA-70's f-holes contrasts attractively with its overall color.

firm's "FA" range of full-body semi-acoustics, which was launched in the 1990s. This example, the FA70-BS (the suffix refers to its "Brown Sunburst" finish), has a spruce top, maple back and sides, and two humbucking pickups.

# DAN ARMSTRONG LUCITE BASS

DAN ARMSTRONG (1934-2004) started out as a professional guitarist, but later switched to designing, repairing and modifying instruments at his workshop in New York City. In 1968, his "see through" electric guitars and basses, with bodies made of transparent Lucite, and bolted-on maple necks, were put into production by the New Jersey-based Ampeg company, best known for its amplifiers.

Dense, easy to work with, and strongly resistant to damage—minor scuffs and scratches could be

*Below: The instrument's pickup housing contains two separate transducers, maximizing the tonal range.*

*The Lucite body is entirely free of unwanted vibrations or resonances.*

removed with a soft cloth and some toothpaste!— Lucite seemed like an ideal material for solid electrics, and the Armstrong/Ampeg axes gained something of a cult following. Keith Richards of the Rolling Stones is known to have played one, and the "see-through" bass in our photos, dating from the late 1960s, carries the autograph of another celebrity Armstong user: Jack Bruce of Cream.

Ampeg ceased to make these intriguing guitars in 1971, but briefly revived them in the late 1990s; various cheaper copies of them have also been manufactured.

*Right*: The rosewood bridge saddle and the metal plate beneath it are designed to optimize sustain.

# ALAN ARNOLD "BJS LEGEND"

Alan Arnold lives and works near Godalming, a small town in the southern English county of Surrey. He made his first guitar in 1994, after having spent the previous two decades working as a joiner, and now produces a very impressive range of standard models, including 6- and 12-string flat-tops, resonator instruments, and an acoustic bass.

The Arnold guitar seen here, however, is more unusual: dating from 2002, it is a custom, limited-edition arch-top, created to celebrate the career of one of Britain's most accomplished and versatile session musicians, Big Jim Sullivan. During a career that spans

PHOTOGRAPHS COURTESY OF GUITAR JUNCTION, WORTHING

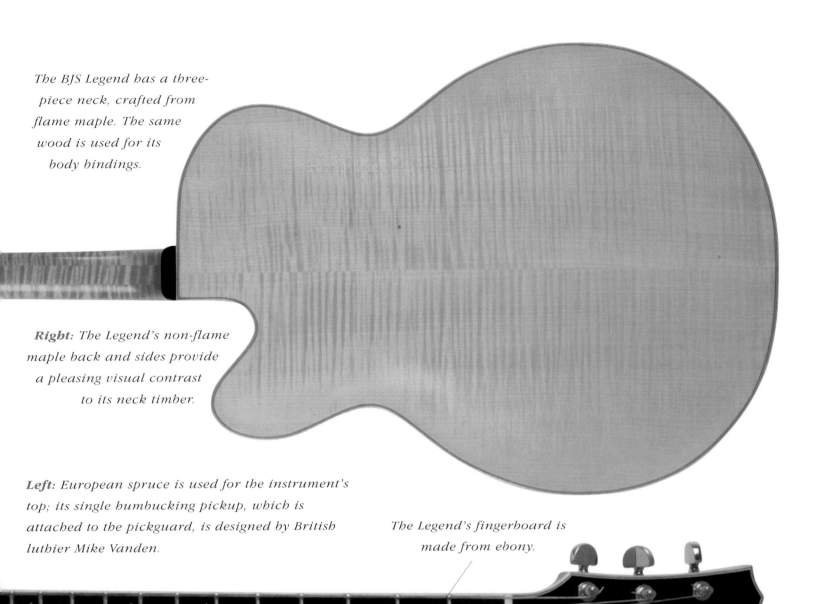

*The BJS Legend has a three-piece neck, crafted from flame maple. The same wood is used for its body bindings.*

**Right:** *The Legend's non-flame maple back and sides provide a pleasing visual contrast to its neck timber.*

**Left:** *European spruce is used for the instrument's top; its single humbucking pickup, which is attached to the pickguard, is designed by British luthier Mike Vanden.*

*The Legend's fingerboard is made from ebony.*

**Below:** *These tailpiece inlays, like those on the rest of the guitar, are abalone.*

more than half a century, Jim is believed to have played on over 1,000 hit singles—and is also famous for giving lessons to future Deep Purple axeman Ritchie Blackmore! He remains active as a performer and teacher, and has expressed his delight with Alan Arnold's fittingly named "BJS Legend," commenting recently that "[its] sounds, both electronic and acoustic, are out of this world."

# ART & LUTHERIE CEDAR CUTAWAY

THE ART & LUTHERIE line of guitars, designed and manufactured in La Patrie, Canada, is the brainchild of Robert Godin (the creator of several other major guitar brands, such as Godin itself, and Norman—see individual entries for these), who established it to produce what he describes as "entry-level acoustics that would bring the key attributes of pro-quality [instruments] within the reach of novice players." Only a few decades ago, such an aim would probably have been doomed to failure; but recent high-tech developments in manufacturing have helped to bring about dramatic improvements in the once dire quality of many inexpensive flat-tops, and Art & Lutherie models such as the Cedar Cutaway seen here are among the very best of their kind.

Like many of the company's acoustics, it has a solid

*Below: The cedar top that gives the model its name is finished in "Transparent Blue."*

**Above:** *The nut on this guitar, like its bridge saddle, is made from the bone substitute Tusq.*

Rosewood is used for the A&L's fingerboard.

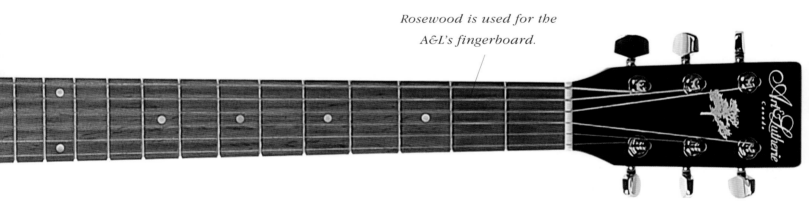

**Left:** *Pickup systems are now commonly found on cheaper acoustics. This preamp unit is fairly simple, but effective.*

top (a feature once almost unheard of in a modestly priced guitar), and its pleasing sound and easy action will serve as an inspiration and encouragement to the beginner. The silver-leaf maple used for its neck is grown in Canada itself, as are 95% of all A&L's tonewoods, and the Cedar Cutaway also boasts a built-in Godin-designed Quantum undersaddle pickup and preamp. Various finishes are available.

# BENEDETTO BRAVO

SINCE ROBERT BENEDETTO built his 7-string guitar for Bucky Pizzarelli, many other prominent players, including the late Chuck Wayne, Kenny Burrell, Jimmy Bruno, and British jazzman Martin Taylor, have adopted his instruments; he has also made a number of violins (one of which was owned and used by Stéphane Grappelli) and cellos. Benedettos tend to be lighter, and often slightly narrower, than many earlier American archtops; Bob believes that, as he told this author in 1999, "big isn't necessarily better or louder," and his approach to construction, as well as his choice of woods, are key contributory factors to the warmth and richness of tone (described by him as "the sound of today") for which his guitars are famous.

For many years, the only available Benedettos were those hand-made by Bob himself. However, in 1999, he began a collaboration with Fender that resulted in some of his models being produced by the company's

*Below: The Bravo has a laminated spruce top, and flamed maple back and sides.*

*The guitar is 16 inches wide, and 2 inches deep.*

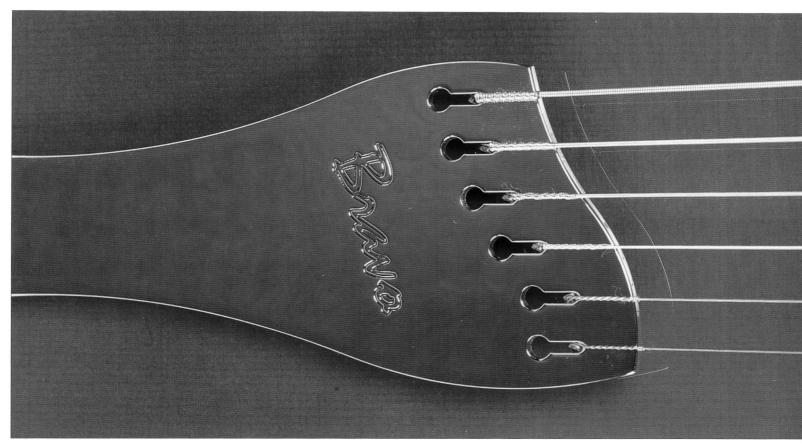

*Above:* The gold-finished tailpiece complements the Bravo's "Claret" coloring.

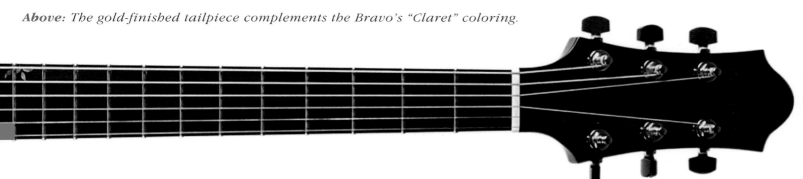

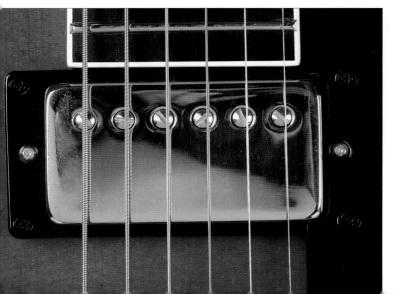

*Left:* The Bravo is fitted with a single Benedetto A6 humbucking pickup, made by Seymour Duncan.

Custom Shop luthiers. The Bravo shown here (like the Pizzarelli on the previous two pages) was one of the fruits of this partnership, which came to an end in early 2006. At the time of writing, Benedetto has just announced plans to establish a manufacturing facility of his own in Savannah, Georgia.

# BLUERIDGE HISTORIC SERIES BR-163CE

**B**LUERIDGE FLAT-TOPS are manufactured for Saga Musical Instruments, a San Francisco-based firm that is one of America's leading importers of guitars, banjos, violins and mandolins; its other brands include Regal (see separate article). Saga was set up in the mid-1970s by musician and storeowner Richard Keldsen; its first products were Japanese-made banjos, and, over the years, it has had its instruments built in a variety of Far Eastern locations. However, what Keldsen described to *Flatpicking Guitar Magazine* interviewer Dan Miller in 2005 as a "favorable investment climate" in China has recently encouraged Japanese, Taiwanese and Korean industrialists to set up new, state-of-the-art factories there, and it is to these facilities that Saga now turns to produce Blueridges.

Thanks to careful design and meticulous quality control, the results of this East-West collaboration have been outstanding. The 000-sized BR-163 shown in our photographs—one of Blueridge's "Historic Series," inspired by classic pre-war Martins—offers exceptional quality at a competitive price, and an equally high standard is maintained throughout the rest of the company's range, which features several other 000s, as well as regular and slope-shoulder dreadnoughts.

*Left: The BR-163CE's piezo pickup and Fishman preamp add to its versatility.*

*Right: These herringbone inlays are inspired by 1930s Martins.*

*Below: The Blueridge sports a high gloss finish, and has an X-braced, solid sitka spruce top, with solid Indian rosewood back and sides. Its bridge is also made from rosewood.*

*A non-cutaway version of this model is also available.*

*Right:* Note the distinctively shaped "butterbean" tuning buttons.

The Blueridge's headstock has a rosewood overlay, and is decorated with abalone and mother-of-pearl.

# BOURGEOIS DS-260

DANA BOURGEOIS comes from Maine, and made his first-ever acoustic guitar while a student at Bowdoin College in Brunswick. He became a professional luthier in 1978, and rose to prominence in the mid-1980s thanks to his involvement with the creation of the Schoenberg Soloist—a cutaway flat-top based on the Martin OM (Orchestral Model) body shape. The Soloist was developed by Bourgeois in collaboration with musician and guitar maker Eric Schoenberg, and manufactured at Martin's factory in Nazareth, Pennsylvania between 1986 and 1993.

In 1995, after spells working for Paul Reed Smith (see separate entries) and Gibson, Dana Bourgeois established his own firm, Bourgeois Guitars, in Lewiston, Maine. Its instruments, though few in number, were soon adopted by several leading players,

*Below: The guitar's top, made from Adrionack spruce, measures just over 15 inches at its widest point.*

*Above:* Indian rosewood is used for the DS-260's back and sides.

including Ricky Skaggs, Steve Earle, and Dan Tyminski, who plays guitar with Alison Krauss's band, Union Station. A custom flat-top made for Tyminski was the basis for the Bourgeois DS-260 production model seen here, which dates from 1997. Thanks to its "12 frets to the body" design, the instrument's sound hole is located nearer to its waist than on a standard, "14-fret to the body" guitar, while the corresponding placement of the bridge close to the widest part of its top helps to create what one commentator has described as "a loose, open quality to [its] sound, [with] lovely warm, balanced tone."

Less than 100 DS-260s were made by Bourgeois Guitars, but the model is currently being constructed in larger quantities by Pantheon, a new company co-founded by Dana Bourgeois in 2000.

# BREEDLOVE SC 25

IN ITS EARLY DAYS, Breedlove employed only a handful of craftsmen; it has subsequently expanded both its staff and its product lines, but retains the adventurous spirit and commitment to excellence that inspired its founders. The company's underlying philosophy was recently defined by its president, Peter Newport, who wrote in an article for Mel Bay's online *Guitar Sessions* magazine in 2006 that his team's "shared vision…goes beyond specifications and time-saving jigs to more of a concept and sensation of building heirloom-quality instruments and believing in the validity of our work."

Both Peter Newport and Kim Breedlove are keen to offer their customers more affordable flat-tops as an alternative to deluxe and custom models. To this end, the firm introduced its "S" (for "simplified") series some years ago; the range, as Newport told Dave Burrluck of *Guitarist* magazine in 2003, is "our hot rod—you take any unnecessary parts off so it's a mean machine." Made alongside the firm's top-of-the-line guitars at its Oregon headquarters, "S" class acoustics have what Breedlove publicity calls an "understated

*Below: Various wood options are offered on SC 25s: our example has a cedar top, and koa back and sides.*

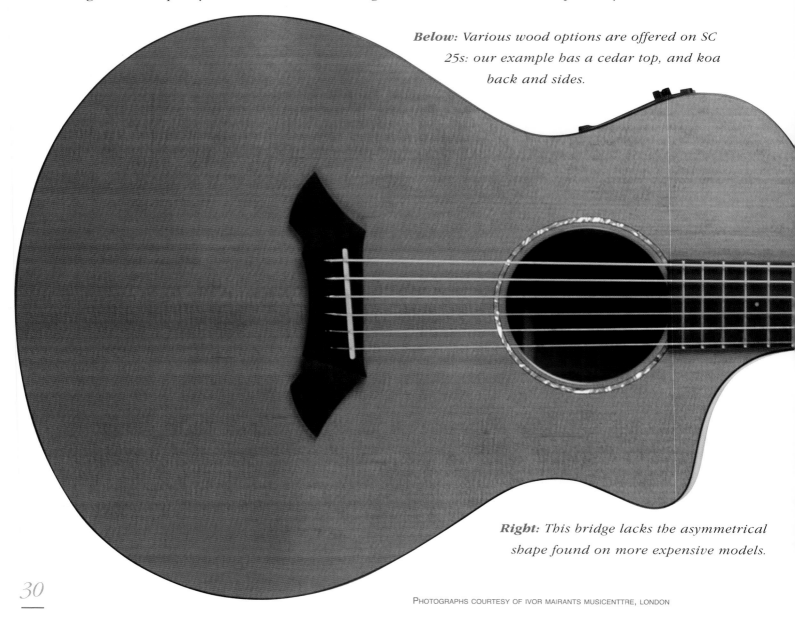

*Right: This bridge lacks the asymmetrical shape found on more expensive models.*

*Right: Fishman preamps are factory fitted to many Breedloves.*

*Above: The edgings on the SC 25 are plain, but its woods are clearly of the finest quality.*

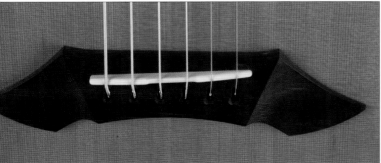

aesthetic," but feature premium tonewoods, as well as meticulous design and construction.

An SC 25 is featured in our photographs: it is a "simplified concert" model, with black bindings and a 15 inch maximum body width, and sports the "soft" cutaway designed in the 1990s by company co-founder Steve Henderson to replace Larry Breedlove's more dramatically angled one.

# BREEDLOVE J 25-12

THE J 25-12 jumbo-bodied 12-string that appears on these pages is part of Breedlove's "Premier Line" of acoustic guitars. Premiers are priced above the "S" series described on the last two pages, and form the basis for the Custom Shop models that represent the company's *crème de la crème*. However, many players will be delighted with the "standard-issue" Premier J 25-12, which can be supplied with or without a soft cutaway, and whose sound has been described by Breedlove as "big, but beautifully well balanced—an elegant combination of power and contro." A companion 6-string J 25 is also available.

Since its formation in 1990, Breedlove has developed into what its president, Peter Newport (quoted by Dave Burrluck in his previously mentioned article for *Guitarist* magazine) has described as "the largest custom shop I know of." It currently produces in the region of 1,000 guitars a year in the USA, and, in

*Alternative versions of the J 25-12 have included a limited edition all-walnut model, produced in 2006.*

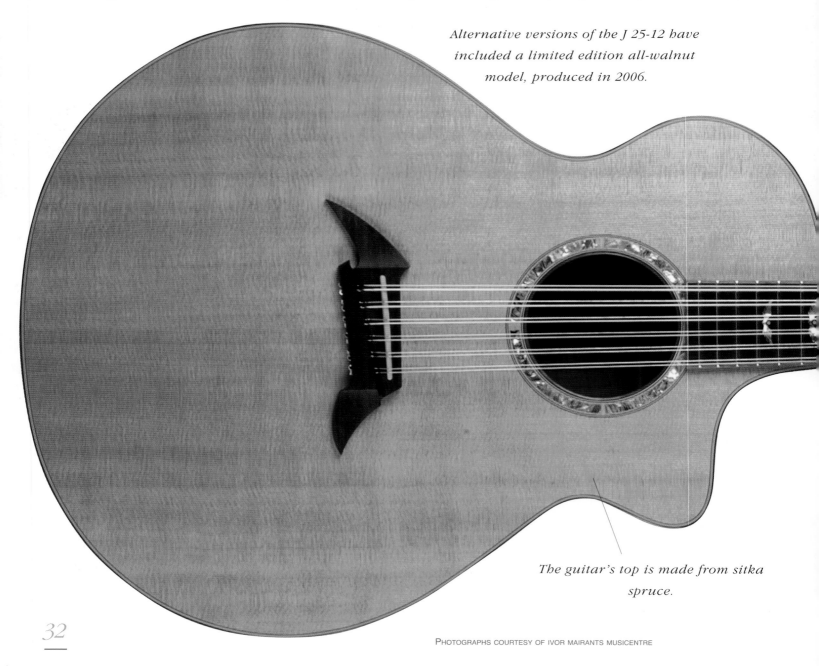

*The guitar's top is made from sitka spruce.*

*Above: The J 25-12's back and sides are made from myrtlewood grown in the region near its Oregon factory.*

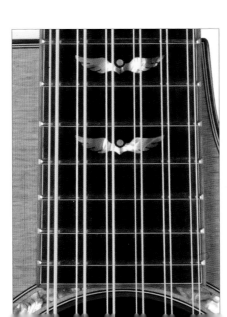

*Above right: This soft cutaway gives exceptional access to the upper frets.*

*Right: "Wings" position markers grace the J 25-12's fingerboard.*

2004, launched its new Korean-built "Atlas" acoustic range. This comprises flat-tops, nylon-strungs and basses, all of which are designed by Kim Breedlove, and subjected to careful quality checks at the company's Oregon headquarters before being shipped to dealers. The Atlas line has been highly acclaimed in the press and by players; it includes the AC200/SM, a solid sitka spruce-topped guitar with laminated mahogany back and sides that sells for under $700.

*Some Creedys are made with cedar tops,
instead of the spruce seen here.*

# BROOK CREEDY 010

BROOK GUITARS operates from a small workshop in the English county of Devon. Its co-owners, Simon Smidmore and Andy Petherick, are both protégés of luthier Andy Manson (see separate entry); before meeting him and becoming involved in guitar building, Smidmore had been a carpenter, and Petherick an engineer. The two men set up Brook in 1995, and went on to spend a number of years making instruments for Manson, although they now concentrate on producing their own

*Above:* The Creedy's *bridge is rosewood.*

designs. These range from dreadnought, jumbo and bass models to small-size travel guitars, each of which is named for a Devonshire river.

The Creedy shown on these pages is a parlor-style flat-top with 12 frets to the body, and a lower bout width of approximately 12.4 inches. It is made from a classic combination of woods: spruce for its top and figured rosewood for its back and sides. Brook guitars are available with two alternative trims: '010'-type instruments like this one have an unbound headstock and fingerboard, mother-of-pearl fingerboard markers, herringbone purfling and chrome hardware, while '015' guitars boast a bound headstock and fingerboard, diamond and dot fingerboard markers, gold tuners, and an abalone rosette.

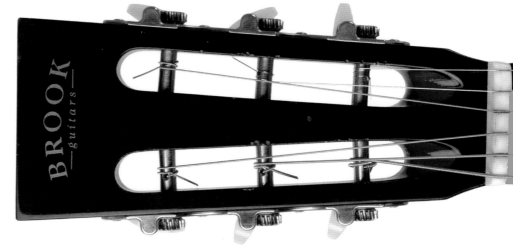

*Right:* This model dates from 2003, and is still in production at Brook Guitars.

# AMALIO BURGUET 1F

VALENCIA, ON THE MEDITERRANEAN coast of Spain, is an important musical center, and a number of leading guitar makers are based near the city. Alboraya, just to its north, is the home of Esteve Guitars (see separate entry), while in the opposite direction lies the village of Catarroja, the birthplace and headquarters of Amalio Burguet.

Born in 1951, Burguet developed a fascination for the classical and flamenco guitar at an early age, and went on to study both music and instrument building before opening his first, small-scale lutherie workshop. In 1994, he and an expanded staff began operating from their current premises, where, as Burguet explains on his website, they now combine modern production techniques with individual craftsmanship to create guitars that will offer "unsurpassed value to the working musician."

Models such as the "1F" seen here are clear proof of the Burguet company's success. A professional quality, though reasonably priced flamenco guitar, it is available with a spruce or cedar top, while its body is made from cypress, a lightweight wood often chosen to give flamenco instruments their characteristic liveliness and vibrancy.

*Below: The 1F has a cedar neck and an ebony fingerboard. A cutaway-bodied version of the guitar can also be supplied.*

*This headstock has a rosewood overlay.*

*Left: A vividly patterned rosette and a high-gloss finish add to the Burguet's visual impact.*

*Amalio Burguet promises his customers "a hand-made Spanish guitar at an affordable price."*

# BURNS MARVIN SHADOWS CUSTOM

JIM BURNS (1925-1998), sometimes hailed as the "British Leo Fender," was an able guitarist who acquired craft and metalworking skills while serving as a Royal Air Force fitter during World War II, and soon applied them to instrument making. By the 1950s, he was focusing on lutherie while supporting himself in other jobs, and in 1959, his solid-body designs became commercially available for the first time, thanks to a partnership with manufacturer Henry Weill. This proved to be short-lived, and in 1960, Burns set up a new company bearing his own name.

Three years later, he persuaded Hank Marvin, lead guitarist with one of the United Kingdom's most prominent pop groups, The Shadows, and previously a dedicated Fender Stratocaster user, to collaborate (with fellow band member Bruce Welch) on the development of a Burns electric carrying his endorsement. The Burns Marvin, a reissued custom version of which is seen here, debuted in 1964, and was warmly received—but despite its success, Jim Burns' company quickly found itself in serious financial trouble, and its founder sold it to the Baldwin Piano

*Below:* The custom Burns Marvin is made in China, and has an alder body with a maple neck.

*Above:* The signatures of Hank Marvin and Bruce Welch appear on the "Rezo-Tube" vibrato of this special edition guitar.

*Right:* Gold-plated locking tuners are fitted to the Marvin's "scroll" headstock.

and Organ Company in 1965. The firm's subsequent history was a chequered one; it shut down in 1970, and although Jim himself went on to make various attempts to re-establish himself, it was not until 1992, when Burns London was formed (see following pages) that his name and designs again achieved the prominence they deserved. Jim did not own this company, but acted as a consultant to it until his death.

# COLLINGS OM2H

MICHIGAN-BORN BILL COLLINGS grew up in Ohio; after considering and rejecting the possibility of becoming a doctor, he relocated to Houston, Texas in 1973. Here, he made his living repairing guitars, before starting to build his own instruments in 1975. At this early stage in his career, he had only a makeshift workshop in the spare bedroom of his apartment, but as prominent local musicians—including future stars such as singer-songwriter Lyle

Lovett—began using Collings guitars, the young luthier's reputation grew steadily. In 1980, he moved west to Austin, where he initially shared premises with two other craftsmen, establishing a shop of his own a few years later, and setting up the company that bears his name in 1986.

Demand for Collings' work received a further boost in 1988 when the respected Nashville guitar dealer and expert George Gruhn placed an order for 24 custom

*Below: Collings OMs are based on the Martin "Orchestra Models" first produeced in 1929. This OM2H has a 15-inch wide body with a spruce top.*

*The Collings' body is bordered with herringbone inlays; its back and sides are rosewood.*

*Like the Martin 1920s and 30s OMs, the Collings' fingerboard has "diamond" inlays.*

***Above:*** *Collings' soundhole label, with the model name written on by hand. A larger reporoduction of this distinctive pen-and-ink drawing of the company's factory is also available on a t-shirt!*

*Collings uses tuners made by Waverly for all its instruments.*

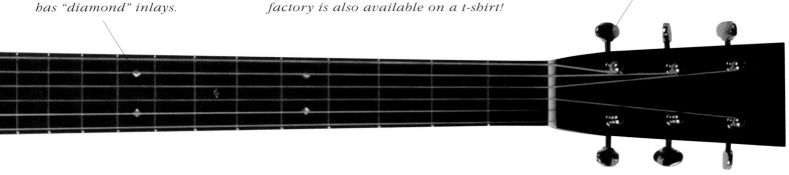

instruments. As the company's official history records, this commission "helped to establish Bill in the national market," and soon his designs were attracting attention of major names such as David Crosby, Emmylou Harris, John Prine, and even Keith Richards of the Rolling Stones.

The growth in orders led, inevitably, to expansion, but Bill Collings has always been determined to maintain the high standards of quality and consistency

he is justly renowned for. At a question-and-answer session at the NAMM (National Association of Music Merchants) show in 2005, he explained that he achieves this by refusing to "break construction [at the factory] up into tiny little pieces…We keep it flowing as if one person is doing the whole guitar."

Collings currently produces eight categories of guitar; the instrument shown here is one of its Martin-inspired OM (Orchestra Model) models.

# CORT SFX 6

WHILE ITS HEADQUARTERS is in Northbrook, Illinois, Cort builds its guitars in Asia, where—unlike some of its competitors—it has its own dedicated manufacturing facilities; as a result, it is able to offer high quality, U.S.-designed instruments at relatively reasonable prices. Founded in 1960, the firm has, in recent years, acquired a number of high-profile endorsees: these include virtuoso jazz-rock fusion guitarist Larry Coryell, star session musician, arranger and bandleader Joe Beck, and veteran bluesman Matt "Guitar" Murphy, all of whom have worked closely with Cort to develop their own "signature" electrics. (After Murphy suffered a severe stroke in 2002, Cort's Director of Artist Relations, Eric Fuchsman, organized a benefit for him that attracted support from Coryell and many other major names; sadly, Fuchsman himself died, at the age of only 51, three years later.)

The company produces an extensive range of other

*Below: Solid spruce is used for the top of the SFX 6.*

**Above left:** *This preamp, connected to the Cort's under-bridge transducer, delivers outstanding results in live concerts.*

**Above right:** *The SFX 6's neck is mahogany; here, it joins the guitar's rosewood back and sides.*

solid-bodies, basses, acoustics and semi-acoustics, aimed at a cross-section of players, from beginners to professionals. Its SFX flat-tops, one of which, the SFX 6, is shown here, were conceived (to quote the company's publicity), as "extra light acoustics with rich tone and resonance either on the stage or [at] home unplugged." They feature solid tops and cutaways, plus built-in pickups designed and made by Fishman Transducers of Wilmington, Massachusetts. The SFX 6 is equipped with a Classic 4 Fishman unit; this offers 4-band equalization and an additional "brilliance" control.

Though unpretentious and unostentatious in appearance, the SFX 6 performs excellently: the busy blues musician who owns the guitar in our photos has described it to the author as the best amplified flat-top he has ever used onstage, and has left the instrument's original price tag on its body to remind him of what a bargain it was!

# D'ANGELICO EXCEL, 1949

JOHN D'ANGELICO (1905-1964) was a New Yorker of Italian extraction. After learning his lutherie skills from his great-uncle, an eminent violin and mandolin builder, he established a shop of his own in the Little Italy district of his home city in 1932. There, he and a small number of assistants and apprentices crafted handmade archtop guitars based around four model types, Style A, Style B, Excel and New Yorker—though individual instruments were frequently customized in line with players' requirements. His output was comparatively small: guitar expert George Gruhn, writing in 1980, estimated that "during the late 1930s, when production was at its peak, D'Angelico was able to make approximately 35 instruments per year."

No more Style As or Bs appeared after the 1940s, but D'Angelico continued to make his other two archtop models until his death in 1964. He built his first cutaway-body guitar in 1947, and the new shape proved highly successful; this elegant, lovingly preserved cutaway Excel dates from two years later.

*Below: The "finial" ornament within the cutout of this headstock is a characteristic D'Angelico feature.*

*Above: High quality Grover tuners were John D'Angelico's first choice for his instruments.*

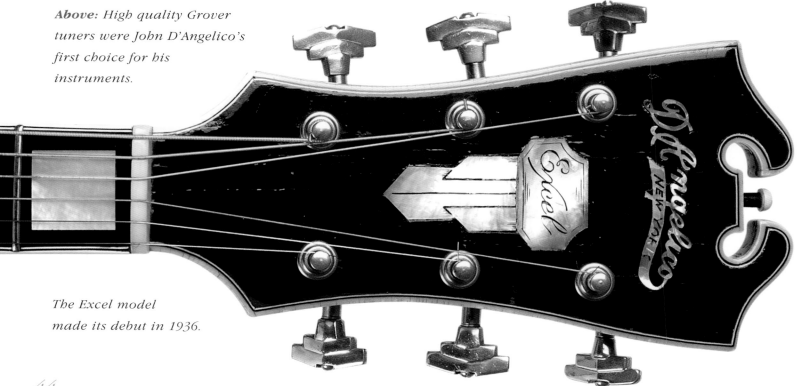

*The Excel model made its debut in 1936.*

The tailpiece
seen below is
not the original
one fitted by
D'Angelico.

This Excel is
17 inches wide,
and has a solid
spruce top.

# D'ANGELICO NYL-2 (NEW YORKER)

THE D'ANGELICO NEW YORKER featured here, like the Excel EXS-1DH, is a modern replica made by D'Angelico Guitars of America. The New Yorker, which debuted in 1936, was John D'Angelico's "top of the

skills and energy of his last apprentice, Jimmy D'Aquisto, whom he had taken on in 1952. Those who knew both men have commented on the strong emotional bond—closer to a father-son relationship than that of an employer and trainee—that clearly existed between them, and there are significant links between D'Angelico's work and the designs produced by D'Aquisto during his own later career. These are explored on the following pages.

line" model; and, like his own guitars, this one combines handsome looks with what a reviewer for *Just Jazz Guitar*, Dr. Ken Ciuffreda, described in 2001 as "a rich and deep jazz tone." Its 17-inch top is an inch narrower than D'Angelico's original New Yorkers, but this and other cosmetic and constructional discrepancies do not detract from the appeal of an instrument that, in the words of another critic, Doug Munro of *Jazz Times* magazine, "has all the classic D'Angelico trademarks, with the same headstock and tailpiece we fondly remember."

As John D'Angelico's health declined towards the end of his life, he came to rely increasingly upon the

*Right: The inlay at the center of the D'Angelico New Yorker's headstock is a stylized representation of the Big Apple's Chrysler building.*

PHOTOGRAPHS COURTESY OF IVOR MAIRANTS MUSICENTRE. LONDON

# D'AQUISTO NEW YORKER DQ-NYE

JOHN D'ANGELICO'S LAST GUITARS were assembled by his apprentice, Jimmy D'Aquisto. After D'Angelico's death, D'Aquisto (1935-1995) established his own lutherie business, but continued to produce the Excel and New Yorker archtop models created by his mentor. At first, there was little difference between his versions and the originals, but in time, D'Aquisto—who, as his friend and fellow guitar maker John Monteleone told this author in 1999, "was always torn between living the legacy of John and being himself"—began to invest these classic designs with his own distinctive touches. By the late 1960s, his New Yorkers had acquired reshaped f-holes, and D'Angelico's "Chrysler Building" headstock inlay had been replaced with a scroll-type decoration; and by the '70s, he had abandoned his predecessor's brass tailpieces, substituting ebony ones. These and other modifications are visible on the replica D'Aquisto New Yorker in our photographs—and before long, Jimmy's guitars were to demonstrate more radical new ideas.

*Below: The pickguard on this D'Aqusto replica has no D'Angelico-style "stairsteps."*

*Opposite page: D'Aquisto-style f-holes are elliptical, lacking any center stroke.*

*This headstock cutout is quite different from D'Angelico's.*

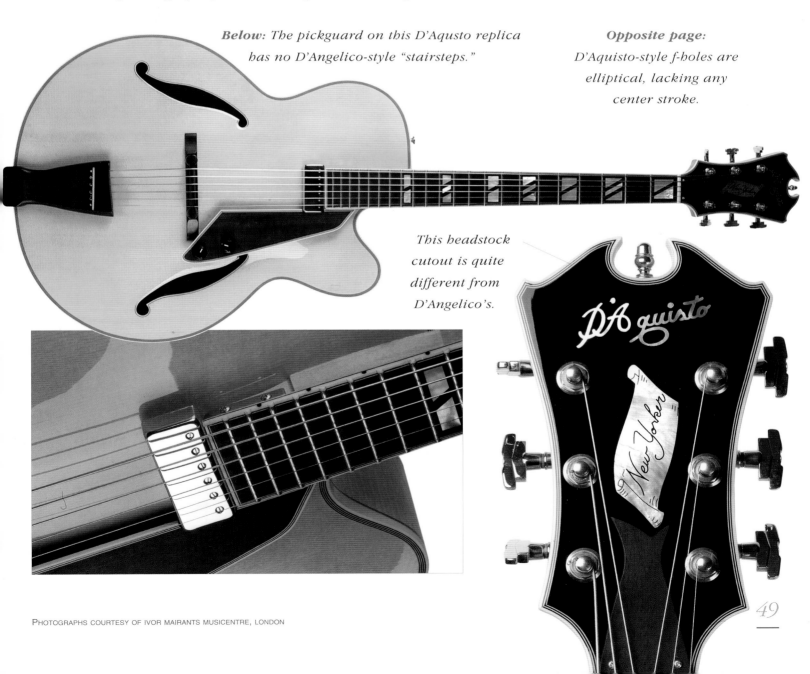

# DAISY ROCK PIXIE

PRODUCING GUITARS FOR GIRLS and women can be a commercially uncertain venture—as Gretsch discovered with its Princess solid-body in 1962 (see separate entry)—but more recently, the California-based Daisy Rock company has been enjoying considerable success with a range of electrics and acoustics aimed specifically at female players.

Daisy Rock was the brainchild of Los Angeles-based Tish Ciravolo, whose experiences as a teenage bass player led her to the conclusion that (as she puts it on the company's website) "standard guitars are often too big and bulky for the female form." Accordingly, the instruments in her company's catalog have lighter bodies and thinner necks than usual, and are designed in shapes and colors intended to appeal to girls and young women. The guitars have been widely acclaimed, and are selling well, thanks in part to high-profile endorsements from a number of prominent female musicians, from Dolly Parton to Sarah Smith of the young Canadian rock band The Joys.

The Daisy Rock acoustic seen here is a Pixie model, finished in "Sky Blue"; "Powder Pink" and "Pixie Purple" shades are also available, and a "sister" version of the model, incorporating a piezo-electric pickup with an onboard tuner, is produced in "Plum Purple" Burst or "Blueberry Burst."

*Opposite page: The Daisy Rock Pixie weights just 4$\frac{1}{2}$ pounds, and is styled to appeal to the company's young female target market.*

*Solid spruce is used for this acoustic's top; it has an oval-shaped back made of composites, and a mahogany neck.*

*This model is also sold as part of a "starter pack" with a tutor book and accessories.*

*Appropriately, the Pixie has "daisy" fret-markers on its rosewood fingerboard.*

PHOTOGRAPHS COURTESY OF PEACH, BLAKE END, BRAINTREE

# DAISY ROCK HEARTBREAKER BASS

THE AVERAGE BASS GUITAR tends to be considerably less "woman-friendly" than its 6-string counterpart—and even iconic female bassists such as Suzi Quatro, whose appearances as Leather Tuscadero in the classic TV series *Happy Days* inspired Daisy Rock founder Tish Caravolo to take up the instrument, have sometimes complained that their favorite "axes" are very often dauntingly large and heavy. Caravolo herself described the first bass she tried out in her teenage years as feeling "like a bat in my female-sized hands," but the US-designed, Far Eastern-built models she now offers to her Daisy Rock customers have no such drawbacks: their scale lengths, necks and bodies are all optimized for use by girls and young women, while their shapes and colors give them fashion appeal as well as practicality.

The current range of Daisy Rock basses includes relatively conventional-looking solid, double-cutaway models such as the Elite and the Rock Candy, and the semi-hollow Retro-H. There are also more *outré* stylings, with bodies resembling stars, butterflies and (of course) daisies. The Heartbreaker shown here steers a middle course between these extremes. It boasts a cordiform body produced in a variety of shades (this one is "Princess Purple"), and has a bolted-on, rock maple neck. The instrument weighs just under 8 pounds, and its single pickup is a Seymour Duncan-designed unit with split pairs of upper- and lower-string pole pieces similar to those found on Fender Precision Basses.

With its impressive performance and striking looks, the Heartbreaker has sold well, and is now, according to Daisy Rock's publicity, proving increasingly attractive to male as well as female players.

*Below: Like many Asian-made solid-bodies, the Daisy Rock Heartbreaker's body is built from basswood. Alternative finishes include "Red Hot Red" and "Cheetah", and a matching Heartbreaker 6-string guitar is also available.*

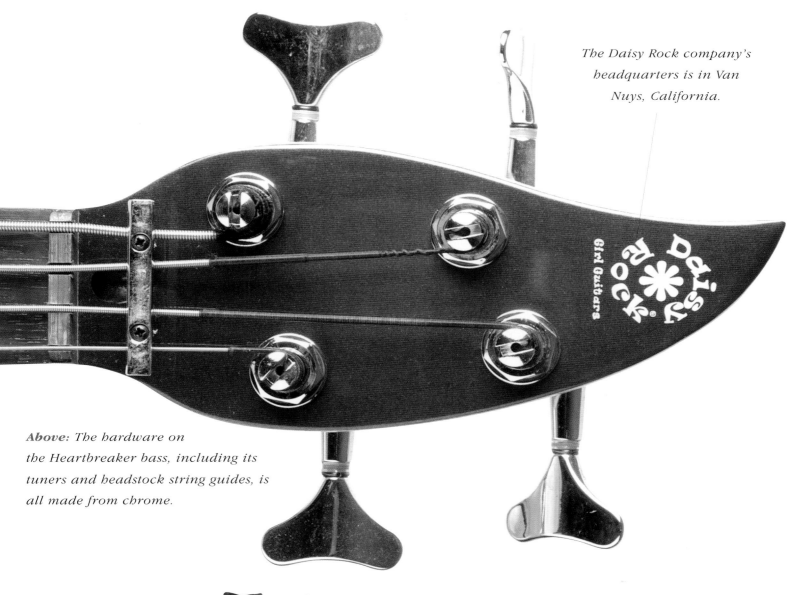

*The Daisy Rock company's headquarters is in Van Nuys, California.*

**Above:** *The hardware on the Heartbreaker bass, including its tuners and headstock string guides, is all made from chrome.*

**Left:** *Seymour Duncan, the company that makes the Heartbreaker's pickups, is one of the USA's most respected transducer designers.*

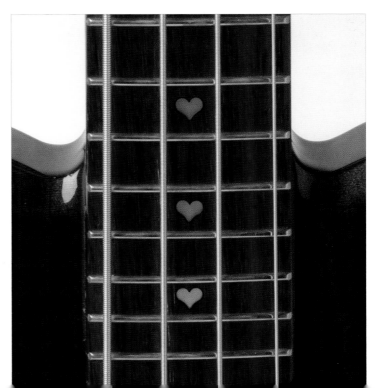

**Right:** *The "heart" motif extends to the markers on this model's 22-fret, rosewood fingerboard.*

# DANELECTRO SOLID-BODY

NATHAN DANIEL (1912-1994) made his initial reputation as a designer and manufacturer of guitar amplifiers in the 1930s and 40s. He specialized in budget models, and, by the mid-1950s, was also producing electric guitars at his factory in New Jersey. These included Silvertones sold by Sears, Roebuck & Company, and Danelectros marketed through a number of other catalog companies and wholesalers.

This mid-1960s Danelectro is a typical example of Daniel's "cheap and cheerful" approach to design and construction. Its body is made from poplar, topped and backed with stapled-on Masonite hardboard, and its single pickup is mounted inside a chrome-plated lipstick casing; Daniel bought up surplus stocks of

*Below: The body shape of this guitar is in what Nathan Daniel named his "shorthorn" style, with a double cutaway. Its top is 13.25 inches wide.*

these metal tubes and used them on all his electrics from about 1956 onwards. The guitar's sides are coated with Naugahyde (more familiar as a furniture covering), and it has a rosewood-faced, 21-fret fingerboard. It would originally have boasted cream-colored control knobs; the black ones seen here are later substitutions.

Though originally regarded as beginners' guitars, Danelectros have been used by famous players,

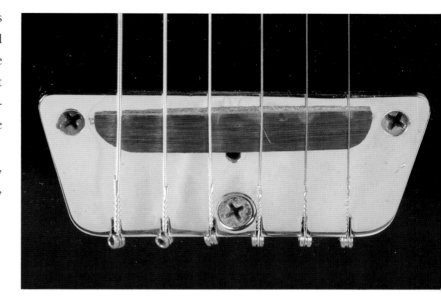

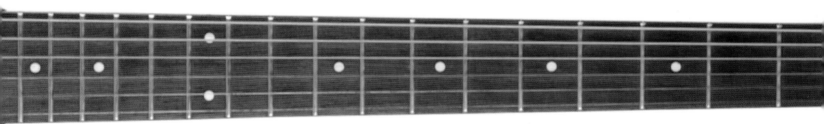

*Left: The Danelectro is simply and cheaply built, with a bolted-on neck and "3-a-side" tuners..*

*Top: With a sliver of rosewood serving as a bridge saddle, little or no adjustment is possible.*

including Jimmy Page of Led Zeppelin, and Tom Petty, and models that once sold for under $100 are now collectors' items. New, inexpensive instruments bearing the Danelectro name are currently being made in the Far East, while more upmarket Daniel-inspired electrics are available from Nashville-based luthier Jerry Jones, a long-time admirer of these quirky, unpretentious "axes."

# DEAN "DIMEBAG" TRIBUTE ML

ON WEDNESDAY DECEMBER 8 2004, "Dimebag" Darrell Abbott, guitarist with the leading heavy metal band Damageplan, was gunned down on stage in Columbus, Ohio. His murderer, a 25-year-old man later named as Nathan Gale, went on to kill three other people in an apparently motiveless attack before himself being shot dead by police. Dimebag, who had formed Damageplan with his brother, drummer Vinnie Paul Abbott, after the breakup of their previous high-profile group, Pantera, in 2003, was very much admired in hard rock circles, and among the many memorials to him is the instrument seen in our photographs—one of a series of "Tribute" guitars produced by the Dean company. Dimebag had signed a new endorsement deal with Dean only weeks before his death, having used its axes exclusively in his younger days.

The guitar shown here has an "ML"-type body, named for the late Matt Lynn, a childhood friend of Dean founder Dean B. Zelinsky. It is intended, as the firm's publicity puts it, "to spread [the instrument's] mass over a large area," and features a distinctive headstock configuration that extends string length with the aim of creating "a sound like no other."

*Below: The guitar's neck is bolted on, and has a 24³/4-inch cale length. Its body is finished in what Dean call "Vintage Brazilliaburst."*

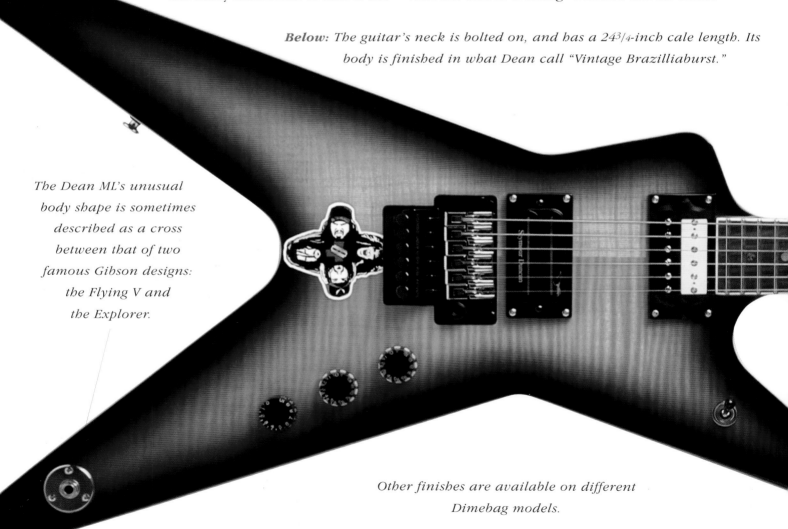

*The Dean ML's unusual body shape is sometimes described as a cross between that of two famous Gibson designs: the Flying V and the Explorer.*

*Other finishes are available on different Dimebag models.*

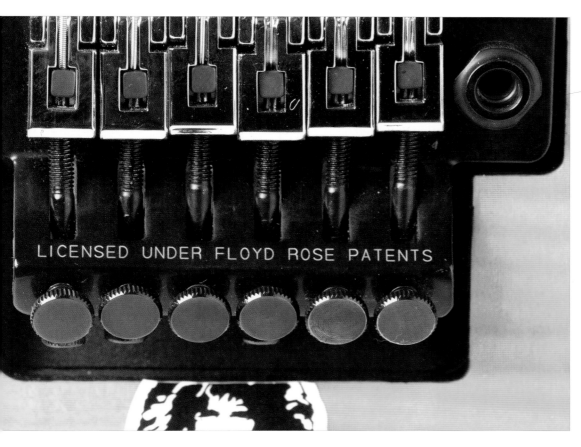

LICENSED UNDER FLOYD ROSE PATENTS

**Above:** *This Floyd Rose-licensed tremolo incorporates tuners (the wheels at its base).*

*The "whammy bar" for the tremolo fits into the hole to the right of the bridge saddles.*

**Above:** *The string locks at the guitar's nut help to ensure tuning stability, even during heavy tremolo use.*

The shape was a favorite of Dimebag's, and this model is designed to resemble the early Dean instruments he did so much to popularize. Its features include a Floyd Rose-licensed tremolo and, in the guitar's bridge position, a "Dimebucker" high-output pickup; its body and neck are mahogany, and its rosewood fingerboard boasts a cream binding. Dimebag Darrell himself is directly commemorated on the headstock graphics, and on the "Dimebag quad" image located below the "trem."

**Left:** *This picture of "Dimebag" Darrell is also avaiable on T-shirts and other merchandise, proceeds from which go to the Dimebag Memorial Foundation.*

# DEAN COPPER RESONATOR

IN 1998, DEAN GUITARS expanded its product range, previously dominated by electric solid-bodies, to feature both acoustics and, even more surprisingly, resonators—a category of instruments often regarded as having only specialist appeal. Dean, however, was evidently committed to them, and the resonator guitars it launched that year included wood- and metal-bodied biscuit-bridge types, as well as a spider-bridge, Dobro-like model, the "SP."

Dean's resonators, manufactured in the Far East and therefore substantially less expensive than classic US-made brands like National Reso-Phonic, have been given a generally warm reception by reviewers. In November 2002, Teja Gerken of *Acoustic Guitar* magazine tested the company's chrome-engraved Resonator S alongside six other metal-bodied resos, concluding that it "stood up pretty well" to all its rivals, and "provided a large dose of resonator vibe at a budget price" (then $899). There is also praise for these guitars from players such as leading blues picker and bandleader Patrick Sweany, quoted on the Dean website as saying that his acoustic/electric

*Below: The Dean Heirloom resonators are single-cone acoustics with 3-inch deep bodies.*

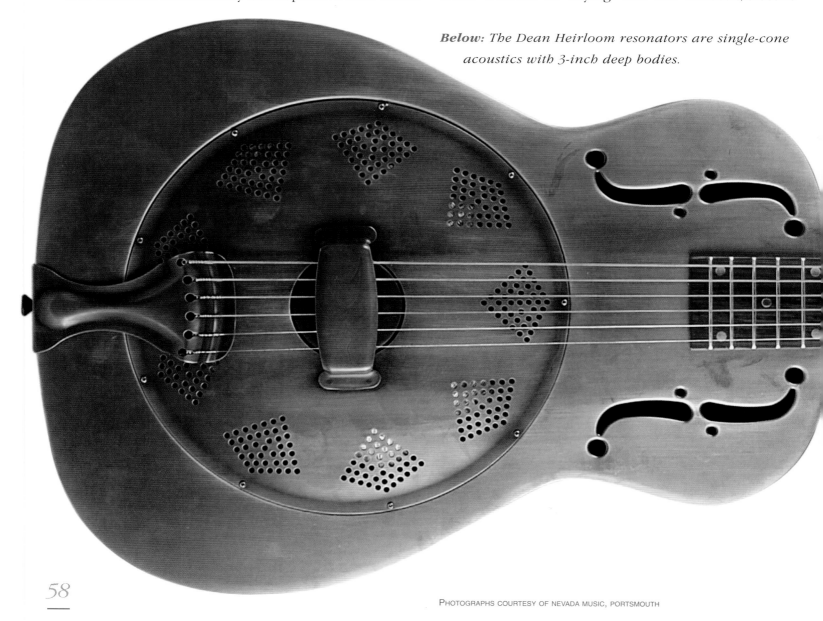

Resonator GCE "has exactly what I'm looking for…no matter what kind of gig [I'm doing.]"

In 2004, Dean introduced two new "Heirloom" resonators: like their predecessors, they are proving popular among blues players with limited funds. Both are single-cones: they share the same basic specification, and differ only in their body materials: "distressed brass," and (as here) "distressed copper."

**Top left:** *The neck on this model (and on its brass-bodied companion) is mahogany, with a rosewood fingerboard.*

**Top right:** *Dean's distinctive logo graces the Heirloom's headstock.*

These rectangles form one of the standard decorative patterns found on Dobro coverplates.

**Below:** The earliest Dobros were all wood-bodied; this model was made under license by the Chicago-based Regal company in the mid-1930s.

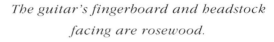

# DOBRO (1)

IN EARLY 1929, John Dopyera (1893-1988) resigned from the board of the Los Angeles-based National company. His departure followed a dispute over the ownership of the design for a single-cone resonator providing mechanical amplification for guitars and other instruments (see the National entries).

*Like many Regal Dobros, this instrument has 14 frets to the body.*

Dopyera and his brother Rudy had previously collaborated on the development of these resonators for National, and, together with their other siblings Emil, Robert and Louis, they now formed a rival resonator guitar making firm named Dobro. Its name is an abbreviation of "Dopyera Brothers," and also means "good" in Slovak, the Dopyeras' native language.

Prevented from using the single-cone resonator they had devised during their time at National, John and Rudy Dopyera invented an alternative one, whose specification is explained overleaf. Rudy filed a patent application for it in June 1929, though, according to some experts, Dobro instruments incorporating the new design were already on the market by this time.

*The guitar's fingerboard and headstock facing are rosewood.*

*The guitar's engraved body is made from nickel-plated brass.*

# DOBRO DM 36: "THE ROSE"

REGAL NEVER RESUMED production of Dobros after 1945, and no further instruments were made until the mid-1950s, when two of the Dopyeras, Rudy and Emil, began assembling guitars using spare parts left over from before the war. These models were labeled "DB Originals:" the Dobro name itself was still owned by Louis Dopyera, a partner in Valco (the successor to National—see National Cosmopolitan entry). In 1958, Louis ceded the trademark to some of his brothers, who applied it to a range of new Dobros they launched soon afterward. For a short period in the 1960s, however, the Mosrite company, based in Bakersfield, California, gained possession of the marque, obliging a different group of Dopyera family members, who had founded the OMI (Original Musical Instrument) firm at Long Beach, California, in 1967, to give yet another name, "Hound Dog," to the resonator guitars they manufactured there. Following Mosrite's bankruptcy in 1969, though, the Dopyeras were able to buy back the Dobro brand, whose logo they continued to use on their OMI resonators until the firm was sold to Gibson in 1993.

*Below: "The Rose," one of a series of Dobros with floral engravings, went on to be produced by Gibson after its takeover of OMI.*

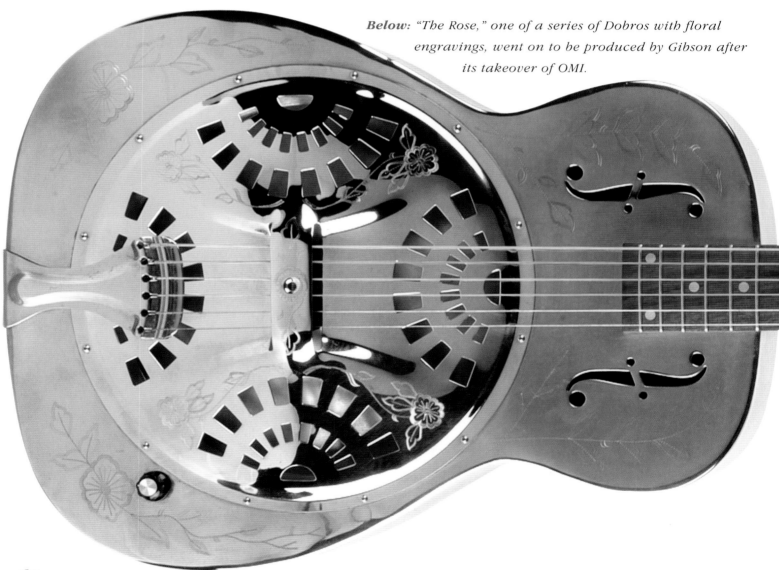

*Above: Engravings like these have featured on Dobros since the 1930s; Rudy Dopyera was responsible for designing many of them.*

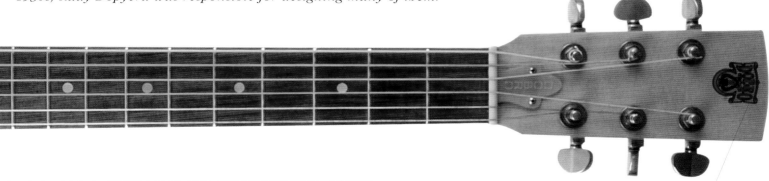

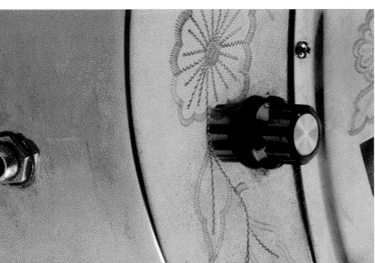

**Left:** *The DM 36 has an unobtrusively built-in piezo pickup.*

*Dobro's logo has scarcely changed since the 1930s.*

A Gibson-made Dobro is featured on pages 352-3: the pictures here show a Californian-built OMI DM 36 model, named "The Rose," and dating from 1971. Unusally for a Dobro, it has a "biscuit" bridge.

63

# PATRICK EGGLE NEW YORK

**B**RITISH-BORN GUITAR MAKER Patrick Eggle first became involved with lutherie as a schoolboy, and, by the late 1980s, was already gaining a reputation for his distinctive designs and expert repair work. His first major breakthrough came in 1990, when his instruments caught the eye of businessman Andrew Selby at a trade fair in the English Midlands. A year later, Patrick Eggle Guitars, a firm set up by Selby to manufacture Eggle's designs, opened in the city of Coventry. Among its early successes were models such as the Berlin and the New York; both appeared in a

variety of configurations, and a 2-pickup, "Fire Engine Red" New York from this period is shown here.

By the middle of the decade, Patrick Eggle Guitars was turning out up to 2,000 instruments a year, but in 1995, Eggle himself left the firm to return to smaller scale guitar making. Patrick Eggle Guitars has continued without him, and is now based in Birmingham, where it currently produces an impressive range of electrics, including a revived New York with slightly different specifications to the one featured in our photos.

*Left: This New York dates from the mid-1990s; the model was originally produced from 1994 to 1997.*

*Right: The guitar has a bolt-on, maple neck with a rosewood finger-board. Its body is made from alder.*

**Left:** *The tone control on the New York incorporates a pull-out coil tap for the bridge humbucker. The switch below is a two-way pickup selector.*

**Above:** *This headstock has been designed to give the strings a completely straight path from nut to machine heads.*

*New Yorks were made in "Standard," "Plus" and other versions.*

Patrick James Eggle (who uses his full name on his current instruments to differentiate them from those made by Patrick Eggle Guitars) now concentrates on building flat-top and archtop acoustic guitars. After a spell working in the English county of Bedfordshire, he has relocated to North Carolina; examples of his recent output can be seen on the next four pages.

# EPIPHONE MASTERBILT

THE NEW-YORK BASED House of Stathopoulo was set up by a Greek émigré, Anastasios Stathopoulo, in 1873. The company switched from violin making to fretted instrument building under the management of Anastasios' son Epaminondas ("Epi"). Renamed Epiphone, it introduced its first archtop acoustic guitars in the 1920s, and within a decade, these were rivaling Gibsons in terms of both sales and quality.

Among the firm's most successful models were its Masterbilts, launched in 1931. The sunburst-finish Masterbilt shown here dates from about this time, and has an interesting history: in 1954, it was acquired by singer Wee Willie Harris, a seminal figure on the early

*Left*: *The Epiphone guitar factory was located in New York's Long Island City.*

*1930s Epiphone users included leading jazzmen such as George Van Eps, Allan Reuss and Dick McDonough.*

*Above:* Note the binding around the mock-tortoiseshell pickguard.

*Left:* The Masterbilt's solid spruce top delivers a pleasingly rich tone.

*Left:* Many years of stage work have left the Masterbilt with more than a few "battle scars!"

British rock and roll scene, who appeared regularly at the "2 i's" coffee bar in London's Soho (alongside such famous names as Cliff Richard and the Shadows), and went on to use the guitar throughout a lengthy subsequent showbusiness career.

*Marks like these are part of the inevitable ageing process, and do not detract from the resale value of vintage guitars like this one.*

# EPIPHONE CASINO

L IKE THE GRANADA SEEN ON OUR PREVIOUS PAGES, the Epiphone Casino, introduced in 1961, is a close copy of an existing Gibson model—in this case, the ES-330, which had made its own first appearance some two years previously. Outwardly, both guitars somewhat resembled the Gibson ES-335 (see separate entries), although the 330 and Casino were true hollow-bodies, lacking the 335's center block. They were also fitted with single-coil, P-90 pickups, rather than the 335's humbuckers.

The distinctive "dog-ear" pickup covers on the first Casinos were black, and the instruments also boasted "dot" fret markers and mock-tortoiseshell pickguards. These features were all changed within a few years: the Casino shown in our photographs, dating from 1964, has a white pickguard, nickel-covered P-90s, and "parallelogram" neck inlays.

The Casino is sometimes described as "the guitar that put Epiphone on the map," and while this statement takes no account of the company's distinguished earlier reputation, its modest "ES-330 clone" was certainly to prove highly successful with jazz, country and (increasingly) rock players.

*Mahogany is used for the Casino's neck; it has a rosewood fingerboard.*

*White pickguards first appeared on the Casino in 1963.*

*Right: Like its Gibson counterpart, the Epiphone Casino has a 16-inch wide, 1³/4-inch deep body. Its spruce top and maple back and sides are all laminated.*

The 1965 is finished in "Vintage Sunburst."

John Lennon bought his Casino in 1966, but it was made in 1965—hence the date on this replica.

# EPIPHONE CASINO (JOHN LENNON 1965)

FOLLOWING ITS INTRODUCTION in 1961, the Epiphone Casino sold well in the USA, and subsequently attracted the attention of some high-profile overseas customers: The Beatles. It was actually Paul McCartney (nominally the group's bassist) who first used one during a Beatles recording session in London in 1965. The following year, however, George Harrison and John Lennon purchased their own Casinos, and while Harrison did not play his very frequently (he was more closely associated with Gretschs), Lennon almost immediately adopted the Epiphone as his principal electric guitar, and continued to feature Casinos on live gigs and recordings for the rest of his life.

In both 1999 and 2005, Gibson celebrated John Lennon's links with this classic instrument by producing limited edition replicas of the first Epiphone Casino he owned. These have appeared in two forms: the 1965 (seen here), and the Revolution, a version of the same model with its sunburst finish stripped off; Lennon's own guitar underwent this transformation in 1968.

*Left: The Casino is fitted with two P-90 picksups; their nickel-plated covers have characteristic "dog-ears."*

*Below: The commemorative guitar's tuners, like those on John Lennon's own model, are made by Kluson.*

*This guitar is one of the "John Lennon" limited edition models issued in 2005.*

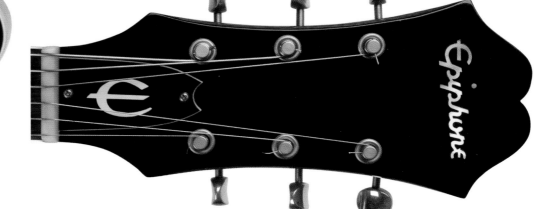

# EPIPHONE SORRENTO

*These distinctive oval fret position markers were added to the Sorrento in 1962; earlier versions of the instrument had standard dot inlays.*

**G**IBSON'S ES-125T, a thinline electric with a single P-90 pickup, was introduced in 1956. It had been conceived as a relatively low-price addition to the company's range, but, for musicians on a tight budget, an even less costly alternative model was provided four years later: the Epiphone Sorrento, whose exotic-sounding name was "borrowed" from a port town in southwest Italy.

There was certainly nothing Mediterranean about the styling of the guitar: in fact, like other Epis of the period, it closely replicated its Gibson original, and was, of course, manufactured alongside it in Kalamazoo, Michigan. Both the ES-125T and Sorrento had bodies constructed from maple plywood, and a single, sharp-horned cutaway, though the Epi (available in one- or two-pickup versions) lacked the Gibson's P-90 transducers, which were replaced with mini-humbuckers. The earliest Epiphone Sorrentos also boasted vibratos, but these were discontinued several years before the 1967 example seen in our photos was made.

***Below:** Despite the Epiphone logo, the Sorrento is essentially a slightly modified Gibson design.*

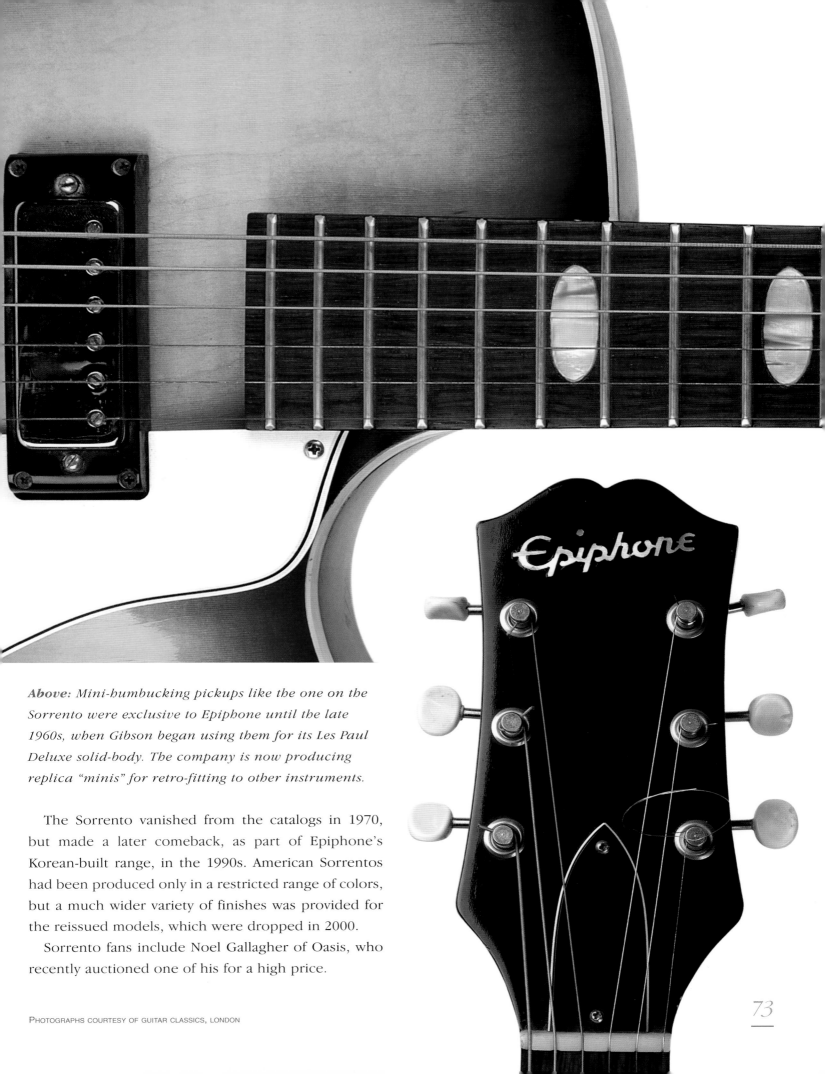

**Above:** *Mini-humbucking pickups like the one on the Sorrento were exclusive to Epiphone until the late 1960s, when Gibson began using them for its Les Paul Deluxe solid-body. The company is now producing replica "minis" for retro-fitting to other instruments.*

The Sorrento vanished from the catalogs in 1970, but made a later comeback, as part of Epiphone's Korean-built range, in the 1990s. American Sorrentos had been produced only in a restricted range of colors, but a much wider variety of finishes was provided for the reissued models, which were dropped in 2000.

Sorrento fans include Noel Gallagher of Oasis, who recently auctioned one of his for a high price.

# EPIPHONE OLYMPIC

THE ORIGINAL Epiphone Olympic was an acoustic archtop from the company's pre-war glory days. Almost a decade after its discontinuation, its name was given to a solid-body electric that debuted in 1960. The new Olympic was almost identical to the Melody Maker electric then being produced by Epi's owners, Gibson; both had single-cutaways, "3-a-side" headstocks, and pickups built into their pickguards. The next stage in the Olympic's evolution occurred in 1962, when the single-cutaway model was joined by the Olympic Special—a guitar closely resembling the double-cutaway Gibson Melody Maker introduced a year earlier and shown in the Gibson section of this book.

*Above:* The removal of this Olympic's vibrato unit has left indelible marks on its top.

*Below:* Olympics could be supplied with standard or three-quarter size bodies.

*Epiphones such as this one command lower prices than Gibsons from the same period.*

PHOTOGRAPHS COURTESY OF GUITAR CLASSICS, LONDON

*Above:* Both single and dual pickup Olympics were available. Each had these distinctive control knobs.

In 1963, the "Mark 1" 1960-style Olympic was replaced by a wholly different design sporting an asymmetrical body, with a Greek "epsilon" Epiphone symbol emblazoned on its pickguard. It retained its old, Melody Maker-like headstock for another year before acquiring a "6-a-side" tuner arrangement. It is this incarnation of the Olympic that is shown here, although our example has lost the epsilon from between its pickups, and its vibrato (added to the model as standard in the mid-60s) has been removed. Both the "regular" Olympic and the Olympic Special went out of production in 1970.

# EPIPHONE JOE PERRY LES PAUL

GIBSON'S TAKEOVER by Norlin Industries in 1969 led to major changes for Epiphone. Within a year, Epi manufacturing had been switched from Gibson headquarters at Kalamazoo, Michigan to the Far East, and the few surviving remnants of the brand's former distinctiveness were soon to vanish as it became little more than a conduit for cheap copies of existing Gibson models.

While Epiphone still serves as Gibson's lower-cost "companion marque," it has, nevertheless, recently regained a character of its own, and is currently producing a range of imaginatively designed guitars—some adapted from Gibson instruments, others wholly original. The Joe Perry Les Paul shown here falls into the former category: launched in 2004, it was inspired by a 2003 Gibson Signature Model endorsed by the Aerosmith star, and shares its predecessor's striking "Aged Tiger" finish, which was created by Perry's wife

*Right: The Joe Perry Boneyard sports classic Les Paul-style trapezoid fingerboard inlays.*

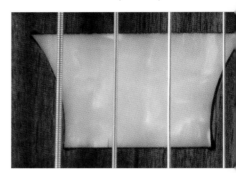

*Below: The guitar's "Aged Tiger" colored top is made from maple.*

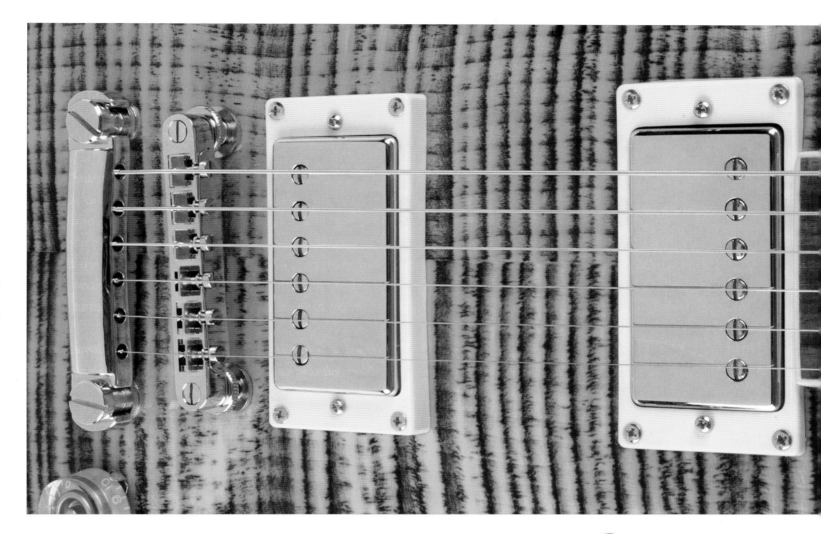

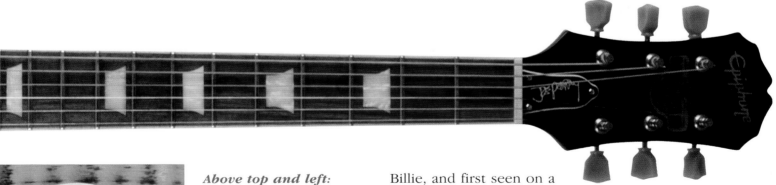

***Above top and left:***
*Cream mountings for the guitar's pickups and selector switch contrast effectively with the surrounding yellow-green body pattern.*

Billie, and first seen on a Gibson Custom Shop axe she gave him as a birthday gift. The Epiphone's other distinctive features include a "Boneyard" headstock logo: this can also be found on bottles of Perry's "Rock Your World Boneyard Brew" hot sauces! Its pickups, like those on the Signature Les Paul, are USA-made Burstbucker II and IIIs.

RHYTHM
TREBLE

# EPIPHONE BOB MARLEY LES PAUL

IN 2002, GIBSON SALUTED the late Bob Marley with a limited edition model based on his Les Paul Special (see separate entry), and a year later, Epiphone launched its own Marley guitar, "enhanced," as Epiphone President Jim Rosenberg put it at the time, "with the image, the colors and the words" of the much-missed reggae star.

The instrument's mahogany body is overlaid with a picture of Marley's face, while the rectangular position markers on its fingerboard are red, gold and green—widely regarded as Jamaica's national colors, although, contrary to what Epiphone states in its publicity, they are not precisely those of the country's official flag, which is black, gold and green. The headstock carries the words "One Love," the title of the classic Marley song featured on his 1977 *Exodus* LP (famously chosen by *Time* magazine as "the album of the [20th] century)," and there is a mocked-up "signature" on its truss-rod cover. Like its more expensive Gibson counterpart, the Epiphone Marley Commemorative Les Paul has a deliberately "worn-in" brown finish; however, pickups and hardware differ between the two models, and the Epi boasts a pleasing extra: a soft carrying case made (appropriately!) from hemp.

*Below: The Commemorative Les Paul Special (to give it its full name) has replica 1957 Alnico-V humbucking pickups, and a mahogany neck with a rosewood fingerboard.*

*Right: Unusually, the Marley is fitted with a metal nut.*

PHOTOGRAPHS COURTESY OF NEVADA MUSIC, PORTSMOUTH

**Above:** *This "seal" on the back of the Epi's headstock proclaims its special status.*

**Right:** *The instrument's "stop" tailpiece and bridge, like its tuners, are chrome-plated.*

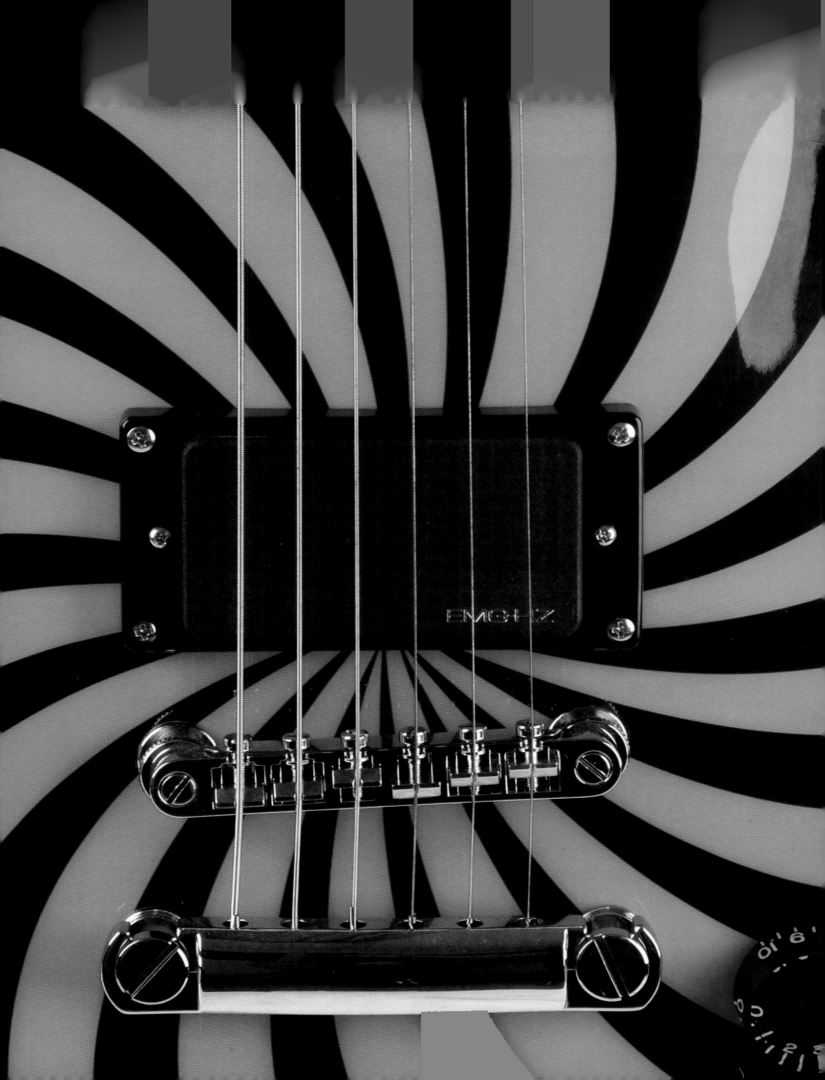

# EPIPHONE ZAKK WYLDE "BUZZSAW"

GUITARIST ZAKK WYLDE first came to prominence in the late 1980s as a member of hard rock legend Ozzy Osbourne's group, and has gone on to enjoy massive success with the band Black Label Society. Epiphone currently produces three Les Paul Specials carrying his name: all have similar specifications, but boast different, though equally flamboyant finishes.

The "Buzzsaw" model shown here is based on one of Zakk Wylde's own instruments: the design covering its top was inspired by a pattern on a cigarette lighter belonging to Black Label Society's tour manager, Tim Bolin, while the guitar's background color was chosen to match the "General Lee" automobile featured in one of Zakk's favorite TV shows, *The Dukes of Hazzard*!

*Below: Like many Les Pauls, this guitar is maple-topped, with a mahogany body.*

*Below: The instrument's neck is made from maple, and has a rosewood fingerboard.*

*Left: The Zakk Wylde "Buzzsaw" Les Paul Special has EMG humbucking pickups, and a chromed bridge and tailpiece.*

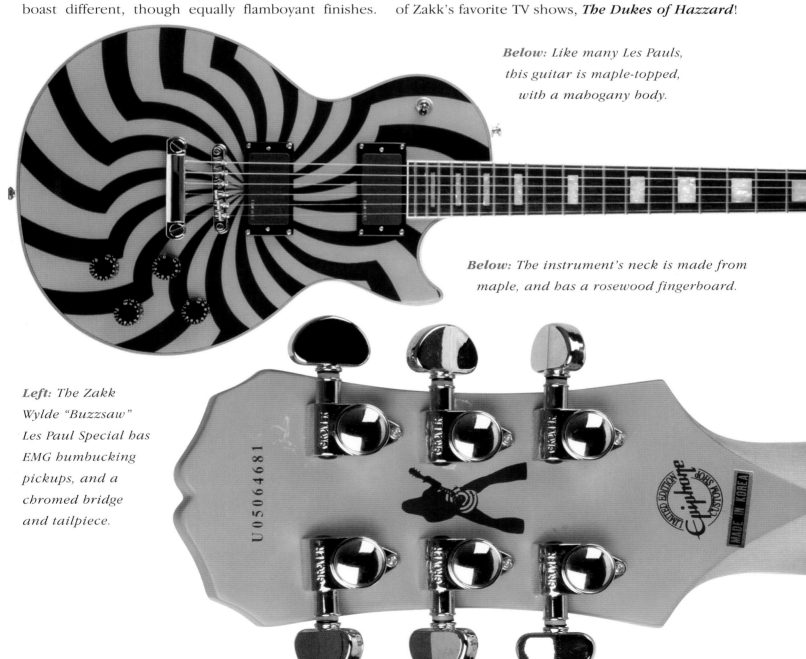

U05064681

These pickups are Alnico-V humbuckers; the bridge transducer is designed to provide an extra high output.

A new selection of "worn-in" body finishes has recently been introduced for the DOT Studio.

PHOTOGRAPHS COURTESY OF NEVADA MUSIC, PORTSMOUTH

# EPIPHONE DOT STUDIO

THE EPIPHONE DOT, launched in 1996, was closely based on the classic Gibson ES-335 "semi-hollow" electric (see separate entries). The DOT Studio, while retaining the shape and basic attributes of its predecessor and the Gibson original, is simpler and more streamlined than either of them. Its two pickups have no individual volume and tone controls, and the traditional 335-style pickguard and fretboard position markers (the "dots" for which the model was named)

have vanished, while the sunburst, cherry and natural finishes provided for the older DOT have been replaced with a choice of striking new colors. These include "Lemon" (as seen here), "Tomato," "Ice Blue" and "Dolphin Gray."

In spite of its pared-down features, the DOT Studio, which is made in China, succeeds in retaining a good deal of the magic of the 335, and is undeniably stylish; it also represents remarkable value for money.

*Right: Black (instead of chrome) hardware is an unusual but effective design choice for this model.*

# ESP LTD TRUCKSTER

ESP—THE INITIALS STAND for "Electric Sound Products"—began in 1975 as a retail outlet in Tokyo, selling audio gear and, later, high-performance replacement parts for guitarists wishing to 'hot-rod' their instruments. As the company's fame spread, particularly among the heavy metal fraternity, it started marketing its products more widely, and eventually switched from manufacturing components to full-time production of guitars and basses.

In 1991, Megadeth founder member James Hetfield began using ESP instruments, and for the group's 2003/4 "St. Anger" tour, the firm built him a heavily modified version of its successful Truckster solid-body. Its specification and appearance were used as the basis

*Below: The switch beside the neck is a dummy, as it is on James Hetfield's own Truckster. The real picksup switch is beside the volume and tone knobs.*

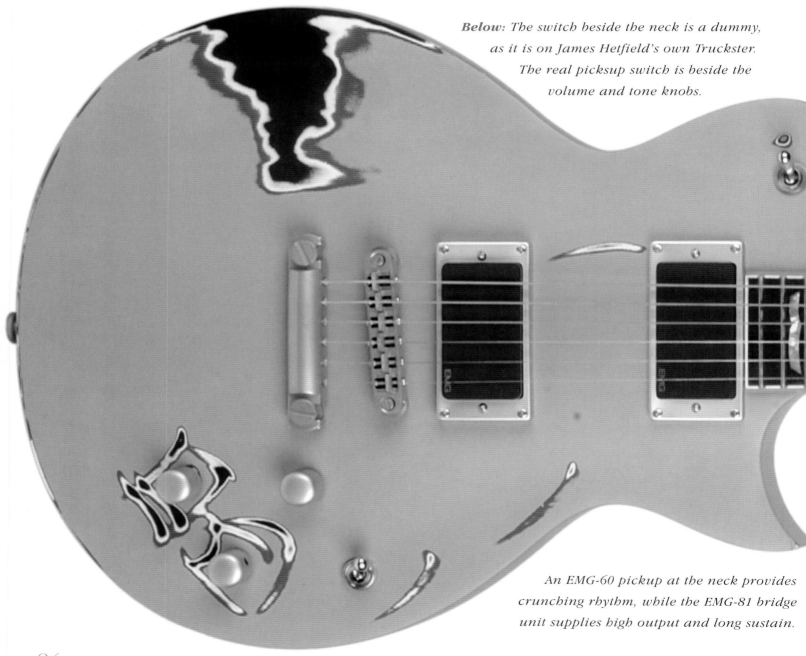

*An EMG-60 pickup at the neck provides crunching rhythm, while the EMG-81 bridge unit supplies high output and long sustain.*

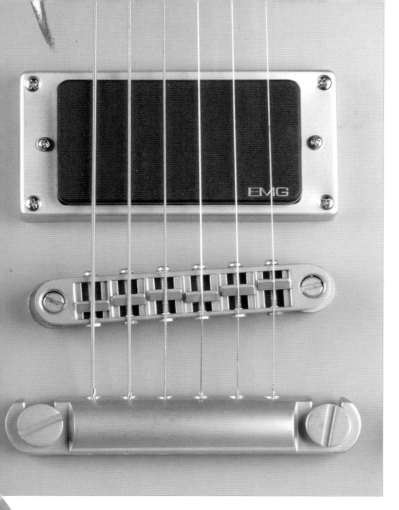

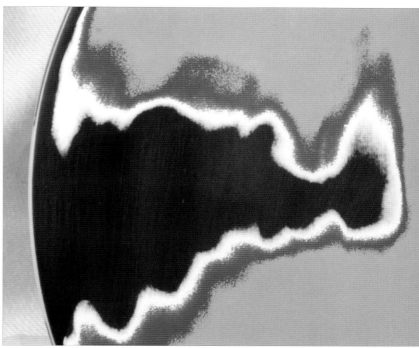

*Above:* The "stud"-style tailpiece seen here is a locking model made by TonePros and was designed to increase tuning stability—which is also enhanced by the guitar's locking tuners.

*Above:* One of the simulated blemishes on the instrument's gray primer finish. These replicate the ones on James Hetfield's own "axe," and certainly supply an authentically "road-worn" look!

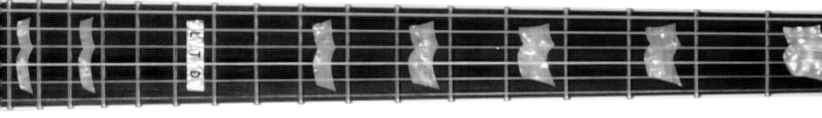

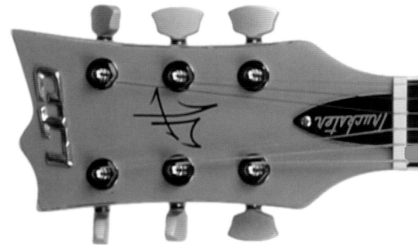

for ESP's Hetfield "Signature Model" Truckster, which debuted in 2005, and is available under the ESP marque and as part of the firm's less expensive LTD range (as seen here).

The "axe" has a mahogany body and neck, and pickups made by EMG ("Electro-Magnetic Resonator") of Santa Rosa, California. Its 22-fret neck has a rosewood fingerboard and "extra-jumbo" width frets, and its Sperzel locking tuners help to ensure that the guitar stays in tune however vigorously it is played!

# FENDER "NO-CASTER" REPLICA

LEO FENDER (1909-1991) had been fascinated by electronics since boyhood, and, after a brief stint working as an accountant, he set up a radio repair shop in his hometown of Fullerton, California, in about 1939. One of his customers, local musician Clayton O. ("Doc") Kauffman, was also a skilled inventor and soon he and Fender were collaborating on the production of Hawaiian guitars and amplifiers. These were sold under the K&F brand name, and after the partnership ended in 1946, Leo founded his own Fender Electric Instrument Company, also based in Fullerton.

Three years later, Fender began developing a solid-bodied electric for "Spanish-style" playing. Unlike the elegant archtop models then being made by other

*Above: This method of fastening strings inside the Fender guitar's body is straightforward and secure.*

*The Fender's "six-a-side" headstock was a novelty in 1950.*

*Above: Ash was used for the bodies on early Fender electrics. The first prototypes had no truss rods; these were added later to prevent the instruments' necks from warping.*

firms, this guitar had an almost crude appearance, but, with its wooden-slab body and bolted-on neck, was easy to manufacture and repair. Named the Esquire, and fitted with a single pickup, it was first shown to the music trade in 1950. Leo subsequently changed various aspects of its specification, and added a second pickup; the revised model, rechristened Broadcaster, went into production in late 1950. However, in February 1951 the Gretsch company, which made Broadkaster drumkits, demanded the removal of the word "Broadcaster" from the guitar on the grounds of trademark infringement. For a while, therefore, new instruments left Fullerton with no names on their headstocks: these were later termed "No-casters," and a modern replica of one is shown here.

*Right:* The simplicity of the Fender guitar's construction took the firm's rivals by surprise— but many were soon copying Leo's innovations.

# FENDER 1952 TELECASTER REPLICA

T HE DISPUTE WITH GRETSCH over the use of the word "Broadcaster" left Leo Fender without a name for his innovative solid electric guitar. The decision to christen it Telecaster is usually attributed to Don Randall, whose Santa Ana-based Radio & Television Equipment Company acted as Fender's distributors. Thanks to the efforts of his sales force, the Tele was soon the talk of the music business—where some traditionalists reacted with distaste (and even outrage) to the spartan simplicity of its design, while others, including many professional players, were thrilled by its convenience and practicality.

Leo Fender himself continued to modify and refine the guitar's features throughout its early life; one significant change, introduced in 1952, removed its "deep soft rhythm" circuit, and the "blend" function for its two pickups, substituting the simpler switching described in the caption below.

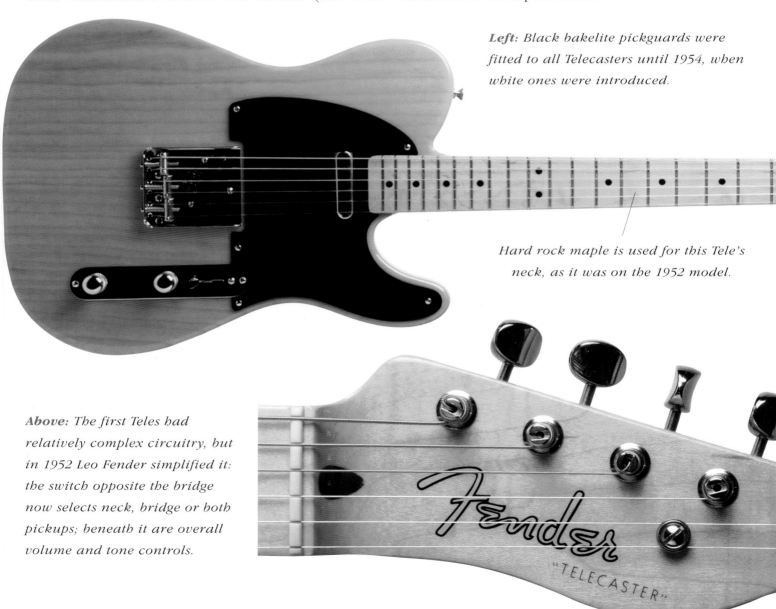

*Left: Black bakelite pickguards were fitted to all Telecasters until 1954, when white ones were introduced.*

*Hard rock maple is used for this Tele's neck, as it was on the 1952 model.*

***Above:*** *The first Teles had relatively complex circuitry, but in 1952 Leo Fender simplified it: the switch opposite the bridge now selects neck, bridge or both pickups; beneath it are overall volume and tone controls.*

PHOTOGRAPHS COURTESY OF PEACH, BLAKE END, BRAINTREE

*Right:* Genuine 1952 Fender Telecasters are rare, and sell at many times the instrument's original price of just under $190. However, this skilfully aged replica is an effective "stand-in."

One of the Tele's selling points was its "modern styled head...with a stright pull for all strings."

These tuners closely resemble the Kluson units used by Fender in the 1950s.

# FENDER PRECISION BASS

THE STAND-UP DOUBLE BASS, played pizzicato, had been a fixture in many popular music combos for much of the first half of the 20th century. However, it had three major drawbacks. The first was its limited volume: against a brass or sax section, let alone a drum kit or an electric guitar, a string bass would frequently struggle to be heard. Secondly, its size and unwieldiness created headaches (and backaches!) onstage—while in transit between gigs, the only space that could often be found for it was on the roof-racks of musicians' cars or tour buses. Last, but not least, were its intonation problems: novice bassists, with no frets to guide their left hands, could play excruciatingly out of tune; and even their more experienced colleagues sometimes struggled to stay in pitch when unable to hear themselves properly amid

***Above:*** *The Precision's metal pickup cover is sometimes removed by players who find it obtrusive.*

***Below:*** *The "Dakota Red" finish on the 1961 model shown here has been expertly renewed.*

*The Precision Bass's fingerboard is made from rosewood.*

PHOTOGRAPHS COURTESY OF GUITAR JUNCTION, WORTHING

*Over this instrument's long life, its tortoiseshell pickguard has very slightly shrunk.*

**Above:** *A close-up of the area where the Precision's maple neck meets its alder body. Screwed to the pickguard adjacent to the strings is a plastic finger rest.*

the noisier instruments on the bandstand.

Leo Fender solved all three difficulties with his Precision bass guitar, launched in 1951. Its slim, solid body was far smaller and lighter than its "stand-up" cousin's; its single pickup supplied a clear, sustained sound from its strings; while its fretted neck

guaranteed accurate intonation, and also made it easy for regular guitarists to "double" on the new instrument. The Precision quickly caught on, and soon, rival firms, including some that had initially dismissed Leo's instrument as a gimmick were eagerly designing their own electric basses.

STRATOCASTER

# FENDER STRATOCASTER ("RELIC")

LEO FENDER'S STRATOCASTER appeared in 1954: his company's own publicity hailed it as "a revolutionary new instrument...years ahead in design [and] unequalled in performance," and it quickly took the guitar world by storm. Unlike its predecessor, the Telecaster, it sported a vibrato mechanism controlled by its pivoting bridge section, three pickups, a double cutaway, and a contoured body designed to be more comfortable to hold than the Tele's. (Interestingly, it was this latter feature that seemed to excite some contemporary commentators the most: in May 1954, **Music Trades** magazine observed that it "actually seems to make the guitar a part of the player...and must be seen and tried to be appreciated.")

Early Stratocasters are among the most collectible of all Fenders, and change hands at many times their original $249.50 price. For many enthusiasts, however, the deliberately aged "Relic" models first produced by the Fender Custom Shop in 1995 are pleasing and

*Left: The recessed jack socket was another of the Stratocaster's innovative design features.*

*Below: This Relic Strat dates from 1996; like the original, its body is made from ash.*

*Screws and other hardware are as carefully "aged" as the guitar's body and neck.*

*Right:* One of the pioneers of "aging" guitars is Vince Cunetto, a member of the original team that produced this and other "Relics" at Fender.

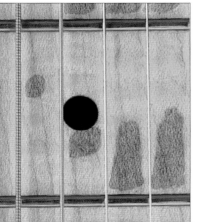

*Left:* These fake "wear spots" replicate the effects of decades of finger pressure and sweat on the Stratocaster's fingerboard.

desirable substitutes for one of these originals. The Relic seen here is a replica of the 1956 "custom-color" Strat with gold fittings used by singer and guitarist Mary Kaye—a major 50s and 60s star, whose trio enjoyed hits with songs such as "You Can't Be True Dear" and "Do You Believe In Dreams?"

*Left:* The Stratocaster's pickups and controls are all directly attached to its pickguard.

This is the 5-way pickup selector mentioned in the main text.

# FENDER MARK KNOPFLER STRATOCASTER

GUITARISTS WERE SOON taking advantage of the Fender Stratocaster's capabilities—and occasionally using it in ways that surprised its creator. Its original pickup switch, for example, was a three-way device that "officially" enabled only one transducer to be selected at a time; however, by careful positioning, it was possible to activate two pickups (neck and center, or center and bridge) simultaneously, creating a characteristic, "out-of-phase" sound that would soon be widely exploited. It was not until 1977 (according to information from A.R. Duchossoir's exhaustive study of the Stratocaster) that the switch was replaced with a five-way component; in the meantime, players often resorted to using matchsticks to hold it in these intermediate settings.

Over the years, some performers have taken more extensive liberties with Leo Fender's design—changing pickups, adding electronics, and sometimes even fitting alternative vibrato units—but for others, the unaltered Stratocaster remains an unsurpassable tool. Among this category of contented musicians is Mark Knopfler, whose 1961 "Fiesta Red" model has featured on many of his classic recordings (including, most famously, Dire Straits' 1978/9 hit "Sultans of Swing"); he also continues to use it extensively onstage and in the studio. In 2003, Fender began producing replicas of Knopfler's Strat, one of which is shown here. Its woods and colors all match those of a '60s instrument, although it does have a 5-way pickup selector!

*Below: The guitar's neck is maple, with a rosewood fretboard.*

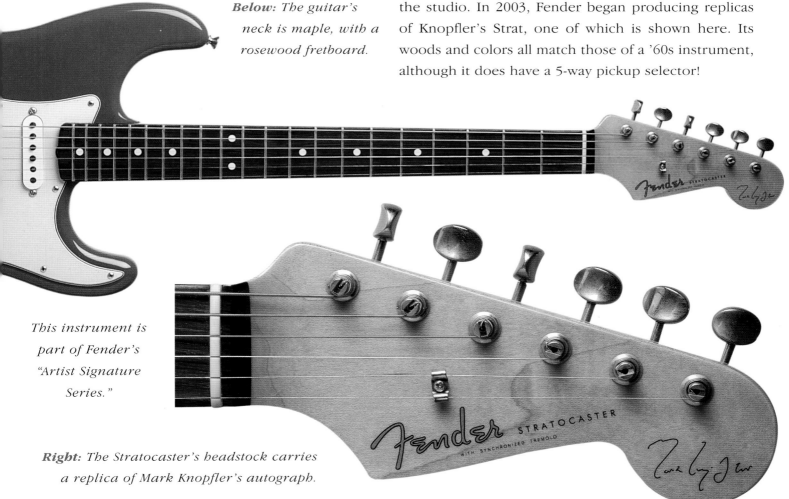

*This instrument is part of Fender's "Artist Signature Series."*

*Right: The Stratocaster's headstock carries a replica of Mark Knopfler's autograph.*

# FENDER JAZZMASTER

WITHIN A FEW YEARS of launching the Stratocaster, Leo Fender was working on a major new electric guitar, the Jazzmaster. As its name suggested, this was aimed at the jazz fraternity rather than the rockers, country pickers and bluesmen that had favored the Telecaster and Strat, and it featured mellower sounding pickups, plus a switchable "rhythm circuit" for the neck transducer, allowing its volume and tone to be preset for playing backing chords. There was also a locking vibrato, and a body that was shaped to maximize comfort for seated players.

The guitar debuted in 1958 (though a prototype survives from the previous year), but failed to win over many jazz performers, and attracted a good deal of criticism for its unstable bridge, excessive weight, and odd shape: Fender plant manager Forrest White once likened it to a "pregnant duck"! Nevertheless, it has had many admirers, especially among "surf" guitarists and (later) punk and indie bands, and is recognized as a genuine, if quirky, Fender classic.

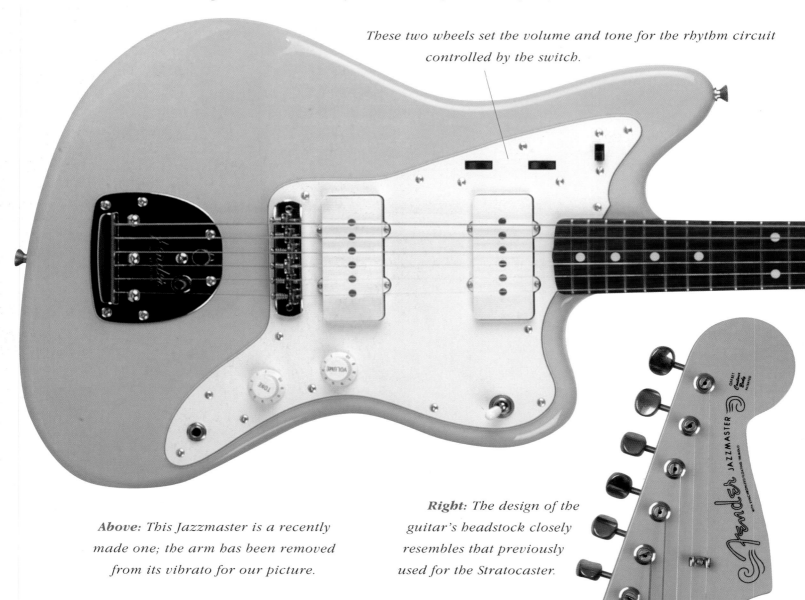

These two wheels set the volume and tone for the rhythm circuit controlled by the switch.

**Above:** *This Jazzmaster is a recently made one; the arm has been removed from its vibrato for our picture.*

**Right:** *The design of the guitar's headstock closely resembles that previously used for the Stratocaster.*

**Below:** *The strange, asymmetrical shape of the Jazzmaster's body was designed principally for the comfort of seated players, but did not improve its popularity with the jazz performers it was aimed at.*

**JAZZ BASS®**
MADE IN U.S.A

# FENDER JAZZ BASS (22-FRET)

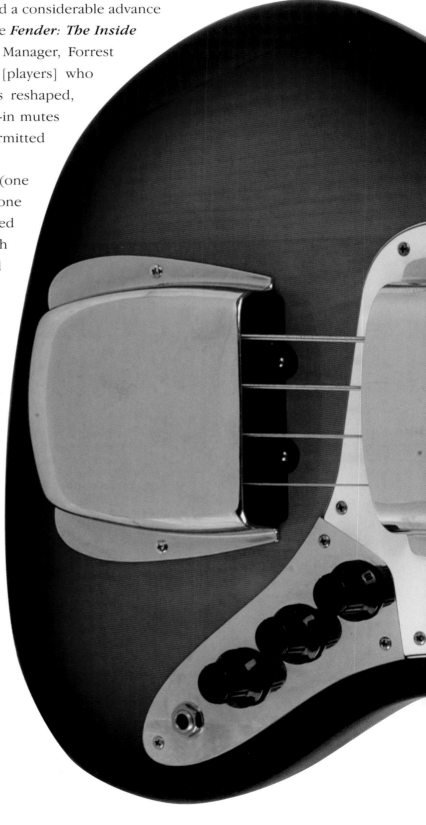

INTRODUCED IN 1960, the Jazz Bass represented a considerable advance on Fender's previous Precision model: to quote *Fender: The Inside Story* (1994) by the company's former General Manager, Forrest White, it "offered that little bit extra for those [players] who desired it." Most immediately noticeable was its reshaped, "off-set" body; there were also two pickups, built-in mutes for each string, and a narrower neck that permitted nimbler fingerwork.

Early Jazz Basses featured two "stacked" knobs (one for each pickup), which combined volume and tone controls on a single shaft. This arrangement proved rather unpopular, and it was later replaced with a three-knob configuration, which provided individual volume and overall tone controls. The

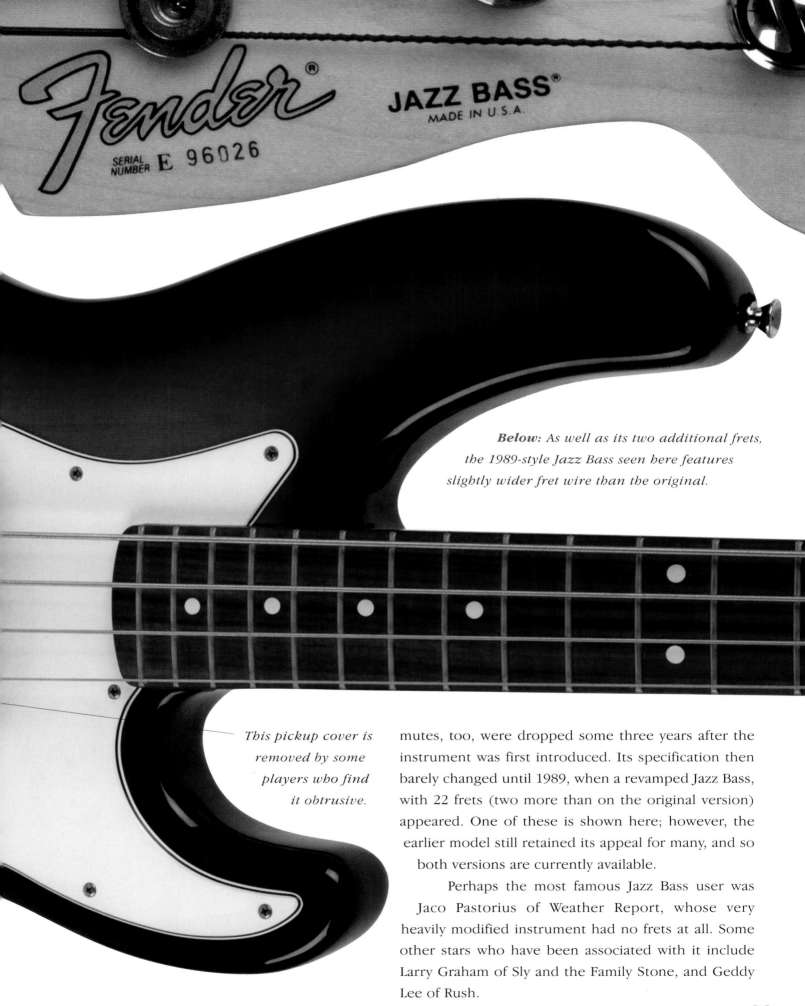

**Fender** ®

**JAZZ BASS** ®
MADE IN U.S.A.

SERIAL NUMBER E 96026

*Below: As well as its two additional frets, the 1989-style Jazz Bass seen here features slightly wider fret wire than the original.*

*This pickup cover is removed by some players who find it obtrusive.*

mutes, too, were dropped some three years after the instrument was first introduced. Its specification then barely changed until 1989, when a revamped Jazz Bass, with 22 frets (two more than on the original version) appeared. One of these is shown here; however, the earlier model still retained its appeal for many, and so both versions are currently available.

Perhaps the most famous Jazz Bass user was Jaco Pastorius of Weather Report, whose very heavily modified instrument had no frets at all. Some other stars who have been associated with it include Larry Graham of Sly and the Family Stone, and Geddy Lee of Rush.

# JAGUAR

# FENDER JAGUAR

IN ITS 1962 CATALOG, Fender proudly announced "the newest addition to [its] line of Fine Electric Instruments;" named the Jaguar. It had a number of novel features, including a neck with a 24-inch scale (1½ inches shorter than a Telecaster or Stratocaster) that was designed to appeal to musicians with smaller hands, and a string mute, installed between the back pickup and the bridge, that could, as the company's publicity put it, "be activated or disengaged by the light touch of a finger."

It was possible to combine either or both of the Jaguar's pickups with what became widely known as a "strangle" switch, which removed most of the

**Above:** *Two of these three switches control the Jaguar's pickups; the third engages the guitar's bass-cut (a.k.a. "strangle") circuitry.*

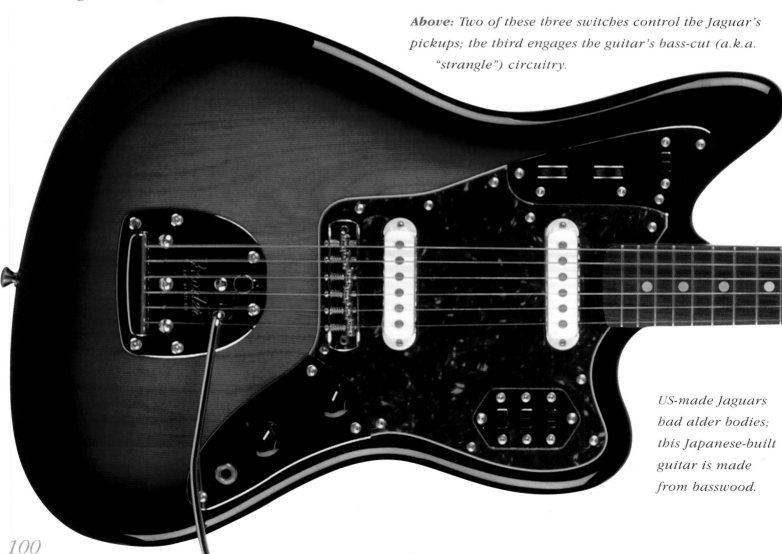

*US-made Jaguars had alder bodies; this Japanese-built guitar is made from basswood.*

PHOTOGRAPHS COURTESY OF AMERICAN GUITAR CENTRE & BASSWORLD, TONBRIDGE

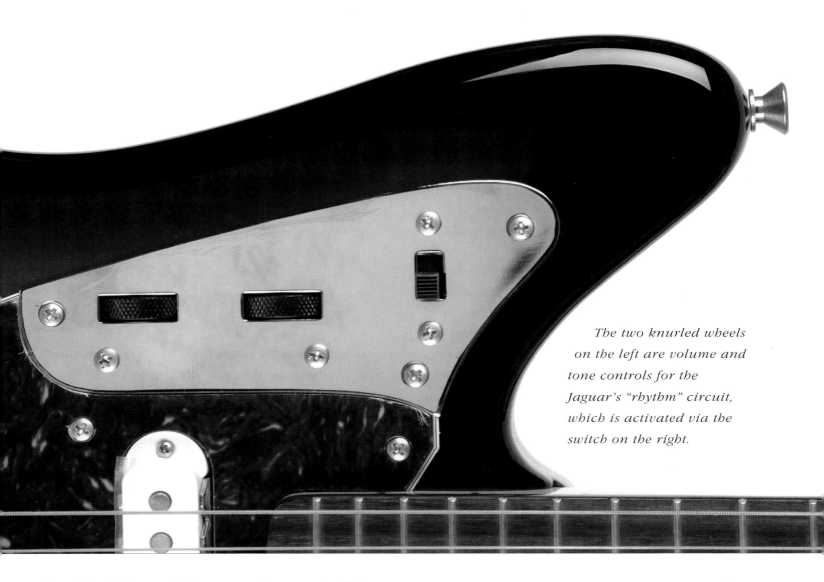

*The two knurled wheels on the left are volume and tone controls for the Jaguar's "rhythm" circuit, which is activated via the switch on the right.*

**Below:** *The 22-fret neck (one more than a typical Tele or Strat) provides an extra helf step at the top of the fingerboard.*

instrument's bass response, while a separate set of controls allowed players to pre-set volume and tone levels for rhythm (see captions). The guitar was also fitted with a "Synchronized tremolo" (like many manufacturers, Fender uses the term "tremolo" as a misnomer for "vibrato"), which could be locked down when not required.

Though the instrument was discontinued in 1974, it has since developed something of a cult following. The model shown here is a modern example, made in Japan; it lacks the bridge cover that would have been found on an original US-manufactured Jaguar.

**MUSTANG BASS**

# FENDER MUSTANG BASS

FENDER'S MUSTANG BASS, designed to match the 6-string Mustang shown on the previous two pages, was introduced in 1966. A beginners' model with a single, split-coil pickup not unlike the one found on the Fender Precision, its chief selling point was its 30-inch scale (a full four inches shorter than the scale length on the Precision or Jazz basses), which, as the

**Left:** *The Mustang bass's split pickup is, to quote Fender, "positioned for maximum string response."*

company explained in its publicity, made the Mustang "ideal for the student and musician with short reach." The bass was initially offered in the same red, white and blue colors as the Mustang guitar; by 1970, however, both instruments had been restyled in what Fender termed "competition colors," with three stripes overlaid across the upper edges of their bodies, near where the player's right forearm rests. These bold finishes were replaced by more conventional ones in the middle of the decade.

Despite its lowly status in the catalog, from which it was temporarily dropped in the early 1980s, the Mustang bass has attracted a surprising number of high profile players, including Tina Weymouth of Talking Heads, and, on at least one occasion, Bill Wyman of the

**Below:** *The model is currently made in "Fiesta Red" (as seen here) or "Vintage White."*

*The instrument's body is made from alder.*

PHOTOGRAPHS COURTESY OF NEVADA MUSIC, PORTSMOUTH

**Below:** *The bass has a maple neck, with a 19-fret rosewood fingerboard.*

Rolling Stones. Many other musicians, amateur and professional, have also retained a soft spot for it, and Fender's decision, in 2002, to start producing the model again was warmly welcomed.

The Mustang featured in our photographs was built by Fender Japan in 2005.

# FENDER "FLORAL" TELECASTER (JAPAN)

THE FENDER TELECASTER is among the least "fancy" of instruments, and its long-established status as the guitar of choice for unpretentious, hard-gigging musicians can lead us to picture it only with plain (and often somewhat battered) finishes. In the wake of the 1967 "Summer of Love," however, Fender made the surprising decision to start producing Telecasters and Telecaster basses decorated in hippy-influenced "blue floral" and "pink paisley." These appeared in 1968, and the paisley model achieved considerable prominence when James Burton, lead guitarist for Elvis Presley, began using it on live shows and TV appearances with "The King." Despite this extensive exposure, the unusually finished Teles did not sell in large numbers, and they were discontinued in 1969.

Since then, a combination of nostalgia for the 1960s and changing tastes has led to original examples of these instruments becoming highly sought after; those in the market for one have included country star Marty Stuart, who told **Vintage Guitar** magazine in 1995, "I've got three paisleys right now, but I'm really in search for a classic floral Tele." Unfortunately, finding an immaculate specimen can be difficult, as the guitars' polyester-coated finish tends to fade with the passage of time, except around the area covered by their transparent pickguards. A possible solution to this problem (though obviously not one for purists!) is to abandon the search for a 1968/9 model and settle, instead, for a "reissue" floral or paisley Telecaster like the one here, which is produced by Fender's Japanese division. These debuted in the mid-1980s, but then disappeared from the catalog before being reintroduced in 2002/3.

*Left: This replica Tele has a 1969-style headstock with larger lettering than was used on pre-'69 instruments.*

*Above: Like many Far-Eastern made Fenders, our floral Telecaster has a basswood body; its neck and fingerboard are maple, and its "vintage-style" bridge is chrome-plated.*

The Electric XII's body is made of alder, and this example has a sunburst finish. Various other colors were obtainable at a surcharge to its standard price of $339.

**Below:** The guitar's pickups can be used singly or together, and there is also a "deep-tone" setting which can be switched into circuit via the selector knob on its top.

# FENDER ELECTRIC XII

BY THE MID-1960s, the rich, jangling timbre of the 12-string guitar was the sound of the moment, and Leo Fender hoped that his Electric XII solid-body, introduced in 1965, would give more established 12-string manufacturers such as Rickenbacker a run for their money. The new guitar had a strikingly shaped headstock (nicknamed "the hockey-stick" by admirers and detractors alike), and a pair of pickups whose split groups of pole-pieces were intended to enrich the tone of the lower strings and add additional edge and clarity to their treble counterparts. It also boasted an ingeniously designed bridge, patented by Fender the following year, that offered more scope for string adjustment than the units fitted to many other 12-strings, improving intonation and making the guitar easier to finger. Sadly, although the Electric XII attracted several leading players, including The Who's Pete Townshend, and Jimmy Page of Led Zeppelin, who used it memorably on "Stairway to Heaven" (1971), it failed to sell well, and was discontinued in 1969.

*The Electric XII's pickups are mounted on its bound plastic pickguard.*

*This metal guide straightens the path of the inner strings as they approach the nut.*

# FENDER CORONADO II ANTIGUA

IN JANUARY 1965, Columbia Broadcasting System (CBS) purchased the Fender Electric Instrument Company for just over $13,000,000. The change of ownership was precipitated by Leo Fender's indifferent health, and the need to fund his business's expansion; he was retained as a consultant to the firm, but played little or no role in its future development, and was prevented, by the terms of his deal with CBS, from setting up any guitar- or amplifier-making enterprises of his own until 1970. His subsequent career is detailed in the Music Man and G&L entries later in this book.

With new management came new products, among the most striking of which were the Coronados—the firm's first-ever non-solid body electrics, designed by Roger Rossmeisl, who had previously worked for Rickenbacker. The Coronado I and II (with one and two pickups respectively) were launched in 1966, together with a 12-stringer. For a while, these were produced in both regular and stained-beech "Wildwood" versions, and in 1968, a further color

*Above right*: The "6-a-side" headstock is one familar feature retained on the hollowbody Coronado.

*Right*: Antigua coloring was later applied to several Fender solids, including Telecaster and Stratocasters.

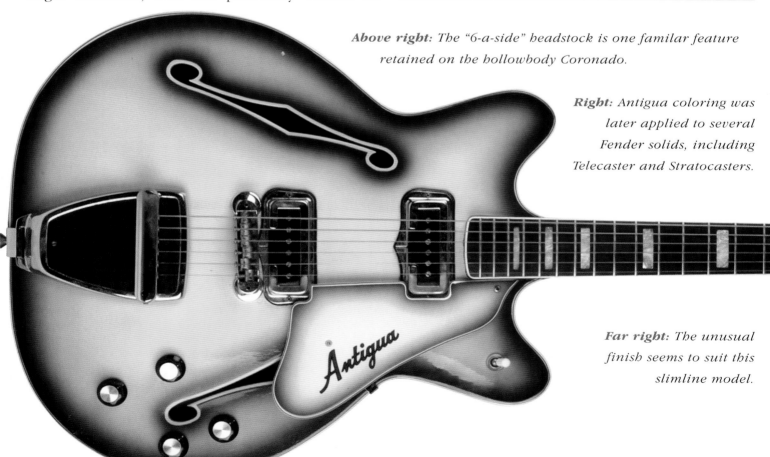

*Far right*: The unusual finish seems to suit this slimline model.

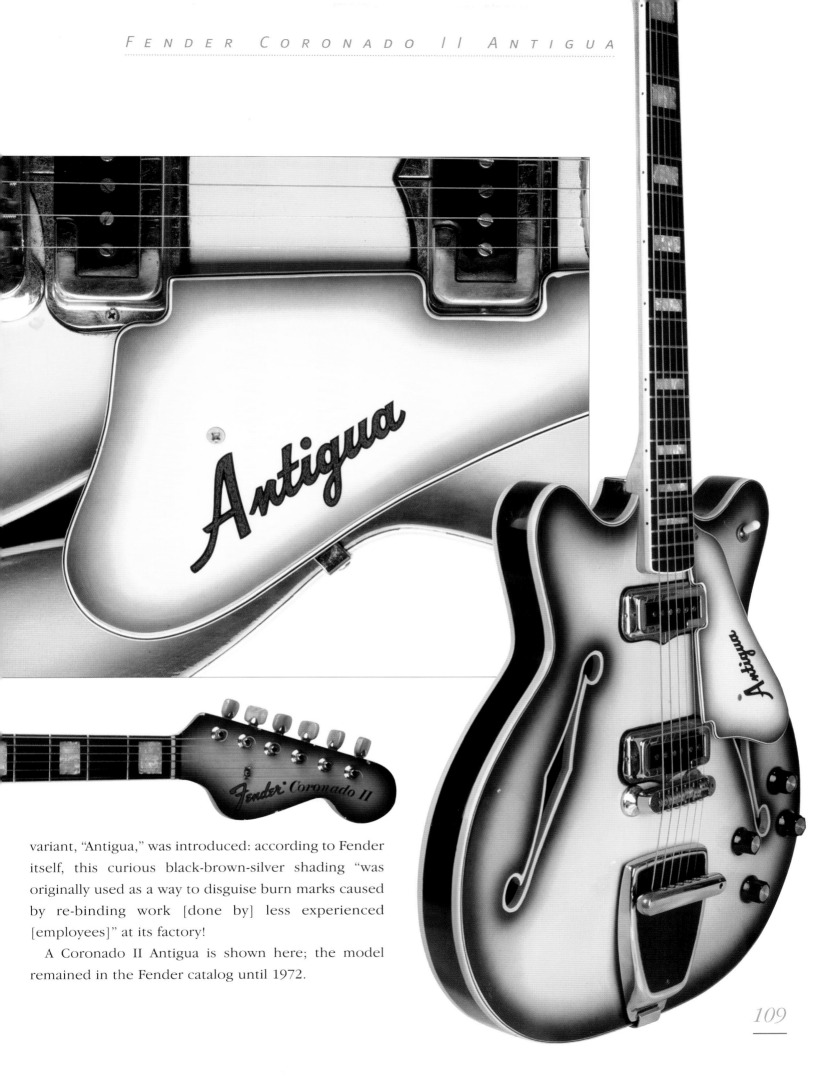

variant, "Antigua," was introduced: according to Fender itself, this curious black-brown-silver shading "was originally used as a way to disguise burn marks caused by re-binding work [done by] less experienced [employees]" at its factory!

A Coronado II Antigua is shown here; the model remained in the Fender catalog until 1972.

# FENDER FRETLESS PRECISION BASS

FRETLESS BASSES WERE RARITIES during the mid-to-late 1960s: the highest profile model then in circulation was Ampeg's AUB-1, introduced, along with its fretted cousin, the AEB-1, in 1966. Ampeg aimed the AUB-1 primarily at stand-up players who wanted to make the transition to bass guitar, but it was also adopted by a handful of rock performers, including Rick Danko of The Band, a former Fender Jazz Bass devotee. Though still relatively small, the fretless market was one that Fender soon decided to involve itself in, and it introduced a fretless option on its classic Precision bass in 1970.

This instrument (an example of which, from the mid-70s, can be seen here) initially sold steadily rather than spectacularly, but its profile received a boost when John Paul Jones of Led Zeppelin began using one onstage in 1972. It is now regarded as a classic, though, inevitably, it has been overshadowed by the fame of the fretless Fender Jazz bass, due to the latter's associations with the late Jaco Pastorius—who himself

*Below: Aside from its fretless neck, this instrument is a standard Precision model.*

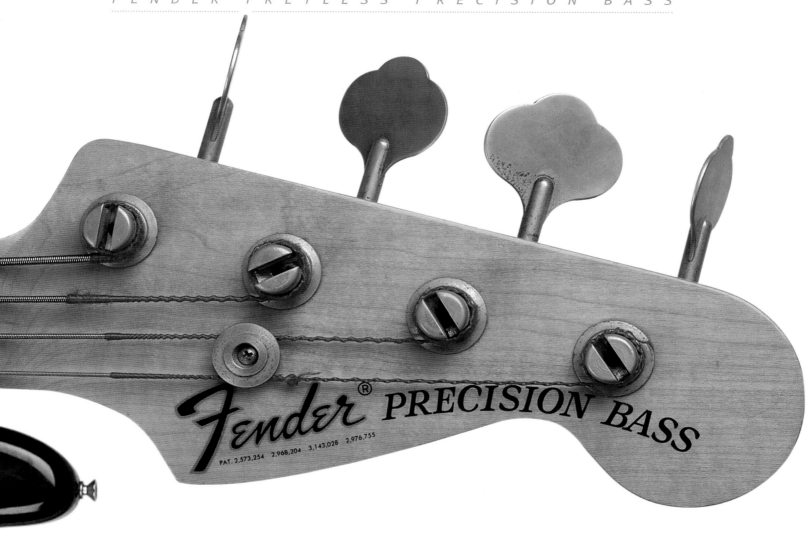

**Bottom:** *The Fretless Precision has a curved rosewood fingerboard; the neck beneath it is made from hard rock maple.*

**Above:** *A 1970s Fender catalog described the Precision as "the most well-known and widely used electric bass in the world."*

removed the frets from his own standard Jazz model, and went on to feature it with the great jazz-rock band Weather Report, as well as on his own solo albums and session dates.

In 2006, Fender launched a new fretless Precision: it carries the signature of Tony Franklin, the English-born musician (famous for his work with Paul Rodgers and Jimmy Page in The Firm) who is also the company's Artist Relations Manager.

# FENDER TELECASTER THINLINE

IN THE MID-TO-LATE 1960s, Fender and its CBS masters were hungry for novelty—and the increased profits that it could bring. Having already ventured into unfamiliar territory with its hollowbody Coronado range (see separate entry), the company now began experimenting with one of its staple products, the Telecaster. There had been concern that some players found the Tele too heavy, and in 1968, an attempt was made to solve this problem by routing out substantial sections of its body, adding an f-hole, and marketing the result as the Telecaster Thinline. Offered in a choice of "natural" finishes (mahogany or ash), the adapted Tele underwent a further modification in 1972, when its single-coil pickups were replaced with humbuckers designed by former Gibson staffer Seth Lover (these are fitted to the Thinline in our photos). The instrument was discontinued some six years later.

*Right*: The classic Fender pickup controls look rather different when surrounded by a glossy, smartly bound pickguard.

*Below*: The Thinline shown here dates from 1972, and has an ash body.

*Thanks to its carved out body, the Thinline is about 50% lighter than a standard Telecaster.*

*The classic Tele neck remains unaffected by the changes that created the Thinline.*

**Below:** *This Telecaster Deluxe's alder body is finished in three-color sunburst, an option costing an extra $50. The model's "regular" colors are black and walnut.*

*Like the original Deluxe, the modern replica has a smart, three-ply black pickguard.*

# FENDER TELECASTER DELUXE

THE SETH LOVER "WIDE RANGE" humbucking pickups installed on the Thinline Telecaster (see previous pages) reappeared on two other early-70s Teles: a new version of the Custom, fitted with a neck-position humbucker; and the Deluxe, which boasted twin double-coil units, and debuted in 1972. Like the revamped Custom, the Deluxe had individual volume and tone knobs for its transducers, with a small pickup selector on its upper bass bout replacing the chunky, but eminently practical "lever-switch" designed by Leo Fender. However, it differed from its predecessor in several key respects: its maple neck incorporated a Stratocaster-style headstock instead of the regular, narrower Tele one; it had a more sophisticated, fully adjustable bridge; and it was, for a while, available with a vibrato.

The Deluxe was discontinued in 1981, but made a comeback in January 2004: a recently-made example is shown here. Though the reissue's specification is similar to its predecessor's, its pickups have been re-designed.

*Above: The all-maple neck and fingerboard on the Tele Deluxe are authentic features derived from the 1972 model.*

*Bridge, pickup covers and other hardware on this instrument are chrome-plated.*

# FENDER TELECASTER, 1976

AMONG CONNOISSEURS of vintage guitars, Fenders made before 1965 are widely regarded as superior to those produced during the period in which CBS owned the company (1965-1985). This judgment fails to recognize the fine quality of many CBS-era instruments; the 1976 Telecaster in our photos, with its elegant sunburst finish, fast neck, and gutsy tone, is an excellent, highly collectible model. Nevertheless, it is a fair generalization that, to quote music historian Richard E. Smith, the firm's "older guitar[s] were not necessarily better, [but] most of the better guitars were old;" and by the mid-70s, ongoing problems at Fender's Fullerton, California headquarters were leading to an undeniable decline in standards.

Lack of investment, remote and sometimes rather misguided management, and stiff competition from Far Eastern manufacturers have all been cited as contributing factors to Fender's difficulties, and in 1981, CBS brought in a team of experienced music business executives (including Bill Schultz, who became president of Fender that year) in an attempt to sort matters out once and for all. Their arrival represented a turning point for the troubled company, and in 1985, Schultz headed the group that purchased it from CBS in a deal worth $12.5 million.

Bill Schultz went on to serve as Fender CEO for the

*Below: This Tele's "Three-tone Sunburst" finish is still in pristine condition.*

*Left: The Fender "F" was registered as a trademark in 1967, but first used several years earlier..*

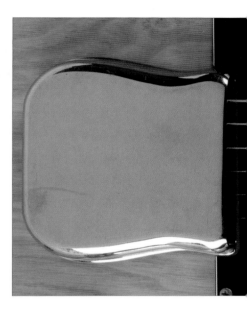

*Above: The Telecaster's bridge cover is often removed by players... and sometimes used as an ashtray!*

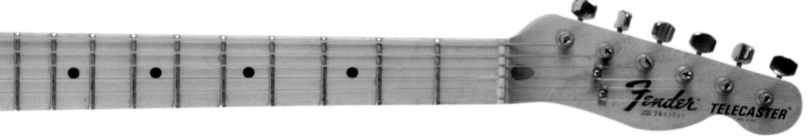

next two decades; during this period, the firm has prospered and expanded, establishing a new manufacturing base in Corona, California, as well as a corporate headquarters in Scottsdale, Arizona.

*Left: The first two digits of this serial number are an abbreviated indication of its year of manufacture.*

# FENDER BULLET

THOUGH THE "CBS YEARS" are generally regarded as difficult and even bleak ones for Fender, the company continued to employ and train some outstanding craftsmen during this period. Among them was John Page, who began his career at the firm in 1978, and was quickly promoted to its Research & Development Department, where he worked for a while alongside one of Leo Fender's most distinguished former lieutenants, Freddie Tavares.

In the early 1980s, Page was given the task of developing a replacement "student" guitar for the Mustang (see separate entry), which had recently been discontinued. His design needed to be inspiring for beginners, robust, and, perhaps most of all, cost-

effective—as by then, Fender, like other US-based instrument manufacturers, was under threat from the growing number of cheap Far Eastern imports flooding into the domestic market. Page responded by creating the Bullet, a two-pickup model with a Telecaster-style neck and a Stratocaster-like body. It sold for $189, and debuted in 1981.

The first Bullets, including the one in our pictures, whose serial number indicates a manufacturing date of 1981 or 1982, were officially "made in the USA." However, some sources have claimed that the initial batches of these guitars were constructed, at Fender's headquarters in Fullerton, California, using components supplied from Korea—a situation that

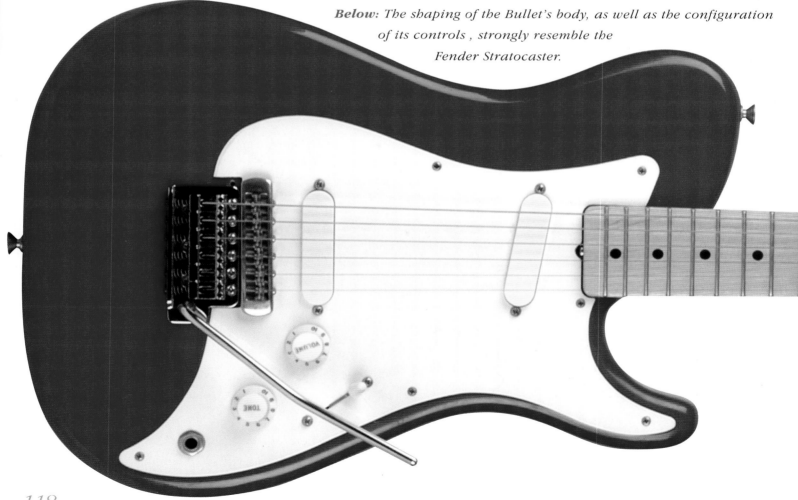

*Below: The shaping of the Bullet's body, as well as the configuration of its controls, strongly resemble the Fender Stratocaster.*

*Above:* According to available records, the very first Bullets did not have vibratos; the unit seen above is probably a later addition.

This "letter and six digit" serial number allows us to date the Bullet to within a year (see main text).

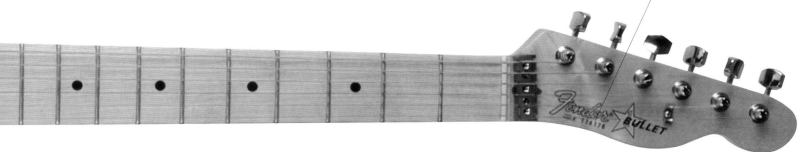

allegedly changed when John Page expressed dissatisfaction with the quality of the bought-in parts, and arranged for Fender USA itself to produce them.

The Bullet's subsequent history is scarcely less confusing. By 1983, the model was being manufactured in Japan as part of the Squier range, but about four years later, Fender's new management team, which took over from CBS in 1985, discontinued it, although they were soon to start using the Bullet name on budget-priced, Far Eastern-made Stratocasters! The original Bullet's designer, John Page, went on to set up the firm's famous Custom Shop in 1987; he left Fender, after 21 years' service, in 1998, and is now a successful artist.

STRATOCASTER
ZED TREMOLO

# FENDER CUSTOM CLAPTON STRAT

CHRIS FLEMING is a Senior Master Builder at Fender's Custom Shop: this example of his work is one of a limited edition run of ten gold leaf covered Eric Clapton Signature Stratocasters made in 2003. It closely resembles the EC-1 guitar that Clapton himself ordered from the Custom Shop in the mid-1990s; he went on to use EC-1 extensively in the studio and onstage, before auctioning it in 2004 for over $400,000.

Like many top players, Eric Clapton favors Fender Noiseless pickups, and on this model, these are combined with active electronics. Consequently, the instrument's two tone controls, though they look standard, function rather differently from those fitted to passive Strats. The first of them is a center-detented TBX (T=treble, B=bass, X=cut) knob that has no effect in its middle position, but delivers a high- or low-

*Below: Note the metal bridge cover; though supplied with some Strats, it is rarely used by players.*

*Custom Shop Clapton models such as this are highly collectible.*

*Above: Gold tuners match this unique Strat's body!*

*Right: This stylish logo appears on all Fender Custom Shop instruments.*

frequency boost when turned. The other tone control is a "master active mid boost," providing up to 25 decibels of additional mid-range power!

The guitar's body weighs just $7\frac{1}{2}$ pounds, and, as is customary on Fender Master Built guitars, carries its maker's signature on the back of its neck heel (this is not visible in our photos) and also boasts a certificate of authenticity. Shortly after we photographed it, it was sold for just over $7,400.

# FENDER "TELE 52"

**W**ELL OVER HALF A CENTURY since its first appearance, the Fender Telecaster remains a favorite with players at every level, and is currently available in a bewildering number of versions. It is hard to know what Leo Fender himself would have made of the guitar's continuing popularity. While undoubtedly proud of his creation, he was also eager to develop new, more impressively specified solid-bodies intended to outperform and (he hoped) outsell it, and is quoted in Richard R. Smith's book ***Fender: The Sound Heard 'Round the World*** as saying that his second great guitar, the Stratocaster, was meant to "obsolesce the Telecaster." Such a prospect was

unlikely then, and is unthinkable now: different performers may express a preference for the more sophisticated Strat or the raw, basic Tele, but each has a special place in the pantheon of popular music, and deserves to be celebrated for its own, utterly distinctive qualities.

The "Tele 52" in our pictures is a modern homage by Fender to the Telecaster as it was in its early days. Though its color is an anachronism (black Teles did not appear until some years later), and the frugal Leo Fender might have looked askance at its gold hardware, it captures something of its ancestor's spirit, and is both elegant and functional.

*Below: This limited edition model has now been discontinued.*

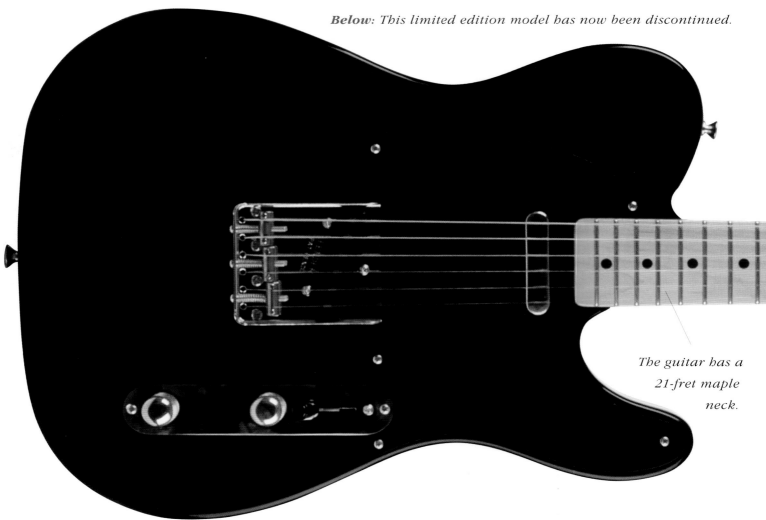

*The guitar has a 21-fret maple neck.*

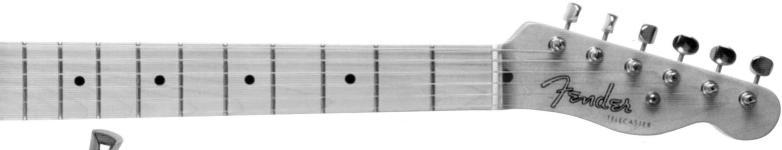

**Left:** These gold tuners are made by Gotob.

**Above top:** The pickup controls and other hardware are shaped and positioned like their 50s counterparts.

# FENDER SHOWMASTER

THE TELECASTER and Stratocaster are classics, but both are now well over half a century old, and Fender, while obviously committed to keeping them in the catalog, is naturally anxious to expand its range by developing exciting new electric guitars. This is a difficult task for all manufacturers, given the undeniable conservatism of many players, who tend to "know what they like, and like what they know;" but over the last few years, a handful of recently introduced instruments have started to look as though they may, in time, become hardy perennials—and one of these is certainly the Fender Showmaster.

Launched in 1998 as a Custom Shop model, it had a significant difference from other, longer established Fenders: its neck was "set" (glued in), rather than bolted on, providing a smoother feel (especially for guitarists who exploit the upper reaches of the fingerboard), and, according to many experts, superior sustain. Hot pickups and attractive stylings won the Showmaster many admirers, and it was soon being mass-produced in a variety of versions: the example in our pictures was made in the Far East, and features a flame maple top over a basswood body (other tops, including quilted maple and bubinga, are also available), plus Seymour Duncan pickups and a 24-fret fretboard. Striking a careful balance between novelty and tradition (it retains a Strat-type headstock), the Showmaster seems destined for even wider popularity.

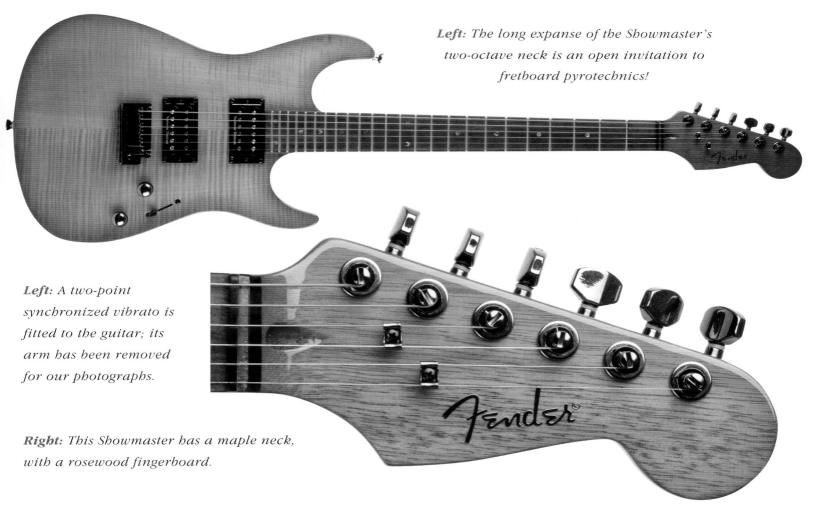

*Left:* The long expanse of the Showmaster's two-octave neck is an open invitation to fretboard pyrotechnics!

*Left:* A two-point synchronized vibrato is fitted to the guitar; its arm has been removed for our photographs.

*Right:* This Showmaster has a maple neck, with a rosewood fingerboard.

# FENDER TORONADO

THE TOWN OF ENSENADA lies some 70 miles down the Pacific Coast from Tijuana, in Mexico's Baja California region. Fender opened a small packaging plant there in 1987, but within a few years, the company's operations south of the border had grown significantly, and the Ensenada factory was producing large quantities of guitars, amplifiers and strings for its US parent: it now occupies over 200,000 square feet of manufacturing space, employs over 1,000 people, and even boasts its own soccer team!

Most of the instruments made by Fender's Mexican division are mid-price versions of Telecasters, Stratocasters, and other classic designs (the cheapest models, including the company's Squier series, are made in the Far East), but in 1998, the first-ever Fender guitar to be both designed and constructed at Ensenada made its debut. Named the Toronado, it was a solid-body electric with an offset waist and, rather usually for a Fender, two humbucking pickups. Four different finishes were available ("Arctic White," "Black," "Brown Sunburst," and "Candy Apple Red"), and the instrument was well received by customers—though a number of them commented that the guitar sounded more than a little like a Gibson!

In 2002, Fender USA paid the Toronado a significant compliment when, in a reversal of the usual order of

*Below: This "American Special" Toronado is fitted with humbucking pickups.*

*The guitar's 24¹/₂-inch scale length is noticably shorter than the 25¹/₂ found on Telecasters and Stratocasters.*

*Above:* The Toronado has an alder body and
a bolted-on maple neck with abalone inlays.

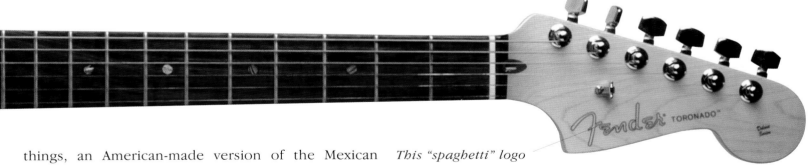

things, an American-made version of the Mexican Toronado was introduced. At the time, the company's vice-president of marketing for guitars and amplifiers, Richard McDonald, commented that the instrument represented "an entirely new direction for Fender guitars in looks, feel, and sound." It featured a choice of pickups (single-coil or Atomic II humbucker) and

*This "spaghetti" logo*
*lettering is a favorite Fender feature.*

two alternative colors, "Butterscotch Blond" and "Crimson Transparent." One of these US-built Toronados is shown here: a revamped Mexican model with slightly different specifications appeared in 2004.

# FENDER CUSTOM SHOP JAGUAR STRAT

THIS FENDER CUSTOM SHOP Stratocaster dates from 1999, and is one of a limited edition of only 25 produced in partnership with Jaguar, Britain's world-famous sports car maker. The guitars are adorned with Jaguar logos, have a "British Racing Green" finish, and feature inlays and headstock facings crafted from walnut burl supplied by the automobile company's Coventry factory. Even their gig bags have a Jaguar connection: these were made out of the soft white leather used for the firm's car seats! They also boast deluxe Fender features, including Lace Sensor pickups and gold hardware.

The idea for the instruments came from the late Ivor Arbiter, managing director of the firm that distributed

*Below:* *Unusally, this Strat's elegant pickguard is attached to its body without screws.*

PHOTOGRAPHS COURTESY OF NEVADA MUSIC, PORTSMOUTH

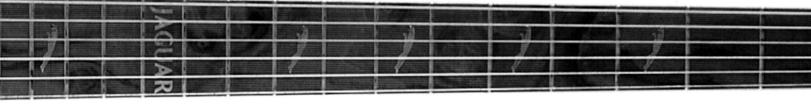

**Right:** *This "leaper" logo is Jaguar's most famous symbol.*

*All the guitar's headstock embellishments are gold.*

Fender products in the UK, and their creation was supervised by Jaguar's Director of Styling, Geoff Lawson. Sadly, Lawson died before the Strats appeared, but had previously told the UK's **Guitarist** magazine how much he had relished being involved in the development of this "very British take on the world's most famous guitar."

**Right:** *A very limited edition...the Jaguar Strat seen here was one of the very last to be produced.*

# FENDER JAG-STANG

KURT COBAIN OF NIRVANA was a devotee of both Fender Mustangs and Jaguars, and longed for a single guitar that would combine their best features. In 1992, he commissioned Californian-based luthier Danny Ferrington (whose other clients include Ry Cooder) to build him a Mustang-influenced axe, which he went on to use mainly in the studio, and about a year later, he began discussions with Fender over the creation of what would become the Jag-Stang.

This curious guitar is, quite literally, a Jaguar-Mustang "fusion:" at an early stage in its development, Cobain cut up photographs of the two models, and stuck them together in the shape he wanted, with handwritten notes detailing neck dimensions, pickup types, and finishes. Larry Brooks of Fender's Custom Shop supervised the process of transforming these ideas into two finished instruments, one of which was featured on Nirvana tour dates in early 1994. Following the star's suicide in April that year, it was decided to

*Above:* The Jag-Stang's neck (front) pickup is a Stratocaster-type unit; Kurt Cobain had originally asked for one from a Fender Mustang in this position.

*Below:* The guitar's body is made from basswood.

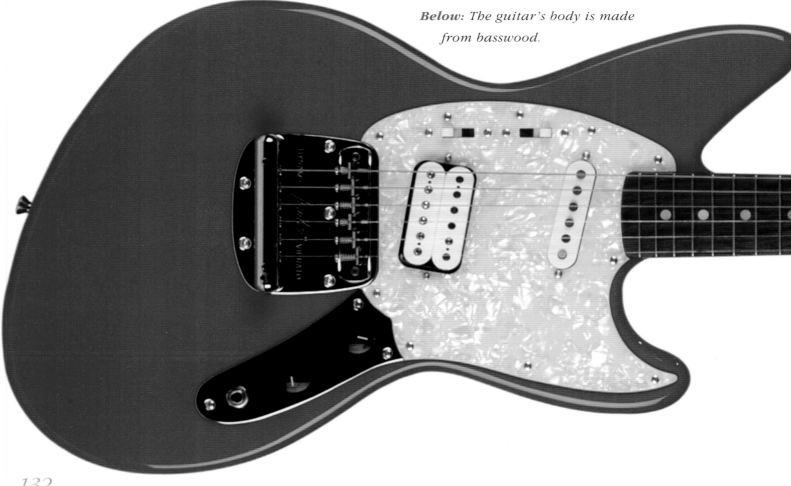

*Above: This chromed bridge/tailpiece incorporates a Fender Dynamic vibrato, whose "whammy bar" has been removed.*

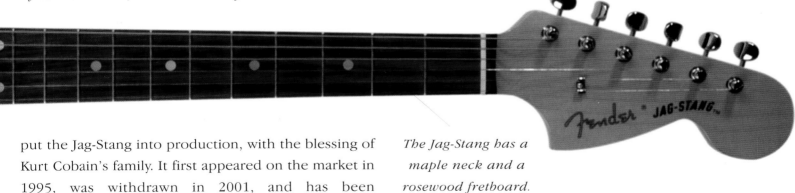

put the Jag-Stang into production, with the blessing of Kurt Cobain's family. It first appeared on the market in 1995, was withdrawn in 2001, and has been sporadically available since.

*The Jag-Stang has a maple neck and a rosewood fretboard.*

The Jag-Stang's odd-looking body divides opinion, as does its idiosyncratic pickup configuration, featuring a bridge humbucker, a single-coil neck unit, and a switching set-up that allows them to be used singly, or combined either in- or out-of-phase. However, a substantial number of players have fallen for its charm and versatility: they include the author, whose Jag-Stang is pictured here.

# FENDER SPLATTER STRATOCASTER

IN SUMMER 2003, Fender announced the introduction of a limited edition of Mexican-made Stratocasters with unusual, even bizarre finishes. These were applied to the instruments' bodies and pickguards, prior to their necks and electronics being installed, by rotating them on turntables while spraying them with a combination of colored paints; the resultant swirls, blobs and lines were later sealed into the wood when its finish was applied. The random nature of this operation meant that no two "paint jobs" were exactly the same, although the color mixes used in each case were, of course, pre-selected.

After the first "Splattercasters" (as they were quickly nicknamed) were displayed at that year's NAMM (National Association of Music Merchants) show, interest from dealers exceeded expectation, and consequently, an initial run of 300 was extended to 3,000, with the guitars selling at a recommended retail price of just over $570. While many purchasers now cherish their Splatter Stratocasters as collectors' items, the likelihood of these strange, though striking models ever becoming sought-after classics is doubtful.

*Below:* Beneath its "splatter" finish, this Stratocaster is a regular production instrument, with an alder body, maple neck, and rosewood fingerboard.

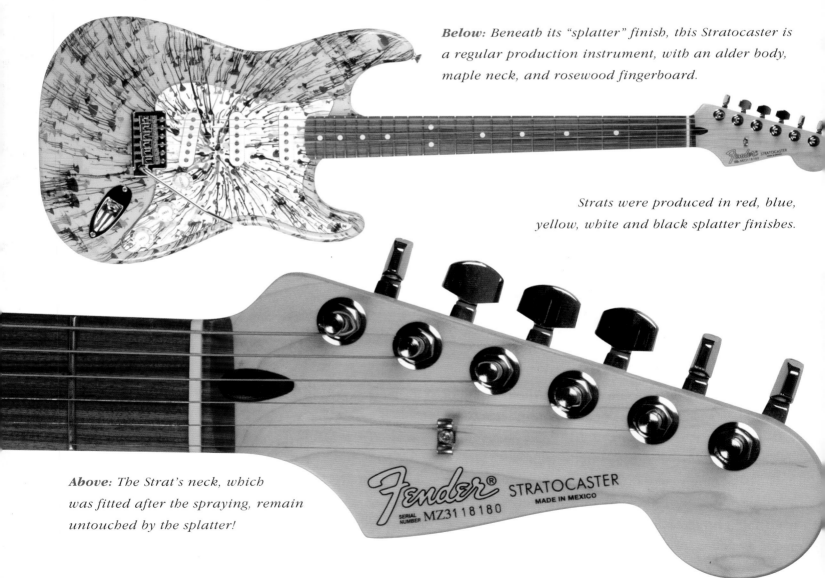

*Strats were produced in red, blue, yellow, white and black splatter finishes.*

*Above:* The Strat's neck, which was fitted after the spraying, remain untouched by the splatter!

PHOTOGRAPHS COURTESY OF AMERICAN GUITAR & BASSWORLD, TONBRIDGE

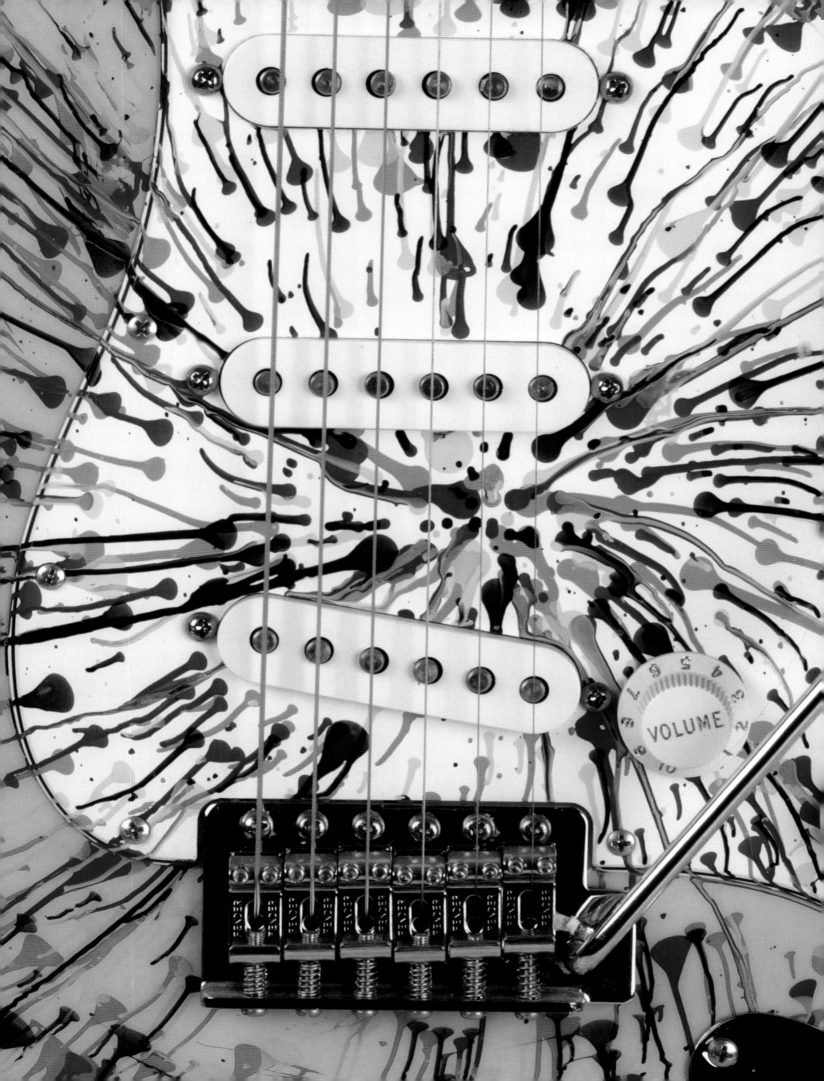

# FRET-KING COUNTRY SQUIRE

TREVOR WILKINSON is one of the most respected figures in British and international guitar making circles, and his high quality vibratos, pickups and other hardware have been widely used in America and Europe for many years. Among Wilkinson's current projects is the Fret-King range of electrics: these began appearing in the late 1990s, and their design draws on his three decades of experience as a luthier and restorer. There are eight Fret-King models (including two basses), most of them based on body shapes reminiscent of classic 1950s and 60s instruments.

The Country Squire shown here is Wilkinson's tribute to the Telecaster. It is produced in three versions: the one in our photos is the "Classic," which has a solid two piece swamp ash body. Significantly, all the Squires feature three-saddle bridges similar to those used on early Teles; Wilkinson considers that "with…two strings holding each [saddle] down, less of

*This model has a "Signal Red" finish.*

*Above: The guitar's neck is made from maple, and its 21-fret fingerboard is rosewood.*

*The Country Squire's pickups are Alnico V-type units made by Trevor Wilkinson.*

the string's energy is wasted stopping the saddles rattling about, allowing the string to sustain more." The other Country Squires are the chambered "Semitone," and the Jeff Beck-inspired "Yardbird."

*The Classic's bridge pickup has
raised pole pieces for additional "bite."*

# FRET-KING CORONA 60SP

THE FRET-KING CORONA is described by its creator, Trevor Wilkinson, as "homage to the classic double cutaway guitar of all time." Like the Fret-King Country Squire on the previous two pages, this Fender Stratocaster-inspired design is available in three alternative configurations, named 50, 60 and 70.

The Corona 60 has a neck profile similar to a 1960s Strat, though, as Wilkinson explains, the radius of its fingerboard has been altered "to facilitate bending notes whilst keeping a low action." The example seen on these pages sports a "soapbar" pickup (with a look and sound reminiscent of Gibson's classic P-90 transducer) in its bridge position; 60s can also be supplied with humbuckers at their bridges, while the Corona 70 has them at both its neck and bridge. The 50 lacks these options, retaining a more conventional Stratocaster-style pickup arrangement. All the Coronas are provided with locking, height adjustable tuners, and Wilkinson/ Gotoh VSV vibrato units.

*Left: A single volume knob controls the Corona's overall output level.*

*Below: The Coronas have alder bodies, with maple necks and roswood fingerboards.*

*This model can be supplied with either 21 or (as here) 22 frets.*

PHOTOGRAPHS COURTESY OF IVOR MAIRANTS MUSICENTRE, LONDON

The Fret-King range has been very widely praised for its skilful blend of old and new. When the first models in the series (the Korina-bodied Esprits) debuted back in 1998, they won the coveted "Best Guitar of the Show" award at that year's Frankfurt Music Fair; and more recently, a number of leading musicians have all declared themselves delighted with the instruments.

*Above top: The VSV*
*vibrato is seen here without its controlling arm.*

They include the veteran British rocker Mick Abrahams, who has commented that "the first time I played my Fret-King, it felt like I'd been playing it for twenty years."

# FURY BANDIT

THE CITY OF SASKATOON, in the Canadian province of Saskatchewan, lies some 400 northwest of Winnipeg and about 300 miles southeast of Edmonton. Since 1962, it has been the home of Fury Guitars, a firm founded by instrument designer Glenn McDougall, and still run by him and his wife, Janet. In the 1950s, Glenn had combined an interest in guitar construction with dreams of becoming a professional player. However, a serious accident in 1958 put paid to his hopes of a performing career, and, a few years later, while still holding down a day job as a commercial artist, he set up Fury in order to start manufacturing the Fireball electric guitar he had been developing.

Glenn was unable to devote himself to full time lutherie until 1966, and, as a profile of Fury published recently in **Vintage Guitar** magazine revealed, the first decade of the new company's existence was "an uphill struggle." Nevertheless, many of the design features developed during those early years are still found on today's Furys—and significantly, the firm's current catalog includes modernized versions of both the Fireball and another 1960s instrument, the Bandit. A recently made example of the latter model appears in our photographs.

*Below: The Fury Bandit has an uncontoured, 1 1/2-inch thick body. Its bridge and other hardware are chrome plated; gold-plating is available as an optional extra.*

*This deep cutaway makes high position playing easy and comfortable.*

*Above: The switches on the left of this photo are coil taps for the two humbucking pickups; near them are the volume knob and pickup selector.*

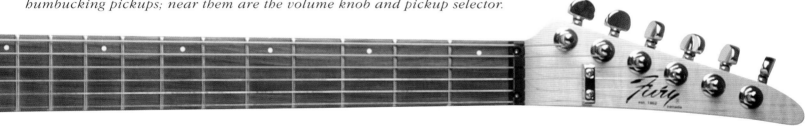

Though new technology has boosted and speeded up Fury's instrument production—its output now includes six regular models, including a bass, an electric 12-string, and a baritone guitar—Glenn McDougall's personal aims have changed little in over four decades. As he states on the company's website, he remains "committed to designing and manufacturing guitars that...produce pure, balanced tone [and] high output power...In short, guitars that are easy to play." The Bandit displays all these qualities: made from maple and available in three different pickup configurations (the instrument featured here is fitted with two humbuckers), it incorporates a high-mass truss-rod for optimum neck rigidity, as well as Fury's patented "Uninut" acrylic nut, designed to improve sustain and playing action.

# G&L F-100

G&L STANDS FOR "GEORGE & LEO": the firm was set up in 1980 by Leo Fender and his long-standing friend and colleague George Fullerton. They had recently left Music Man (see separate entry), and were seeking a new outlet for Leo's latest guitar design innovations. G&L established itself in Fullerton, southern California, where the original Fender Electric Instrument Company had been based, and its first product was the F-100 solid-body, an example of which, dating from 1980, is shown here.

The F-100 came in a number of slightly different forms: the one in our photographs is a Series 1 F-100E model. Series I F-100s have a larger fingerboard radius (12 inch) than their Series II counterparts, and the "E" suffix denotes the presence of active electronics, powered by an onboard battery. The guitar is fitted with two humbucking pickups (plus a coil-tap switch that converts them to single-coil mode), and a vibrato whose operation is described in the caption below. The F-100 series remained in production at Fullerton until 1985.

*The F-100E in our pictures is finished in "Translucent Red."*

**Left**: *This vibrato pivots on two knife-edge fulcrum points. The tension of its operating arm can be adjusted to suit players' preferences.*

**Above**: *The F-100E has an ashwood body (mahogany and maple were also sometimes used) and a maple neck and fingerboard.*

## ASAT™

# G&L ASAT DELUXE

LEO FENDER WORKED AT G&L from 1980 until his death 11 years later. His co-founder George Fullerton still acts as a consultant to the firm, although its ownership and management have now passed to BBE Sound, a business run by Leo's friend and associate John McLaren. McLaren's son, Johnny, is currently G&L's Plant Manager, and he and his staff remain dedicated to the guitar-making goals that Leo Fender spent his life pursuing. Their achievements have been aptly summed up by Kebin Arhens, who wrote recently in **The Music Paper** that "G&L has perpetuated the art of fine instrument making...in the distinguished tradition of its founder."

Among the company's most successful guitars are the ASATs, originally introduced in 1986, and still in production. Their curious name can be explained in two different ways: ASAT may, perhaps, refer to the US Air Force's Anti-Satellite Missile (the F-100 described on the previous two pages also has possible military associations—F-100s were America's first supersonic fighter planes), but is more likely to be a reference to Leo Fender's own remark that the instrument was conceived as "a Strat and a Tele"! ASATs have been used by a substantial number of top players, from Peter Frampton and INXS's Andrew and Tim Farriss to the late Carl Perkins.

The ASAT model seen here is the Deluxe Semi-Hollow. It boasts a figured maple top and a mahogany body, and is fitted with two Seymour Duncan humbucking pickups, which (as on the F-100) can both be coil-tapped.

*The ASAT's headstock, like its neck, is made from bird's eye maple.*

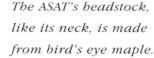

***Left:*** *The ASAT Deluxe Semi-Hollow is slightly reminiscent of one of Leo Fender's earlier designs, the Telecaster Thin Line, but has many innovative features.*

# GIBSON L-5 "MASTER MODEL"

THE GIBSON MANDOLIN-GUITAR Manufacturing Company was founded in Kalamazoo, Michigan, in 1902. It was named for Orville Gibson (1856-1918), a talented and innovative luthier who produced the first-ever mandolins with carved, violin-type tops and backs, and was making large-bodied, steel-strung guitars with arched tops and oval soundholes by the start of the 20th century. "Orville-style" instruments dominated Gibson's early catalogs, but their creator held no executive post within the firm, serving instead as a consultant and a staff trainer. By 1911, however, he had moved away from Kalamazoo due to failing health, and he died seven years later.

In 1919, Gibson bosses recruited Lloyd Allayre Loar (1886-1943) as an "acoustic engineer." Loar quickly became a major force within the firm, and was responsible for the introduction, in 1922, of its F-5 archtop mandolin, which, for the first time, featured f-holes instead of a more traditionally shaped soundhole. The same year saw the launch of the ground-breaking L-5 "Master Model" guitar—the instrument now recognized as the starting point for almost all subsequent archtop acoustic designs. It shared the F-5's f-holes and carved top and back, and had a handsomely finished, 16-inch wide body whose powerful sonic projection was ideal for rhythm playing

*Below: The L-5, finished in "Cremona Brown Sunburst," has a spruce top and maple back and sides.*

in both big bands and smaller ensembles. The new guitar was quickly taken up by many leading jazz performers, and also attracted musicians from other genres, including Maybelle Carter of the famous Carter Family country trio, who bought her L-5 in 1928. The instrument seen here dates from the same year.

*Below: The pointed end on the L-5's fingerboard would become a characteristic feature on Gibson archtops.*

*Left: Much of the Gibson L-5's shape and styling was derived from the design of the company's mandolins.*

# GIBSON SUPER 400

IBSON'S PIONEERING WORK on archtop guitar design was to continue, despite Lloyd Loar's resignation from the company in 1924. By the early 1930s, its "L" range had expanded to include several other f-holed models, and 1934 saw the appearance of an impressive new guitar, the Super 400. This instrument had several striking features: its $400 price; its glamorous, almost ostentatious appearance; and,

most of all, its 18-inch width—though this was later exceeded by Epiphone and, in 1937, by the 19-inch

*Right:* The guitar's name is proudly displayed on its heel...where no one but the owner would have been likely to see it!

*Below:* The Super 400's 18 inch size was intended to provide extra volume, but not all players are convinced that it is very much louder than narrower models.

*Above:* The Super 400's pickguard, like its body, is finely bound.

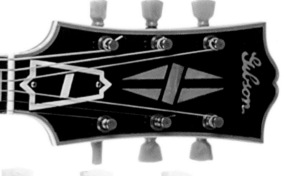

*Below right:* Gold-plated Kluson machine heads are fitted to this Super 400, which dates from 1936.

archtops produced by Stromberg of Boston, Massachusetts. The Super 400 was adopted by a number of high-profile players, but it remained far beyond the reach of most musicians in the Depression-struck USA, and relatively few were made: consequently, it has become one of the most desirable and iconic of all 1930s Gibsons.

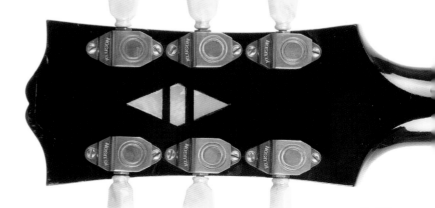

# GIBSON L-5 CUTAWAY

AT THE SAME TIME as the Super 400 was launched in 1934, Gibson unveiled a new version of its L-5 archtop, which now boasted a 17-inch body. Pressure had been mounting on the firm to "advance" the L-5's original, 6-inch size since the appearance of a group of 16³/8-inch wide Epiphones three years previously; and as rivalry between archtop manufacturers grew more intense, the hunt was on for additional features that could steal a march on the competition. One such innovation was the cutaway body, invented by Gibson and introduced as an option on the L-5 and Super 400 in 1939. This "Gibson First," as a contemporary ad explained, would "set the signals for 'Go' all the way up the fingerboard," providing scope for "more notes, more chords, [and] faster, smoother runs." The concept proved so successful that cutaway models like the 1939 L-5 shown in our photographs were soon outselling more traditionally shaped archtops—prompting other companies to produce similarly modified versions of their own guitars.

*Below: Cutaway L-5s were officially known as L-5 Premieres or L-5Ps. This one dates from 1939 or 1940.*

***Above and below:*** *The 1928 L-5 seen earlier had dot position markers; here, these have been replaced with much fancier inlays. Also, the fingerboard on this 1939/40 L-5 lies flat on the body; its predecessor's was slightly elevated.*

# GIBSON ES-150

THE EARLIEST ELECTRIC GUITARS were "Hawaiian" models designed to be laid horizontally on the player's lap, and it was not until 1936 that Gibson introduced its first "Electric Spanish"-style 6-string for standard guitarists; named the ES-150, it was a 16¼-inch wide model with a solid spruce arched top, maple back and sides, and a single "bar-type" pickup. Its entry in the company's catalog contained some words of advice for would-be purchasers unfamiliar with electric instruments: they were told to "strike the strings lightly and you [will] have a tone that can be amplified to any volume you desire." Before long, such guidance would be unnecessary, as electric guitars swiftly caught on among performers—thanks, in no small measure, to the impact of ES-150 user Charlie Christian, who joined the Benny Goodman Orchestra in 1939, and became one of its most outstanding soloists.

During World War II, the manufacture of the ES-150 and many other Gibsons was halted; and when the model reappeared in 1946, its specification had changed. Post-war 150s, like the early 1950s one shown here, were 17 inches wide, made from laminated woods (following a decision that solid timbers were unnecessary for electrics), and featured the company's new P-90 pickup. In this form, the ES-150 remained in production until 1956.

*Right: This adjustable bridge is considerably more elaborate than the basic wooden unit fitted to the ES-150s produced by Gibson between 1936 and 1942.*

*Above: The ES-150, like all Gibson archtops of its period, has its pickguard mounted clear of the guitar's top.*

White binding
on the ES-150
was introduced
in 1946.

The 150's
"trapezoid"
fingerboard
markers are
another post-
war addition.

# GIBSON ES-175D

WHEREAS THE ES-150 was launched as a solid-timbered archtop in the 1930s, and "reborn" in its laminated form after World War II, the ES-175, introduced by Gibson in 1949, had a plywood body from the start, in line with the company's new approach (described on the preceding pages) to the construction of most of its electric hollow-bodies. The 175, whose number reflects its original retail price of $175, also benefited from a cutaway—a feature not found on Gibson's pre-war models.

The first 175s were fitted with a single P-90 pickup and a relatively plain, trapeze-type tailpiece. A two-pickup model, the ES-175D, appeared in 1953, and was given a new, fancier T-shape tailpiece, with zigzag decorations on either side, in 1956; the following year saw the replacement of the P-90 transducers with humbuckers (as seen on the guitar in our photos, which was made in 1968).

The ES-175 has been aptly described by a recent commentator as "one of Gibson's ultimate bread-and-butter instruments," and has been in continuous production since 1949; a slimline version, the ES-175T, appeared in the mid-1970s but was discontinued after only four years.

*The ES-175 has a 16¹/₄ inch wide top, and a 3³/₈ inch deep body.*

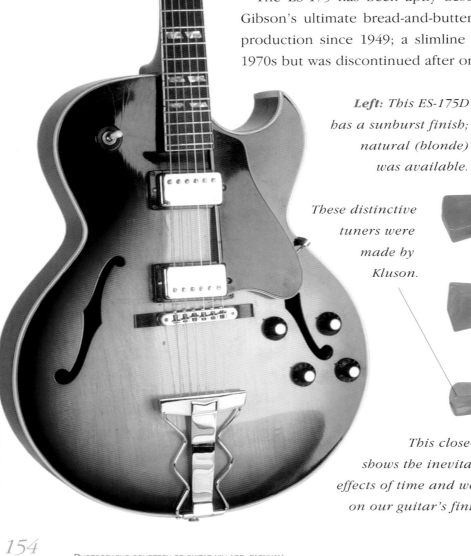

*Left: This ES-175D has a sunburst finish; natural (blonde) was available.*

*These distinctive tuners were made by Kluson.*

*This close-up shows the inevitable effects of time and wear on our guitar's finish.*

PHOTOGRAPHS COURTESY OF GUITAR VILLAGE, FARNHAM

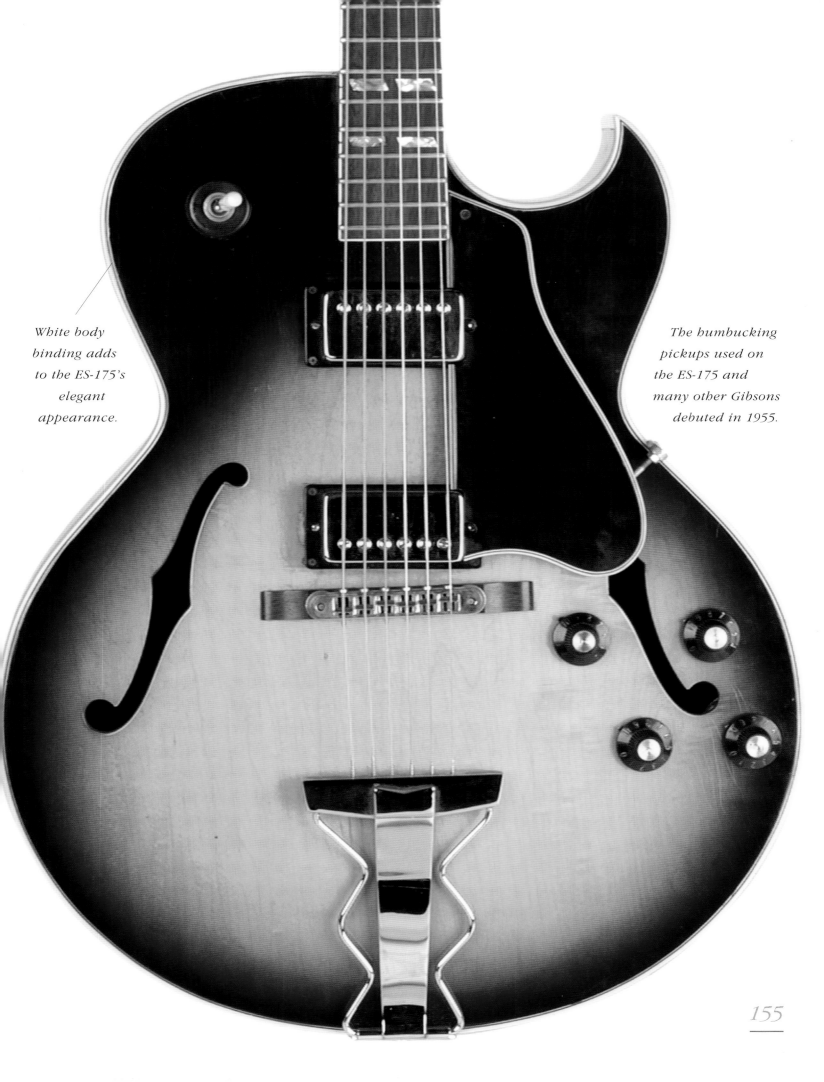

White body binding adds to the ES-175's elegant appearance.

The humbucking pickups used on the ES-175 and many other Gibsons debuted in 1955.

# GIBSON ES-140

THOUGH A THRIVING MARKET existed for reduced-size acoustic guitars suitable for children and those with smaller hands, no similarly scaled-down electrics had ever been produced by a major manufacturer—until the Gibson ES-140 debuted in 1950. The 140 was a three-quarter size version of the highly successful ES-175, and ads for the new model carried a photograph of it placed beside an outline of its "big sister" to demonstrate the extent of the shrinkage. The little guitar went on to sell well, and its profile was further boosted thanks to its association with 1950s child star Larry Collins, one half of the Oklahoma-based Collins Kids rockabilly duo.

Earlier ES-140s, like the one in our pictures, which dates from 1955, retained the 3³/₈ inch body depth of the original ES-175, but in 1956, Gibson slimmed the 140 down to 1³/₄ inches and renamed it the ES-140T; in this form, it remained in production until 1968.

*Left: A side view of the 140's neck, showing the 12th fret position dots, as well as a little wear and tear!*

*Below: The single P-90 pickup on the ES-140 is identical to the one fitted to the full-size ES-175.*

*Above and below:* The ES-140 has a maple body, with a rosewood bridge and a trapeze tailpiece. Its neck is made from mahogany.

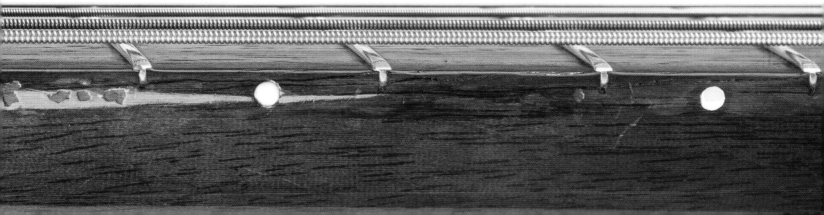

*Surprisingly, this "golden beauty" met with a lukewarm reception from customers.*

**Below:** *This ES-295 dates from 1953, a year after the model's introduction.*

# GIBSON ES-295

*Lighter-colored binding offsets the rich gold of the ES-295's body.*

THE GIBSON ES-295 DEBUTED in 1952; the company's promotional literature, with justifiable pride, called it a "golden beauty" and "a 'royal' instrument," and asserted that "tone and action wise the ES-295 measures up to its outstanding appearance." Visually, the elegant new archtop matched Gibson's Les Paul solid-body, but in other ways, the ES-295 bore close resemblance to the ES-175 described on the previous pages, with the same overall dimensions, and sporting identical "florentine" cutaways and "parallelogram" fret markers. All three models featured P-90 single-coil pickups.

Unlike the Les Paul, the ES-295 never became a best-seller, and it was dropped from the Gibson range in 1958—but it has an enduring place in musical history as the guitar used by Elvis Presley sideman Scotty Moore on "The King's" 1954 sessions for Sun Records in Memphis, Tennessee that produced classic sides such as "That's All Right" and "Blue Moon of Kentucky".

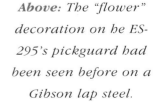

*Above: The "flower" decoration on he ES-295's pickguard had been seen before on a Gibson lap steel.*

**Left:** *The ES-295's control knobs are gold-tinted to match its body's "royal" color scheme.*

# GIBSON L-5 CES

GIBSON'S TWO "FLAGSHIP" pre-war archtop acoustics, the L-5 and Super 400, appeared as electrics in 1951; they kept their original names, but were given the suffix CES (Cutaway Electric Spanish). As befitted their elevated status within the company's product line—reflected in a movie-inspired 1952 Gibson ad proclaiming that the L-5 CES (shown here) "wins the starring roles in every important production"—they also, unlike many humbler models, retained their all-solid wood construction. However, as A.R. Duchossoir explains in his book *Gibson Electrics: The Classic Years*, their tops were now built slightly thicker, and were more heavily braced, "in order to give more rigidity to the sounding board[s] and to inhibit [any] unwanted vibration" that might result from electric use. Unsurprisingly, both guitars were favored by leading jazzmen: the L-5 CES is especially associated with the great Wes Montgomery (1925-

*Below: The L-5 CES has a solid spruce top, and solid maple back and sides.*

**Left:** *This handsome, mother-of-pearl inlaid headstock is complemented by Kluson machine heads with elegantly shaped buttons.*

**Above:** *Each of the six polepieces on the Alnico V pickup seen here is individually adjustable.*

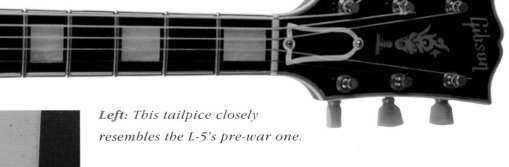

**Left:** *This tailpice closely resembles the L-5's pre-war one.*

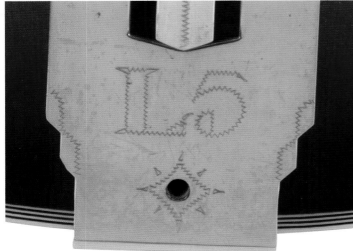

1968), an early disciple of Charlie Christian who later enjoyed huge success as a both a soloist and leader.

Between 1951 and 1953, the L-5 CES was fitted with P-90 pickups; these were subsequently replaced with Alnico V transducers (which can be seen on the guitar in our pictures), and, later, by humbuckers.

# GIBSON BYRDLAND

FOR SOME MUSICIANS, "full-depth" electric archtops like the L-5 CES and ES-175, which measured a substantial 3³/₈ inches from top to back, were a little too bulky for comfort—and when two leading Nashville-based players, Billy Byrd (1920-2001) and Hank Garland (1930-2004), were invited to discuss guitar design with a Gibson representative in early 1955, they suggested that the company should come up with what Garland later described to *Guitar Player* magazine as "an instrument like the L-5, but with a thin body and a bunch of other stuff."

This advice was duly conveyed to Kalamazoo, and the same year saw the launch of the appropriately named Gibson Byrdland, which, although based on the L-5 CES, but was just 2¹/₄ inches deep, and had a slightly shorter scale length and narrower neck than its predecessor. Ads in the music trade press described the Byrdland as "streamlined," and claimed, with some justice, that it "successfully combin[ed] the characteristics of solid body and conventional guitars." Gibson customers concurred, and the new model was quickly followed by other thinlines.

*Below: The 1961 Byrdland in our photos boasts humbucking pickups. These were made standard on the model in 1958.*

*Right: This Byrdland has had its original tailpiece (which carried the model's name) replaced with a Bigsby vibrato unit.*

*Right: Seen fron the front, few differences between the Byrdland and L-5 CES are apparent—however, the former is slimmer, lighter, and easier to play.*

*The ES-335 is 16 inches wide—a comfortably compact size for most players.*

**Below:** *Like the original 335s, this example has a "stop" or "stud" tailpiece, see overleaf for a model with alternative hardware.*

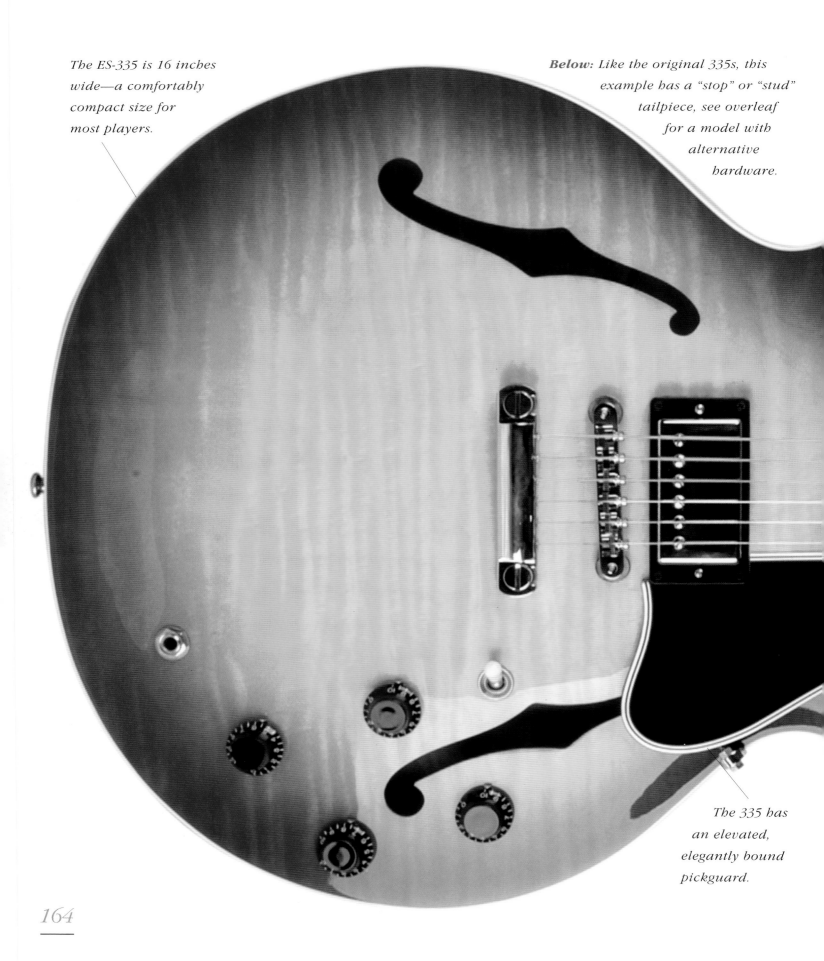

*The 335 has an elevated, elegantly bound pickguard.*

# GIBSON ES-335

*These mounting rings allow precise adjustment of pickup height.*

GIBSON'S ES-335, introduced in spring 1958, had several immediately striking features, including a double cutaway (a first for the company), a thinline body (whose 1³/₄-inch depth matched that of the ES-225, launched three years previously), and a pair of "patent applied for" humbucking pickups, developed by staff engineer Seth Lover (1910-1997), and already seen on several earlier Gibson electrics. But the most revolutionary aspect of the 335's design was invisible from the outside: beneath its laminated maple top lay a wooden block that ran lengthways through the guitar, transforming what would otherwise have been a hollow-body into a "semi-solid;" the only empty cavities inside the 335 were its f-holed side-sections. The instrument's solid center drastically reduced feedback—a frequent bugbear for electric archtops when played at moderate to high volumes—while increasing sustain; and its stylish appearance and comparatively light weight (just over 7 pounds) made it an immediate success with players. The 335 has been in continuous production for well over 40 years.

*Right: The headstock is mounted at a 17-degree angle to optimize the instrument's tone quality.*

# GIBSON ES-335 (2)

IN 1962, GIBSON MADE a purely cosmetic change to the ES-335, substituting block inlays for its "dot" fingerboard markers. A rather more significant alteration occurred some two years later, with the replacement of the model's "stop" or "stud" tailpiece with a trapeze-type unit. The 335 in our pictures dates from 1968, and has been owned since the late 1970s by the British jazz guitarist Charles Alexander, who purchased it after his previous Gibson, a stereo-equipped ES-345 (see next two pages), was stolen.

Like many jazz players, Charles regards the 335 as ideal for his needs, and feels that the sustain provided by its solid center block gives the Gibson ES-335 a "contemporary-sounding" tone more appropriate to his music than the rounder, more "retro" timbre that would be obtained from a hollow-body electric. However, he rarely uses the 335's bridge pickup, preferring the mellower sound of the neck transducer. Aside from some repair work—essential after over two decades of regular gigging!—recently undertaken by Tom Anfield (see separate entries), the instrument has never been modified in any way.

*Below: 1960s Gibson ES-335s are now worth many times their original selling price.*

*These "Gibson-logo" pickup covers are another point of difference between original and later ES335s.*

PHOTOGRAPHS COURTESY OF CHARLES ALEXANDER

**Above:** *Some players feel that the addition of a trapeze tailpiece to the 335 has some effect on the instrument's sound.*

# GIBSON EB-2 BASS

THE GIBSON EB-2 first appeared in 1958; like the visually similar ES-335 guitar launched the same year, it contained an internal center block to improve sustain and reduce feedback. Initially fitted with a single-coil pickup, by 1959, it had acquired a humbucker, together with what a company catalog later described as "the sensational Gibson Bass-Baritone switch," a tone circuit giving an additional "edge" to the instrument's sound. The same feature was included on the Epiphone Rivoli, an EB-2 lookalike that also debuted in 1959. The EB-2 itself was dropped in 1961, but returned three years later, and 1966 saw the appearance of the 2-pickup version seen here. Both basses remained available until the early 1970s.

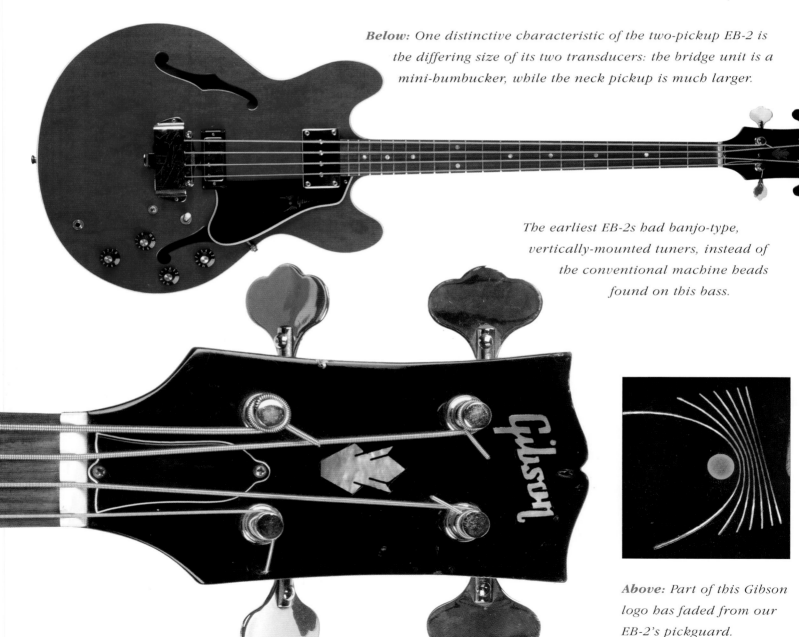

*Below: One distinctive characteristic of the two-pickup EB-2 is the differing size of its two transducers: the bridge unit is a mini-humbucker, while the neck pickup is much larger.*

*The earliest EB-2s had banjo-type, vertically-mounted tuners, instead of the conventional machine heads found on this bass.*

*Above: Part of this Gibson logo has faded from our EB-2's pickguard.*

PHOTOGRAPHS COURTESY OF THE BASS CENTRE, LONDON

*This button activates the EB-2's "Bass-Baritone" circuitry.*

# GIBSON ES-345TD

THE GIBSON ES-345TD was introduced in 1959. While similar in construction and appearance to the ES-335, it had two novel features: stereo wiring, and "Vari-tone" circuitry that, according to the company's publicity, "could produce *any* sound you've *ever* heard from *any* guitar."

Vari-tone settings are adjusted via a rotary knob mounted to the left of the instrument's volume and tone controls. This has six positions: the first of these defeats the Vari-tone, while the other five apply "notch filter"-type cuts to progressively lower frequencies (affecting the deepest notes most at position 6). Opinion has always been somewhat divided over the usefulness of Vari-tone, which lacks the more dramatic frequency shaping capacity of the active EQ circuits fitted to some modern guitars—although many players find it useful, and consider that positions 3 and 4 can make the ES-345's humbucking pickups sound a little like single-coil models.

The guitar's stereo capabilities were considerably

*Below: The ES-345 has a laminated maple body and a semi-solid construction, like its ES-335 cousin.*

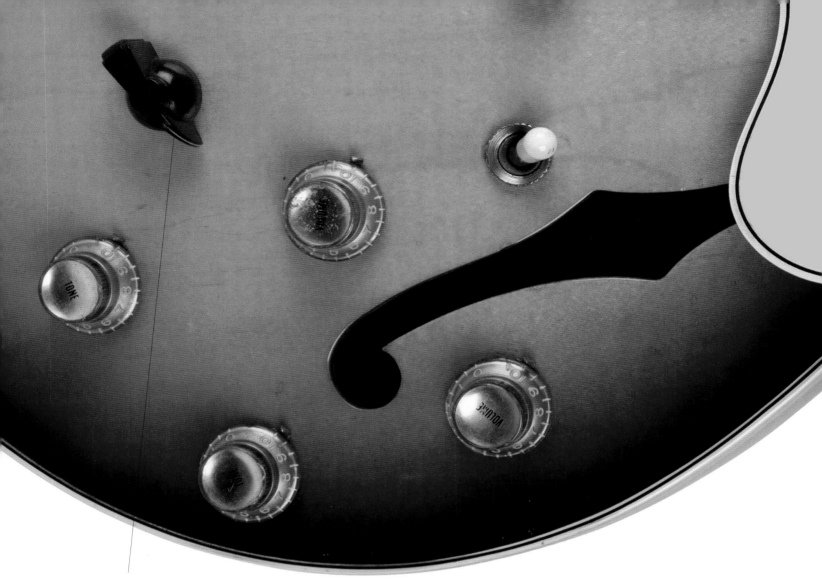

*The 345's Vari-tone switch normally has a circular surround; it has been lost from this instrument.*

simpler than those adopted by Gretsch a few years earlier, which had involved a split between treble and bass strings. Gibson preferred to route each of the 345's pickups to individual channels; their signals could then be connected to separate amplifiers—or, preferably, to the company's own, recently introduced GA-88S stereo guitar amp, which was equipped with two input sockets—via a "Y-type" connecting cord, terminating in a pair of jacks. Musicians with mono amps (the vast majority, both then and now) could use the 345 normally, but would not, of course, be able to enjoy the stereo effect.

The ES-345 remained in the Gibson catalog until 1982, but has subsequently been reissued.

# GIBSON ES-355TD-SV

AS A LUXURY, top-of-the-line reworking of the ES-335, also featuring—in the version seen here—the stereo wiring and Vari-tone circuit found on the ES-345, the ES-355TD-SV (the suffixes stand for "Thinline Double-cutaway Stereo Vari-tone") has frequently inspired purple prose from copywriters. Soon after its launch in 1959, a Gibson catalog called it a "magnificent jazz guitar reflect[ing] all the beauty and skill of the guitar maker's art," while a later ad eulogized it as the embodiment of the "vibrant, vigorous, vital...spirit of

*Below:*"Cherry Red" was initially the only finish in which the ES-355 was available. Other colors were introduced later.

*This vibrato unit is a Gibson Vibrola.*

*Both the headstock
and ebony fretboard
are inlaid with pearl.*

the electric guitar." It is indeed a handsome instrument, though players unimpressed with its ingenious onboard electronics must have been happy that, for a number of years, a mono, non-Vari-tone incarnation of it, named the ES-355TD, could be purchased for rather less money.

Both versions attracted eminent users: they included top Nashville session player Grady Martin who, as Thomas Goldsmith recalls in the book **Classic Guitars of the 50s and 60s**, had string benders fitted to his 355 in order to create "steel-guitar-like pitch shifts." Jazzman Tony Mottola was another devotee—as was blues star B.B. King, who began using the ES-355 in the early 1960s (naming it, like all his instruments, Lucille), but subsequently switched to a version with a sealed top to prevent feedback: this was put into production as the Gibson "B.B. King Model" in 1980. The 355 itself was dropped in 1982, but has since made a number of comebacks, and is currently available as part of Gibson's "Limited Historic" series.

# GIBSON ES-5 SWITCHMASTER, 1959

THE MAJOR SELLING POINT for the original Gibson ES-5, which debuted in 1949, was its unusual pickup configuration. Named "the instrument of a thousand voices" by the company's copywriters, it boasted three P-90s, each of which had its own volume knob; however, there was no selector switch for the transducers, and only a single, overall tone control, positioned on the instrument's upper treble bout. Opinion is divided over the efficacy of this arrangement—top player Ry Cooder has commented that he relishes the freedom it gives him to mix sounds—but during the late 40s and 50s, the ES-5's

*Right:* Like other Gibson archtops, the ES-5 has a "personalized" tailpiece.

*Below:* Humbucking pickups replaced P-90s on the Switchmaster in 1957.

PHOTOGRAPHS COURTESY OF A PRIVATE COLLECTOR

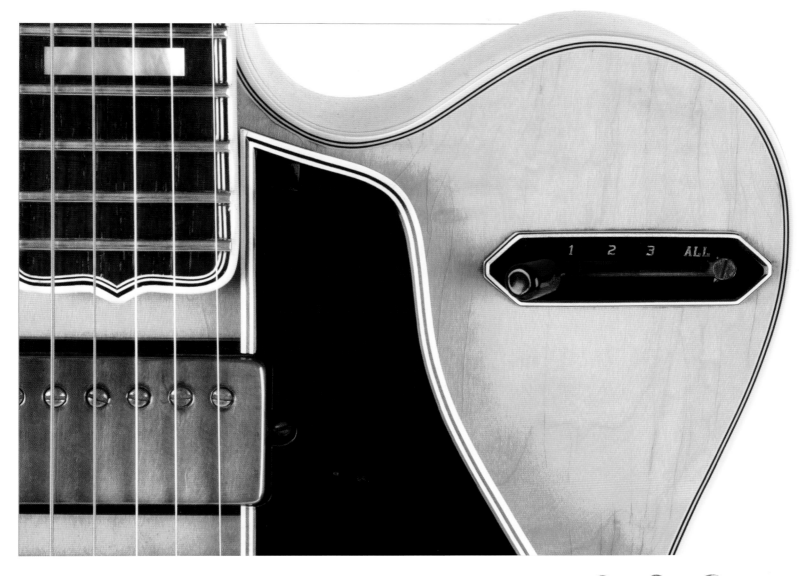

*Above: The provision of a pickup selector on the ES-5 was widely welcomed.*

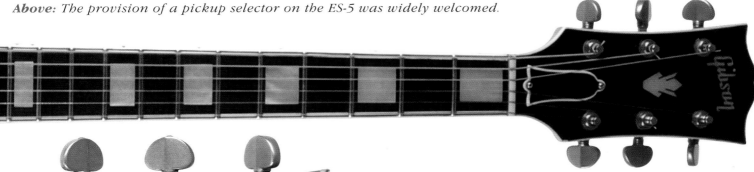

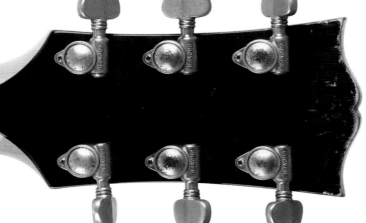

*Left: The reverse side of the Switchmaster's headstock is painted black to match its front.*

circuitry was widely criticized, and in 1955, Gibson altered it, adding a selector, providing individual tone controls for the pickups, and giving the model an additional name: the Switchmaster. An example of the revamped guitar dating from 1959 is shown here.

*Only a small number of ES-5s were made with this Florentine cutaway.*

# GIBSON ES-5 SWITCHMASTER, 1961

IN HIS BOOK, ***The History and Development of the American Guitar***, Ken Achard writes that the ES-5 "heralded the fifties and the start of a new generation of Gibson instruments." By the end of that decade, however, the instrument's future was less certain; thinlines and semi-solids were now the choice of many Gibson archtop users, and the bulky, though elegant Switchmaster was starting to look and sound dated. It had been given humbucking pickups in place of its P-90s in 1957, and it underwent a change in styling four years later, when it acquired a sharp, "Florentine" cutaway. However, by the time this alteration was made, the number of Switchmasters being produced was already beginning to dwindle, and the guitar was eventually discontinued in 1962.

The body of the 1961 Switchmaster shown on these pages conforms to the standard specifications for its year of manufacture, but its neck clearly does not match the comparatively plain, "regular" one found on our previous ES-5, and comes, instead, from an L-5…though it is not known when, or how, this substitution took place!

*Below: Features such as its elaborate headstock binding and "flowerpot" logo reveal that this neck is from a Gibson L-5.*

*Famous Switchmaster users have included Mark Knopfler and the late Frank Zappa.*

# GIBSON L-5 CES, 1963

**S**OME GUITARS enjoy only a brief period in the limelight; but the Gibson L-5, whose original, acoustic version dates back to 1922 (see previous entries) is undoubtedly a hardy perennial. Unlike other classic archtops, its status and sales were largely untouched by the changes of taste and aesthetics that characterized the 1960s, and it was to retain an honored place in the Gibson catalog throughout the decade—and beyond.

The vintage model (seen here in its 1963 CES version) was not, however, entirely untouched by recent trends. By the late 1950s, its single-coil Alnico V pickups had given way to the Seth Lover-designed humbuckers fitted to other top-line Gibson electrics. Their addition made comparatively little visual difference to the instrument, but another new feature—the sharper, Florentine cutaway that replaced the soft Venetian one in about 1960—led to an additional cosmetic change: the shortening of the L-5's pickguard, whose top edge now reached only as far as the last of its 20 frets. On earlier cutaway L-5s, it had extended to the 19th fret or above.

*These tuners, like the guitar's bridge and tailpiece, are gold-plated.*

*The L-5 CES has a spruce top, and maple back and sides.*

PHOTOGRAPHS COURTESY OF A PRIVATE COLLECTOR

# GIBSON L-5, CUSTOM ORDER 1964

THE CONCEPT of a "custom shop" was still unknown to guitar makers and buyers in the early 1960s, largely because manufacturers—even major ones such as Gibson—were still able to accommodate special orders and modifications as part of their mainstream production process. The particular requirements of the unknown musician who commissioned this unusual L-5 would not have been difficult to accomplish: he simply wanted an instrument with a Venetian cutaway instead of the Florentine type then being given to standard models, and asked for a bar-type single coil pickup, like the one

*Right: The L-5 sports elegant, cream-colored binding around its edges.*

*Below: The guitar retains its usual 17 inch width, and its regular features are largely unaffected by the customizing.*

*Above:* The gold-plated bridge permits precise adjustments to be made for individual strings..

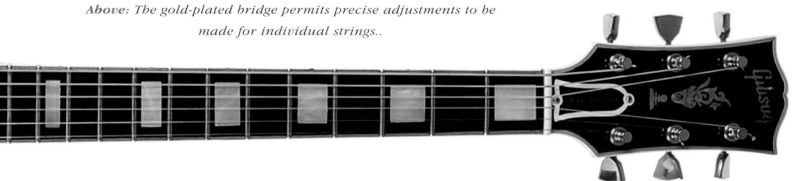

*Left:* The ES-150-style pickup in place on the L-5.

used on pre-war Gibson ES-150s, to be fitted in place of a humbucker. (The latter preference suggests that he was a devotee of Charlie Christian, the 150's most celebrated user.) His order was duly carried out, and resulted in a successful and stylish hybrid.

# GIBSON HOWARD ROBERTS CUSTOM

HOWARD ROBERTS (1929-1992) made his reputation during the 1950s and 60s in Los Angeles, where he worked as a session guitarist, and was especially in demand for movie and TV soundtracks. However, his first love was always jazz, and his many recordings in this genre, both as a leader and a soloist with luminaries such as drummer Chico Hamilton and saxophonist Art Pepper, are treasured by aficionados. He was also an innovative teacher and the co-founder of the prestigious Guitar Institute of Technology (which is now a part of the Hollywood-based Musicians Institute).

In 1961, Roberts was invited by Chicago Musical Instruments, owners of both Gibson and Epiphone, to develop a new semi-acoustic that would bear his name. The resultant instrument debuted as the Epiphone Howard Roberts three years later; a slightly different version, the Howard Roberts Custom, appeared in 1965. Though archtops, the Roberts guitars had distinctive oval soundholes instead of the more usual f-

*Below: The Custom has an all-maple body with a 16-inch wide top. It was available in "Sunburst" (seen here) or "Wine Red."*

*The picksup is attached to the end of the neck, and does not touch the guitar's top.*

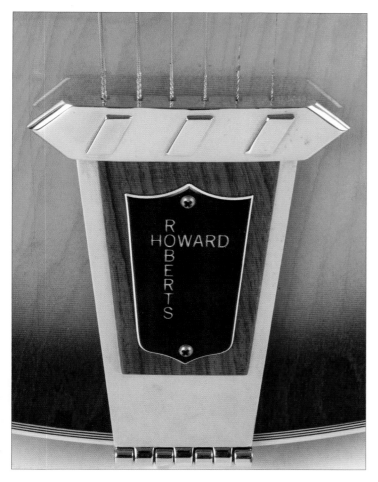

holes, and were fitted with humbucking pickups. Both were discontinued in 1970, but in 1974, the Custom reappeared as a Gibson; this move represented a curious reversal of the normal policy of using Epiphone as a "reissue" brand.

The Gibson Howard Roberts Custom in our pictures dates from about 1974, and is essentially similar to the Epiphone model. One telltale residual sign of its origins is its "wandering vine" headstock inlay, which is very much an Epi feature!

*Left: This tailpiece is similar to the unit used on an earlier "signature" guitar made by Gibson for jazzman Tal Farlow.*

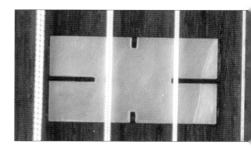

**Above right:** *These unusally shaped fingerboard inlays also appeared on the original Epiphone Howard Roberts Custom.*

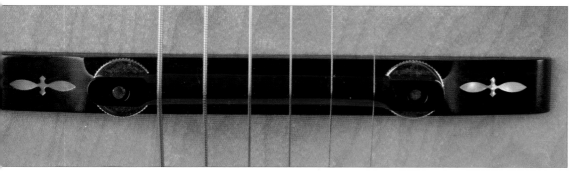

**Left:** *The Roberts's simple ebony bridge is elegant, but offers little scope for adjustment.*

# GIBSON HOWARD ROBERTS FUSION

FOLLOWING THE REINTRODUCTION of the Howard Roberts Custom, Gibson continued to collaborate with the distinguished jazzman (who was known as an enthusiastic modifier of his own instruments), and 1979 saw the launch of a new Roberts model, the Fusion. Its single-cutaway outline is reminiscent of the ES-175, one of the guitars Roberts used regularly before acquiring his "signature" Epiphone (his other favorite was said to be an

Roberts. These included an upgrade from its original TP-6 bridge to a more elaborate, metallic-fingered tailpiece like the one seen on the Gibson Chet Atkins Country Gentleman (see separate entry), as well as a slight repositioning of the guitar's control knobs; while the currently available Fusion III boasts gold hardware and an extended range of finish options. The various Fusions stand as a fitting tribute to Howard Roberts, who died of cancer in 1992, aged 62.

*Below: This Howard Roberts Fusion dates from 1980.*

*Opposite page: The TP-6 bridge/tailpiece allows tuning adjustment, but was replaced on later Fusions.*

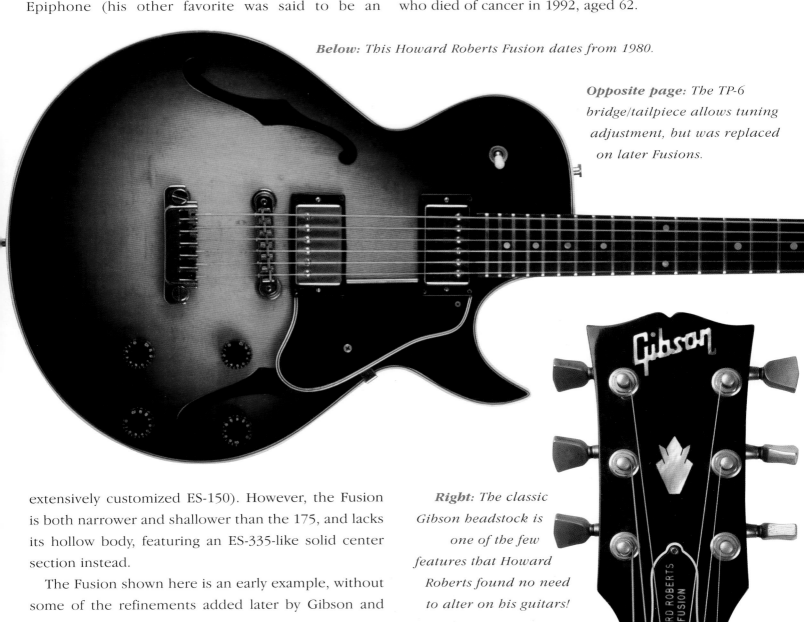

extensively customized ES-150). However, the Fusion is both narrower and shallower than the 175, and lacks its hollow body, featuring an ES-335-like solid center section instead.

The Fusion shown here is an early example, without some of the refinements added later by Gibson and

*Right: The classic Gibson headstock is one of the few features that Howard Roberts found no need to alter on his guitars!*

185

ES 135

# GIBSON ES-135

IN ITS ORIGINAL INCARNATION, the Gibson ES-135 was a non-cutaway archtop with a single pickup: it debuted in 1954, but spent only four years in the catalog. The 135 seen here, first introduced in 1991, is an entirely different instrument, which combines the outline of an ES-175 (with its distinctive Florentine cutaway), and the shallow body and internal center block of an ES-335. Its two pickups are Gibson P-100s—"stacked humbuckers" based on the classic P-90

design, but with an additional, noise-eliminating coil.

The new guitar was immediately successful, and, in 2000, was honored with an "Editors' Pick" award from the influential magazine *Guitar Player*, whose consulting editor, musician Joe Gore, described it as "a super-versatile ax ...with relentless sustain and slap-your-face presence, [whose] gargantuan tones are as easy to ignore as a hippo in your hot tub."

Two years before, Gibson had introduced a

*Below: The 1991-style ES-135 was produced in "Cherry" (as shown here), "Vintage Sunburst" and "Ebony."*

*This pickguard is built up from five layers.*

PHOTOGRAPHS COURTESY OF PEACH, BLAKE END, BRAINTREE

A rosewood fingerboard
tops the 135's maple neck.

**Above:** These P-100 humbucking pickups are
noted for their throaty power and sustain.

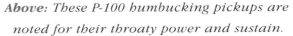

somewhat startling and unusual variant of their popular semi-acoustic: this was the limited-edition, satin-black finished "Gothic" ES-135, part of a series that also included made-over Explorers, Flying Vs and ES-335s. A company press release waxed lyrical over their "darkly deviant good looks," but went on to warn that "these foreboding guitars are not for everyone."

The Goths have come and gone, but in 2003, a further reworking of the 135 appeared, intended (as Gibson puts it), to "bring the [guitar] to a new level of style, performance and affordability." On the new model, the top has been sealed, and the P-100 pickups replaced by two '57 Classic humbuckers; various color options have also been added, and the center section inside the body, made from balsa-like chromyte on the previous 135s, is now mahogany.

187

# GIBSON LES PAUL 1956 REPLICA

LES PAUL (born Lester William Polfus, 1915) has a special place in the history of the electric guitar. A brilliant player, he also took an active interest in guitar design, and, in 1941, built himself a makeshift, partially solid-bodied instrument by sawing up a discarded Epiphone archtop, and giving it a new center section made from a block of wood with two pickups attached. Nicknamed "The Log," this ungainly but ingenious prototype demonstrated many of the qualities that Les Paul had sought in vain from hollow-body archtops (including improved sustain and feedback rejection), but it was not until the early 1950s—after a series of abortive discussions with commercial guitar makers, including Leo Fender—that he agreed to collaborate with Gibson on a mass-production solid-body electric that would bear his name.

The elegantly shaped, gold-topped Gibson Les Paul appeared in 1952, and was described in the company's promotional literature as "the instrument everyone has been waiting for." While Les has frequently stated that

*Right: The 1956 replica is fitted with Gibson P-90 single-coil pickups. Below the P-90 in the picture are the adjustable bridge and "stud" or "stop" tailpiece.*

*Below: This Les Paul has a 12³/₄ inch wide, 17¹/₄ inch long body. Its fingerboard is rosewood.*

*As on many Les Pauls, the pickguard is mounted clear of the guitar's top.*

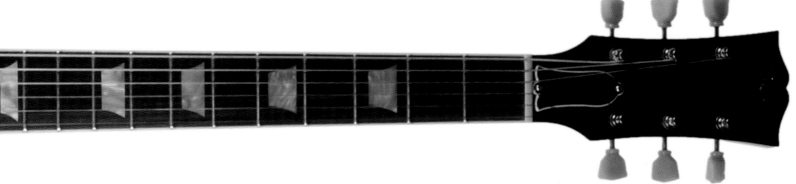

the guitar was all his own work, many experts ascribe a crucial role in its development to Gibson President Ted McCarty (1909-2001). McCarty and his team of designers and craftsmen were undoubtedly involved in choosing the combination of woods (carved maple for the top, mahogany for the body and neck) that helped to give the guitar its unique tone quality; and while Les Paul himself holds the patent for the trapeze-style bridge-cum-tailpiece fitted to the original model, this was dropped after little more than a year in favor of a bridge/tailpiece with adjustable "studs" on either side. A separate, McCarty-designed "Tune-o-Matic" bridge was added in 1955, and the guitar seen here is a Gibson Custom Shop replica of the model's 1956 incarnation.

The Custom's neck, with its sleek ebony fingerboard, is elegant as well as fast-playing.

**Above:** The "Tune-o-Matic" bridge is an effective, widely imitated design. This one is gold-plated, like its adjacent tailpiece.

# GIBSON LES PAUL CUSTOM

THE LES PAUL CUSTOM started out as an upgrade to Gibson's original Les Paul model. Introduced in 1954, it featured the adjustable "Tune-o-Matic" bridge invented by the company's Ted McCarty, and was fitted with two different types of single-coil pickup: a P-90 in the bridge position, and an Alnico V, named for the type of magnet used for its pole-pieces, near its neck. The Alnico transducer, developed by Gibson engineer Seth Lover, offered high output, but performed less well when—as frequently happened—players raised its height excessively. (Lover, quoted in A.R. Duchossoir's *Gibson Electrics: The Classic Years* (1994) explained that guitarists would "get sour notes from that pickup" when it was brought too near the strings, adding, "They should have kept the magnets down the waist.") The other distinctive characteristics of the first Custom were its all-black finish (prompting the nickname "Black Beauty") and the low, wide profile of its frets, which made fast left-hand work easier and earned the instrument another soubriquet: "Fretless Wonder."

The all-black Custom's P-90 and Alnico pickups were subsequently replaced by three humbuckers, and by the early 1960s, the guitar had acquired a new, slimline shape, and was later renamed the SG Custom (see separate entry). Details of the Les Paul-style Custom's subsequent history can be found on pages 300-1, where a 1978 model is shown.

The "Black Beauty" seen here is an early model, preserved in near-perfect condition by its owner, a dedicated collector of vintage Gibsons.

*Left: Gibson described the Les Paul Custom as "the ultimate in a solid body Electric Spanish guitar."*

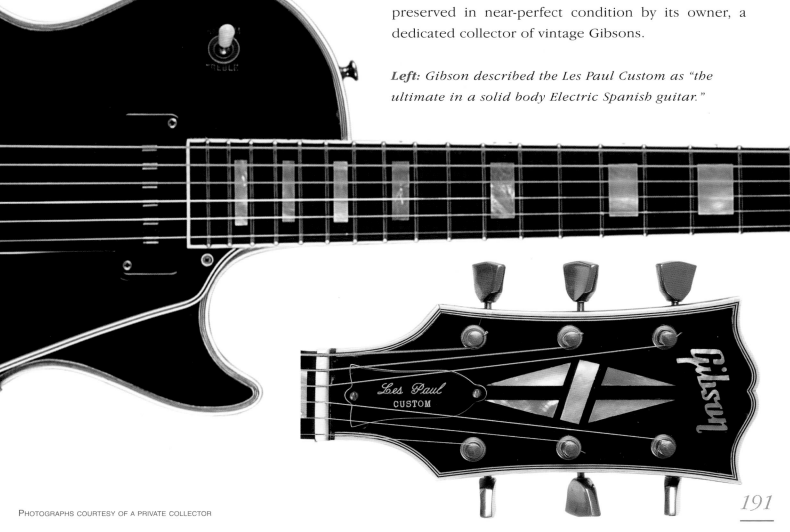

*191*

# GIBSON LES PAUL STANDARD

IN 1957, both the gold-top and Custom Gibson Les Pauls acquired new pickups—the twin-coil, "humbucking" transducers developed a few years earlier by staffer Seth Lover (1910-1997). The rich timbre provided by these units has come to be widely regarded as the "classic Les Paul sound," although some players retain a preference for the P-90s and Alnicos fitted to earlier models.

The next important development in the Les Paul's history occurred the following year, when the original (non-Custom) instrument's gold finish was replaced with a sunburst look; to coincide with this change, the bosses at Kalamazoo decided to give the guitar a new name: the Les Paul Standard. Probably the most famous and highly revered of all the many different types of Les Paul, it was initially available for just three years, during which, according to figures quoted by guitar historian Tony Bacon, only about 1,700 were made. Partly as a result of their scarcity, 1958-60 Standards now have an almost mystical status among some musicians; but at the time of their production, they were not especially big sellers, and were eventually discontinued, along with the rest of the single-cutaway Pauls, to make way for Gibson's new SG-shaped solid-bodies.

Their disappearance was only temporary: a reissued Les Paul Standard debuted in 1968, but it sported a gold finish instead of a sunburst one, and its

*Below: The Les Paul Standard's body is made from layers of maple and mahogany, with a maple top.*

*Above:* The cream-colored surrounds for its pickups are one of the Standard's most distinctive features.

humbucking pickups were much smaller than those found on its predecessor. It was followed by a variety of other new models, but the 1958-style Standard with full-size humbuckers did not return to regular production at Gibson until 1976. It has since been a fixture in the company's catalog, and a recently made Standard is shown in our photographs.

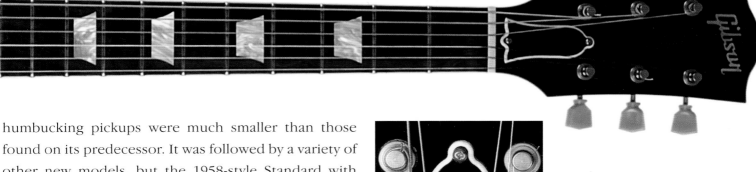

*Left:* Unlike some other Les Pauls, the Standard has no lettering on its truss-rod cover.

The single-pickup Melody Maker shown here dates from 1964; two-pickup versions were also available.

**Below:** The Melody Maker's body and neck are mahogany; it has a rosewood fingerboard.

Versions of this pickup were later used on Gibson's ES-120T and Epiphone's Olympic.

# GIBSON MELODY MAKER

**E**AGER TO CAPTURE A SHARE of the market for less expensive electric guitars as well as premium models, Gibson launched a budget-priced Les Paul in 1954. Named the Junior, it sold for just $99.50, and was fitted with a single P-90 pickup; a ³/₄-size version appeared two years later. 1959 saw the introduction of a new Gibson solid-body, also priced at $99.50. Christened the Melody Maker, it bore a strong resemblance to the single-cutaway Junior—although its body was slightly thinner than its predecessor's, while its headstock was narrower, and its pickup assembly was an all-in-one unit built into its pickguard.

By this time, Les Pauls were undergoing a gradual transformation into SGs; an intermediate stage in this process occurred in 1958 and 1959, when the Junior and TV models, and then the Special, appeared in rounded-horn double-cutaway versions. The Melody Maker acquired the same body shape—seen on the example in our photographs—in 1961, and underwent other minor changes before gaining a full SG styling in 1966.

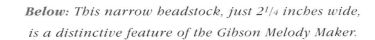

*Below: This narrow headstock, just 2¹/₄ inches wide, is a distinctive feature of the Gibson Melody Maker.*

# GIBSON FLYING V

B Y THE MID-1950s, the success of the Fender Telecaster and Stratocaster—both products from a hitherto obscure firm with no real guitar-making track record—was having a corrosive effect on the reputation of other, longer-established manufacturers. Gibson, in particular, found itself the subject of unwelcome murmurings from its detractors to the effect that, as its retired boss Ted McCarty recalled during an interview published in Rittor Music's authoritative book **The Gibson** (1996) it "was a fuddy duddy old company without a new idea in years." To silence such comments, McCarty urgently needed to come up with some fresh, bold designs, and by 1957 he had devised body shapes for three radical-looking solid electrics, the Moderne, the Futura (soon to be renamed the Explorer) and the Flying V. The Moderne appeared in prototype, but was not

**Above:** *This Flying V was made in 2002. While broadly similar to the original, it is made from mahogany, not korina, and has a number of other minor differences from the 1958 model.*

**Right:** *The Flying V's dramatic shape is perfect for rock star-style posing, but less than ideal for performers who prefer to play sitting down!*

*The 1958-style Flying V boasted a V-shaped tailpiece, not the "stop" unit seen here.*

These tuning buttons match the 1958 model's.

On earlier Flying Vs, the "Gibson" logo was placed on the headstock; here, it has migrated to the truss rod cover.

**Below:** Gibson described the Flying V in 1958 as a guitar that "would be a real asset to the combo musician with a flair for showmanship."

actually marketed until the 1980s; however, the Flying V and the Explorer were unveiled to industry insiders at trade fairs in 1957, before going into production the following year.

These two so-called "modernistic guitars" were both made from West African korina wood, which, according to Gibson expert A.R. Duchossoir, had previously been used only for the firm's Hawaiian models. The assymetrical Explorer was certainly distinctive, but it was the Flying V, with its bold, arrow-like outline, that was to prove more appealing to customers in the long term—despite disappointing initial sales that led it to be temporarily dropped from the company's catalog only a year after its launch.

# GIBSON SG CUSTOM

SINCE ITS FIRST APPEARANCE in 1952, the single-cutaway Gibson Les Paul had become well established, and been highly successful. By the early 1960s, however, sales were declining, as demand grew for lighter-bodied, more streamlined types of electric such as the Fender Stratocaster. The bosses at Kalamazoo responded by giving their Les Pauls a makeover: at the end of 1960, the Standard model acquired a narrower, contoured body with two sharp-horned cutaways, and the following year, an advertisement with the headline "Solid Hit" announced the introduction of a 3-pickup Les Paul Custom with similar restyling. The ad proclaimed the model's new features, which included a vibrato and a choice of finishes, but confirmed that familiar aspects of its design such as the "fretless wonder" neck had been retained. It also pictured Les Paul and his wife Mary Ford playing the revamped instruments. This suggestion of continuity was somewhat misleading: Les Paul's endorsement deal with Gibson was about to come to a temporary end (it was renewed in 1967), and by 1963, his name had vanished from the company's guitars, as "Les Pauls" were rechristened "Solid Guitars" or "SGs."

*Below: SGs are 1⁵/₁₆ inches thick; the Les Paul had a 1³/₄ inch body depth.*

*Right: Body contouring is another new feature found on SGs but not Les Pauls.*

*Like its predecessors, the SG Custom has an ebony fingerboard.*

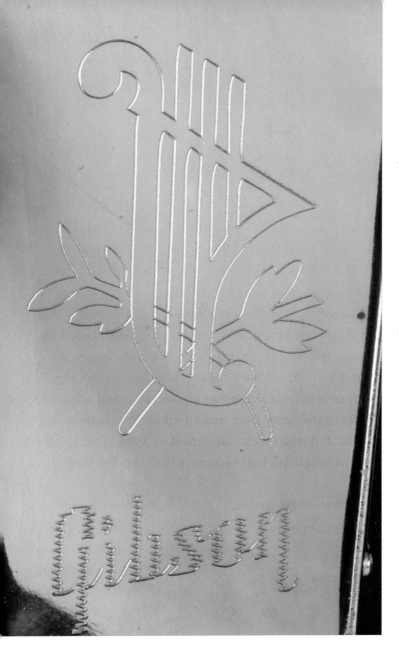

**Above:** *Because of the SG's thin body, its jack socket cannot be side-mounted, and has been repositioned on the instrument's top.*

The 1966 SG Custom shown here has a number of differences from the 1961 Les Paul Custom described above. Some of these are purely cosmetic, like the replacement of the older Custom's smaller scratchplate with a "wrap-around" pickguard; more significantly, the later guitar boasts an "up-and-down" vibrato, instead of the more unusual "side-to-side" device fitted to its predecessor.

**Left:** *On earlier models, this truss-rod cover would have carried Les Paul's name instead of "Custom."*

# GIBSON FIREBIRD III

IN THE EARLY 1960s, Gibson turned to a surprising source in its perennial search for bold, "cutting-edge" solid body designs to keep up the pressure on its rivals. The company's boss, Ted McCarty, admired the work of automobile engineer and stylist Ray Dietrich (1894-1980), whose career had included spells at Chevrolet, Chrysler, Packard, Checker and other major car firms, and invited him to contribute to the development of a radical new guitar, soon to be named the Firebird. Dietrich, however, had no experience of working with instruments, so some of his ideas flew in the face of established convention. Not content with making the Firebirds "reverse bodied" (with their treble horns longer than their bass ones), as the earlier Gibson Explorers had been, he gave them a "neck-through-body" construction instead of a conventional glued-in or bolted-on neck, and turned their headstocks around, so that the bass strings had the longest paths from machine head to bridge. These mirror-image pegheads were fitted with "banjo-like" tuners, whose downward-facing buttons could not be seen from the front of the instruments, adding yet another striking element to an overall visual effect that Gibson's publicity later described as "revolutionary."

Four Firebirds were launched in 1963. The Firebird I was a single-pickup model, while the Firebird III (a

*Below: This Firebird III is finished in "Inverness Green," one of the original custom colors offered to buyers in 1963.*

*These "wings" are attached to the guitar's center neck-body section.*

PHOTOGRAPHS COURTESY OF GUITAR VILLAGE, FARNHAM

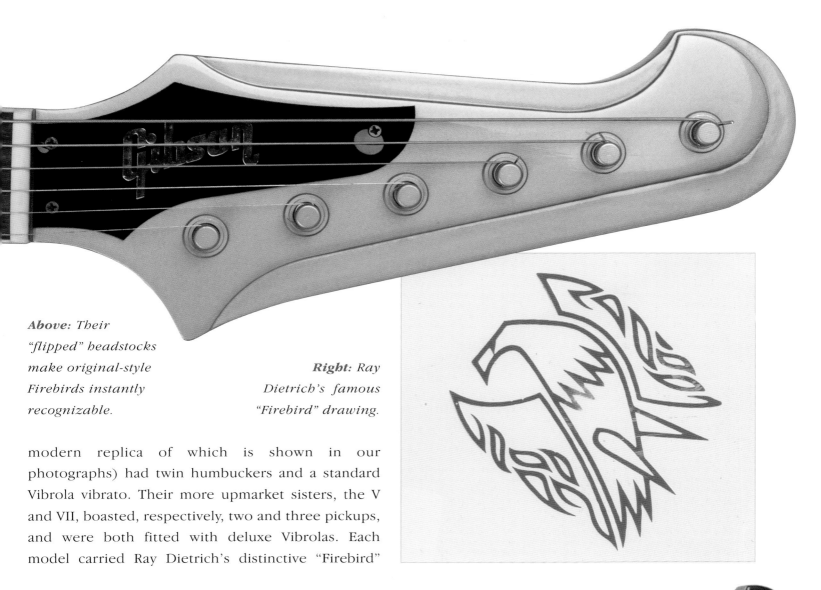

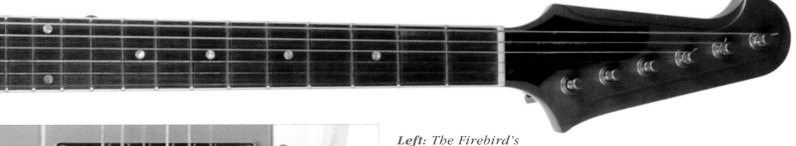

**Above:** *Their "flipped" headstocks make original-style Firebirds instantly recognizable.*

**Right:** *Ray Dietrich's famous "Firebird" drawing.*

modern replica of which is shown in our photographs) had twin humbuckers and a standard Vibrola vibrato. Their more upmarket sisters, the V and VII, boasted, respectively, two and three pickups, and were both fitted with deluxe Vibrolas. Each model carried Ray Dietrich's distinctive "Firebird"

**Left:** *The Firebird's pickups and vibrato are standard components.*

emblem on its pickguard, and two "Thunderbird" basses, also designed by him, debuted at the same time. The new range was fairly modestly priced, with a Firebird I selling for just under $190, and a VII costing $445.

*201*

# GIBSON FIREBIRD V

THE GIBSON FIREBIRDS were not especially well received by dealers or customers, and before long, a more serious threat to their future was looming, as Fender protested that the shape used for the instruments constituted an infringement of its own, patented Jazzmaster and Jaguar designs. Though the issue never came to court, Gibson decided to make some major changes to the Firebird range: in 1965, the guitars' unusual reverse bodies and headstocks were both abandoned, sideways-mounted tuners were fitted, and the "neck-through-body" construction was replaced with a standard neck joint. There were also some hardware changes, such as the substitution of P-90 pickups for humbuckers on the Firebird I and III.

By 1969, these revamped models had been dropped,

*Belov: The center and wings on this Firebird's body are all made from mahogany.*

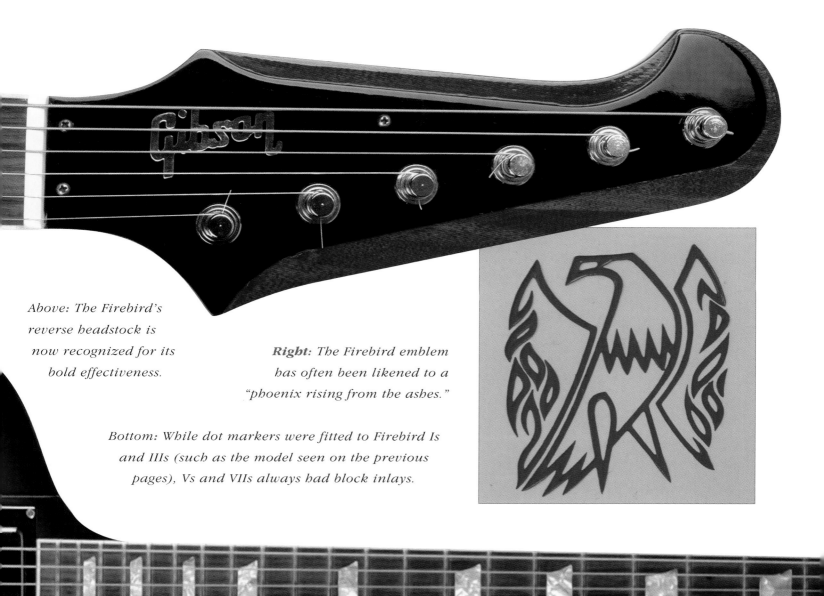

Above: The Firebird's reverse headstock is now recognized for its bold effectiveness.

Right: The Firebird emblem has often been likened to a "phoenix rising from the ashes."

Bottom: While dot markers were fitted to Firebird Is and IIIs (such as the model seen on the previous pages), Vs and VIIs always had block inlays.

These "inline" tuners are manufactured by Grover.

but over the years, affection for the original Firebirds has grown (Gibson expert A.R. Duchossoir suggests that they deserve to be "rank[ed] among [the company's] true classics"), prompting a number of revivals and reissues.

The recently made Firebird V seen on these pages is one of these: part of a series that also includes several three-pickup VIIs and a new "Firebird Studio" model, it has all the "reverse" features of the 1963 models, although it lacks a vibrato.

*Below: The EB-0's unbound mahogany body is 13 inches wide and 1³/₄ inches thick. Mahogany is also used for the neck; the fingerboard is rosewood.*

*This humbucking pickup was designed by Gibson's R&D boss Walter Fuller in 1954.*

# GIBSON EB-0 BASS, 1959

*The EB-0's 30¹/₂ inch scale suits bassists who have smaller hands.*

THE MAHOGANY-BODIED, short-scale Gibson EB-0 bass was introduced in 1959 at a retail price of $195, and early examples—such as this one—share the same body outline as the company's Les Paul Junior 6-string guitar. However, the late 50s and early 60s saw frequent changes in Gibson specifications, and the EB-0 survived for little more than two years in its original form. By 1961, it had been re-styled to match the SG guitar, with sharper, deeper cutaways and contoured sides; the same year saw the launch of a companion model, the EB-3, which had two pickups but was otherwise almost identical to its predecessor. Subsequent specification changes to the EB-0 included the addition of a string mute, and in 1969, a long-scale (30¹/₂ inch) version, EB-0L, made its debut. The EB-0 remained in production until 1979.

This 1959 EB-0 formerly belonged to Jim Kale of the Canadian band Guess Who, which enjoyed chart success in the 1960s and 70s with songs such as "American Woman." The band's original line-up also included guitarist Randy Bachman (later of Bachman Turner Overdrive).

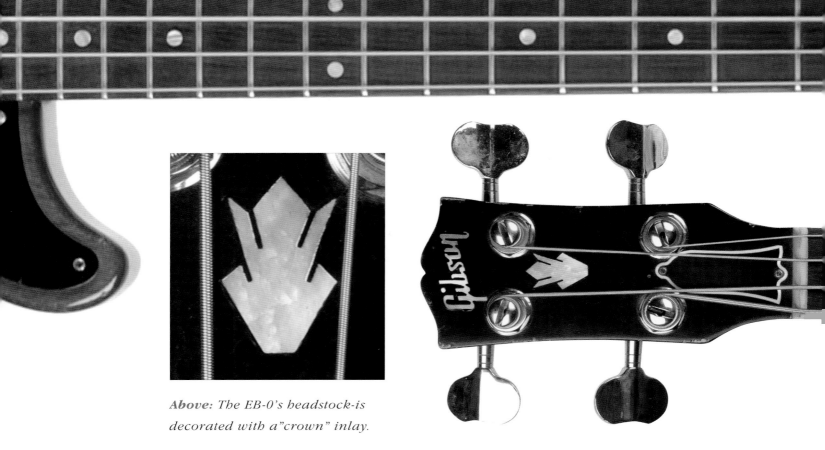

**Above:** *The EB-0's headstock-is decorated with a"crown" inlay.*

# GIBSON PETE TOWNSHEND SG

PETE TOWNSHEND OF THE WHO has used (and abused!) many different guitars during his long career, but the instrument he remains most closely associated with is the Gibson SG Special. As explained earlier, the SG range went through numerous changes following its introduction in 1961; the models used by Townshend as his principal onstage "axes" throughout the late '60s and early '70s were post-1966 Specials. Produced in "Cherry Red" and "Polaris White," these had pickguards that completely surrounded their twin P-90 single coil pickups (pickguards on pre-'66 instruments covered a smaller area). The guitars' factory-fitted vibrato units proved too fragile to withstand Townshend's heavy right-

*Below: A "stud" tailpiece replaces the vibrato found on an original SG Special, otherwise the design is "authentic."*

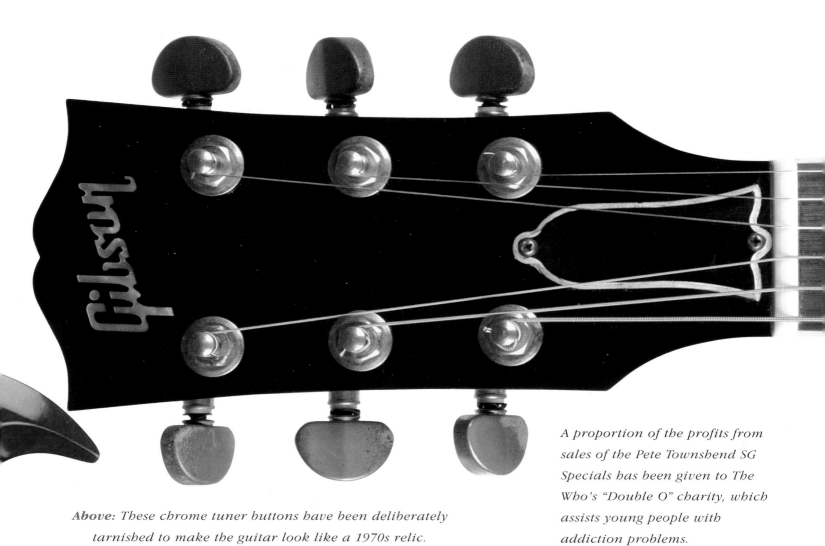

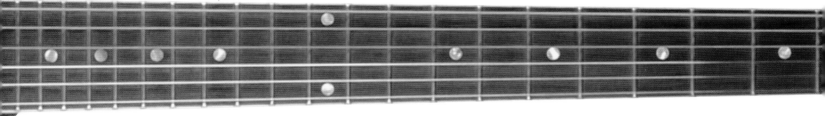

**Above:** *These chrome tuner buttons have been deliberately tarnished to make the guitar look like a 1970s relic.*

*A proportion of the profits from sales of the Pete Townshend SG Specials has been given to The Who's "Double O" charity, which assists young people with addiction problems.*

hand "power chording," and he invariably removed them, often leaving visible screw-holes.

Townshend's favored version of the SG Special was discontinued in 1971, but in 2000, Gibson announced the introduction of a limited edition "Pete Townshend Signature SG," The guitars have the same type of unbound mahogany body as the original 1966–71 Specials, and their hardware has been "aged" to create what Gibson describes a "a truly vintage look."

# GIBSON LES PAUL CUSTOM (1978)

THE OLD-STYLE, SINGLE-CUTAWAY Gibson Les Paul Custom had retained a firm following among many musicians, and by the mid-1960s, second-hand examples—such as the one purchased by Eric Clapton in New York in 1967, and later featured on the recording sessions for Cream's *Disraeli Gears* LP— were fetching high prices. The company responded by re-introducing the pre-SG "Black Beauty" (as well as the Les Paul Standard) in 1968, though it now had two,

rather than three humbucking pickups.

These new models, like their predecessors, were eagerly snapped up by performers: proud owners of 1968 "Black Beauties" have included the late Mick Ronson, who stripped the black coloring off his axe prior to using it on classic 1970s David Bowie albums like *Hunky Dory* and *The Rise and Fall of Ziggy Stardust and the Spiders from Mars*; while another celebrated British rocker, Steve Harley of Cockney

*Left: This Les Paul Custom has a maple top and a mahogany body and neck. It was made in Kalamazoo, MI, a few years prior to Gibson's move to Nashville.*

*In the photo above, the relatively flat profile of the fret wire—a characteristic feature of this model—can clearly be seen.*

PHOTOGRAPHS COURTESY OF GUITAR VILLAGE, FARNHAM

**Above:** *The Custom boasts multi-ply binding around its headstock, gold-plated tuners manufactured by Grover, and pearl inlays.*

**Right:** *Gibson has traditionally named its neck (front) and bridge (back) pickups "rhythm" and "treble," and these terms are used on the legend for the Les Paul Custom's selector switch.*

Rebel, still plays and cherishes his 1969 Custom.

Keen to capitalize on the instrument's enduring popularity, Gibson subsequently produced it in a range of different colors, and have gone on to mark the milestones in its long life with various "Special" models; the earliest of these, a 20th Anniversary instrument issued in 1974, had the distinction of being the firm's first-ever "birthday edition" guitar.

The "Natural," two-pickup Custom featured in our photographs dates from 1978.

# GIBSON EDS-1275

THE GIBSON EDS-1275 6- and 12-string doubleneck electric debuted in 1958. Produced only to special order, it originally sported a hollow body, though this had no f-holes; but by 1962, it had been restyled as an SG-type solid. Early 1275s (or "Double 12s" as they soon became known) of both kinds had spaced pairs of volume and tone controls mounted close to each of their bridges; this arrangement was eventually abandoned in favor of the standard knob grouping seen on the 1989-vintage 1275 in our photos.

The company's 1962 catalog described the Double 12 as "a completely new and exciting instrument," and adventurous guitarists such as UK "prog-rockers" Steve Howe of Yes and Charlie Whitney of Family relished the opportunity it gave them to switch effortlessly between its necks—or, indeed, to use them simultaneously. The 1275's best-known exponent was Jimmy Page of Led Zeppelin, who invariably featured it onstage when playing "Stairway to Heaven." However, the guitar apparently failed to please another eminent musician,

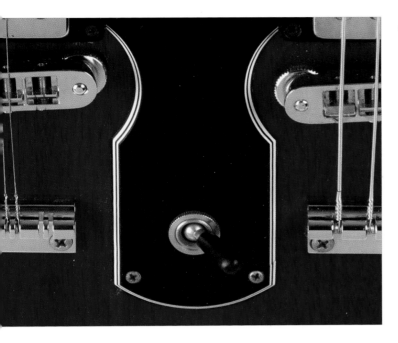

John McLaughlin of the Mahavishnu Orchestra, who tried it out in 1971, but quickly abandoned it in favor of a custom doubleneck made for him by luthier Rex Bogue. A later, more enthusiastic convert was Rush's Alex Lifeson, who began using the Double 12 in about 1977, and can still sometimes be spotted with one—notably on live performances of Rush's classic number "Xanadu," for which fellow band-member Geddy Lee dons a doubleneck Rickenbacker.

The EDS-1275's size and considerable weight may limit its appeal, and it was clearly never intended to sell in the same quantities as a Les Paul or an ES-335; nevertheless, it remains the world's only instantly recognizable doubleneck, and has a special place in the history of rock.

*Above: This switch allows the player to select the pickups for just one of the two necks, or to combine them.*

*The 1275's necks are made from maple, and their rosewood fingerboards have split paralleogram inlays.*

*Left: To avoid a confusing proliferation of knobs, the 1275 has only overall volume and tone controls for the pickups on each of its necks.*

CUSTOM
L-5

# GIBSON L-5S

GIBSON'S FAMOUS L-5 MODEL had already been produced as an acoustic and electric archtop (see preceding pages), but in 1972 it appeared in a surprising new incarnation—as a solid. The L-5S, as it was termed, boasted an elegant maple body, a "Cherry Sunburst" finish (other color options were added later), and two low impedance pickups similar to the type previously used on certain late 1960s and early 70s Les Pauls. Impedance, sometimes referred to as Z, is a synonym for electrical resistance: the tendency of standard, high impedance guitar circuitry to pick up interference and unwanted noise often causes difficulties, especially in the recording studio, and low-Z pickups are much less prone to this problem. However, they also require additional electronics to allow them to work properly with regular, high-Z guitar amplifiers, and tend to produce weaker output signals. Such negative features severely limited the popularity of Gibson's low impedance transducers, and by 1974, they had been dropped from the L-5S in favor of conventional humbuckers. A year later, the guitar's tailpiece, which had been styled similarly to the one found on archtop L-5s, was replaced by a standard, "stop"-type component.

*Below: The L-5S was eventually produced in three finishes: "Natural" (as here), and "Vintage" or "Cherry Sunburst."*

*Access to the L-5S's 22-fret neck is eased by its graceful cutaway.*

PHOTOGRAPHS COURTESY OF GUITAR JUNCTION, WORTHING

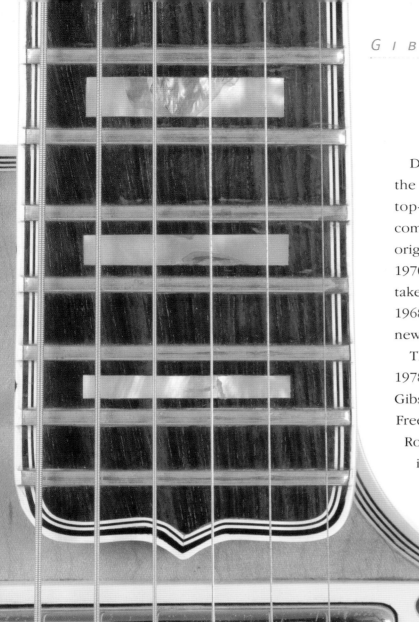

Despite the "Custom" legend on its truss-rod cover, the L-5S was a regular, production instrument, albeit a top-of-the-line one. It was also one of the comparatively few models still being built at Gibson's original factory in Kalamazoo, Michigan; by the mid-1970s, the firm's owners, Norlin Industries (which had taken over from its previous parent company, CMI, in 1968), had shifted most other Gibson manufacturing to new premises located in Nashville, Tennessee.

The L-5S shown in our photographs was made in 1978, six years before the model was dropped from the Gibson range, and was previously the property of ex-Free, Bad Company (and latterly Queen) vocalist Paul Rodgers. Other major names known to be L-5S users include Paul Simon and jazzman Pat Martino, as well as Dave Davies of The Kinks.

*Left: This close-up reveals the fancy binding around the L-5S's ebony fingerboard—whose pointed end has been a feature of L-5 design since the 1920s.*

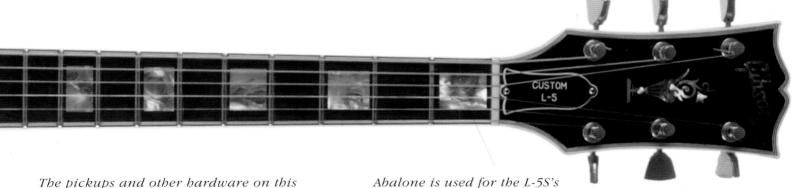

*The pickups and other hardware on this guitar are gold-covered.*

*Abalone is used for the L-5S's fingerboard inlays and headstock decoration.*

Les Paul

# GIBSON LES PAUL BASS

THE FIRST Gibson Les Paul bass appeared in 1970. Like the Les Paul "Personal" 6-string guitar that debuted the previous year, it utilized low impedance circuitry, which offered greatly reduced background noise and an extended frequency response; company publicity claimed that the LP bass's "crisp, clear tones…[would] exceed [those] of any electric bass on the market to date." For most players, however, the undoubted benefits of low impedance instruments were outweighed by practical disadvantages, such as the need to use a transformer when plugging them into standard, high impedance amplifiers. Consequently, these models enjoyed only limited success—although the "Triumph" (as the original LP bass was relabeled in 1971), and a later, semi-hollow high impedance Les Paul bass named the "Signature," both remained in the catalog until 1979.

There were no more Les Paul basses until the 1990s, which saw the launch of a number of 4- and 5-stringers with bodies and looks inspired by the LP Standard and

*Below: Active electronics made by Bartolini are installed on this Les Paul bass. Its four knobs control volume, bass, treble and blend.*

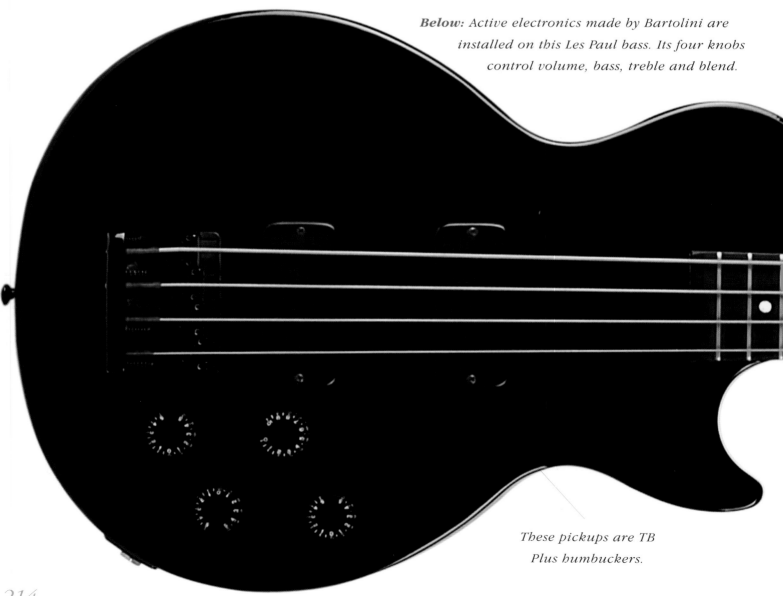

*These pickups are TB Plus humbuckers.*

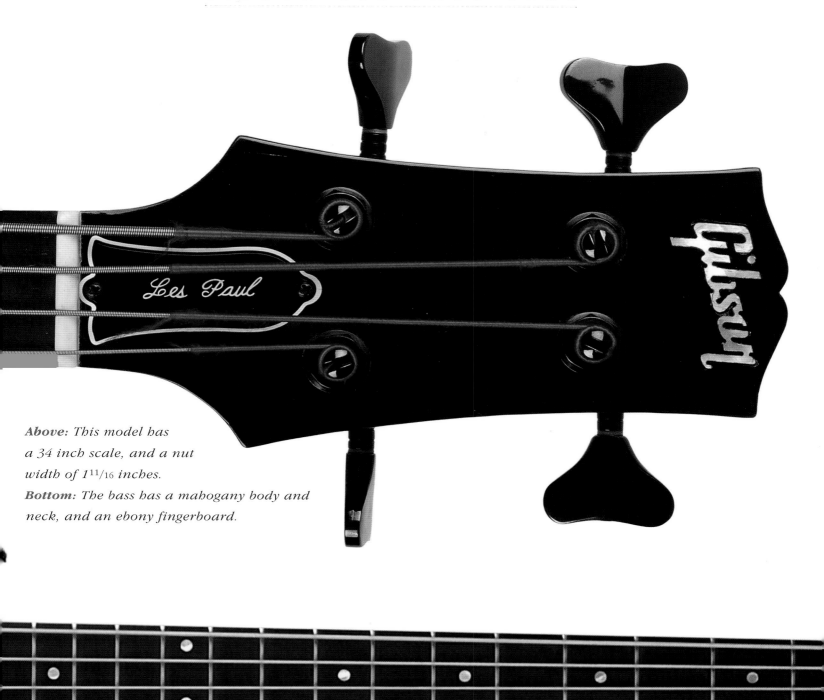

*Above: This model has a 34 inch scale, and a nut width of 1$^{11}$/$_{16}$ inches.*
*Bottom: The bass has a mahogany body and neck, and an ebony fingerboard.*

Special electric guitars. All had normal, high impedance pickups, and several boasted active electronics. The bass shown in our photos is a present-day descendant of these instruments: resembling a Les Paul Special, it is described by Gibson as combining "a classic look and solid performance with basic functionality." It is seen here in an "Ebony" finish, but is also available in "Classic White" and two other colors.

215

Grabbers were initially made in "Ebony" (as here) or "Red;" a natural-finish model appeared in 1976.

This sliding pickup is a humbucker.

# GIBSON GRABBER BASS

**Below:** *The Grabber has an alder body, and a maple neck and fingerboard.*

IN 1973, GIBSON'S L9-S bass appeared—but, within a year, had been given a more memorable—not to say aggressive—new name, the Ripper. This was the start of a trend for Gibsons with a gutsy image: the next bass to come out of Kalamazoo was the Grabber, launched in 1974, and accompanied by a publicity campaign proclaiming that it "had not been hanging around for fifteen or twenty years," and was "not your standard bass in any way."

The Grabber was certainly "non-standard" for Gibson, as, unlike the company's previous basses, it had a bolt-on neck. Its other striking features included a pickup that players could slide up or down to alter the tone it produced, and a very distinctively pointed headstock that was replicated on the Maurader 6-string electric, which appeared the following year, in 1975.

The Grabber remained in Gibson's catalog until 1982.

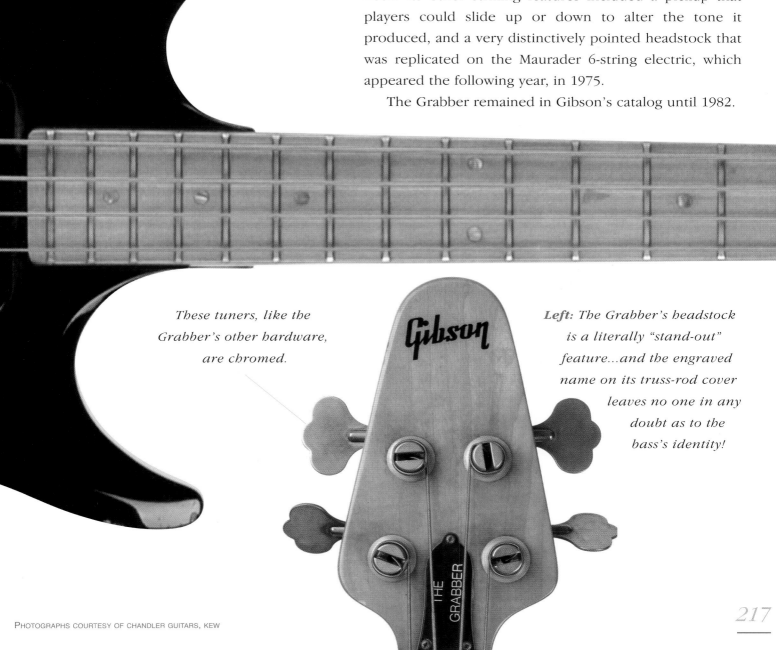

*These tuners, like the Grabber's other hardware, are chromed.*

**Left:** *The Grabber's headstock is a literally "stand-out" feature...and the engraved name on its truss-rod cover leaves no one in any doubt as to the bass's identity!*

# GIBSON "THE PAUL"

IN THE LATE 1970s, Gibson unveiled its "Firebrand" series of electric guitars. This consisted of lower-cost, stripped-down versions of some of the company's most famous designs, and included a solid-body (!) imitation of the ES-335, as well as standard and deluxe reworkings of both the SG and Les Paul—which were differentiated from their full-price counterparts by the use of quote-marks around their names.

The standard "Paul" shown here dates from 1979. Its body is cut from a piece of mahogany, without the maple "crown" found on instruments such as the Les Paul Standard or Custom, and it has little in the way of visual refinement; even the "Gibson" logo is "burned" into the wood of its headstock instead of being inlaid.

*Below: The dimensions of this guitar are almost identical to a genuine Les Paul—though its look and feel are very different.*

*Note the unusual placing of the pickup selector switch, which would normally be on the upper bass bout.*

*Below: The neck, like the body, is walnut; an ebony fingerboard is fitted.*

The guitar's technical specification, in contrast, is surprisingly impressive: humbucking pickups and Grover machine heads are installed, and the owner of the store where this example was photographed comments that it has "very nice action, lovely sustain, and the usual range of Les Paul tones."

The regular "Paul" was available from 1978 until 1982; its deluxe cousin appeared in 1980, and survived until 1986. Neither has since been revived.

# GIBSON LES PAUL (2002)

THE PROLIFERATION of Les Pauls in the current Gibson catalog provides a vast range of choices for players, whether their preference is for vintage-style models of the kind that Far Eastern manufacturers eagerly (and profitably) replicated during the years when the American originals were unavailable, or for striking new versions of the classic solid-body. The instrument shown here falls into the latter category. A Les Paul Standard Mahogany, dating from 2002, it lacks

Humbuckers supplied by the Santa Barbara, California-based Seymour Duncan company—which describes them as "built for aggressive playing styles," and "yield[ing] high output while retaining clarity."

Standard Mahogany guitars of this type are no longer produced by Gibson, and the example in our pictures is something of a rarity; the assistant in the store where it was photographed had not encountered one before, and eventually sold it to a collector.

*Below*: Mahogany, with a "Heritage Cherry" finish, is used for the Heritage Special's carved top and body; its neck is also made from mahogany, and has a rosewood fingerboard.

*Right*: This unusual Les Paul retains a regular headstock.

the maple top found on earlier Standards, and also departs from tradition by having three pickups instead of two. Despite being responsible, over the years, for the creation of a considerable number of classic transducer designs, Gibson occasionally turns to outside manufacturers for its electronics, and the units used on the Standard Mahogany are Distortion

*Opposite page*: This Les Paul boasts a trio of impressively powerful Seymour Duncan pickups.

# GIBSON BLUESHAWK

*The BluesHawk has a mahogany neck with a rosewood fingerboard.*

G IBSON'S "HAWK" SERIES OF ELECTRIC GUITARS was born in 1993, when the solid-body, single cutaway Nighthawk made its debut. It attracted a considerable following (high-profile users included Joe Walsh of The Eagles), and three years later, the range was augmented by the BluesHawk—a thinline, hollow-body design fitted with two Gibson's "Blues 90" pickups. These incorporate a dummy coil to reduce noise and interference, and produce an impressive range of sounds, especially when used in conjunction with the NightHawk's Varitone tone selector. After being switched into circuit by pulling up the tone control, this can then adjusted, via a rotary knob below the pickup selector, to provide preset filter settings that thicken or brighten the BluesHawk's timbre.

Like its predecessor, the BluesHawk proved fairly popular with players, thanks in part to Gibson's shrewd marketing strategy. In 1998, the company offered a limited edition version of the guitar as a prize in the prestigious annual Chicago Bluesfest competition, and, during the 2000–1 hockey season, it awarded a BluesHawk to the best "air guitarist" spotted among the spectators at a Nashville Predators match. However, although such efforts undoubtedly boosted the instrument's profile, its success has never rivalled that of classic solid body Gibsons such as the Les Paul and SG.

*These "Blues 90" pickups, in conjunction with the BluesHawk's Varitone circuitry, can offer eighteen distinct sound settings.*

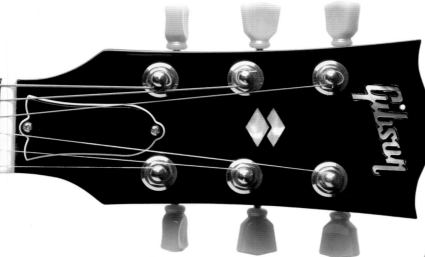

***Right and above:*** *The BluesHawk's back and sides are made from poplar, and it has a maple top. "Diamond" inlays grace its both its headstock and fingerboard.*

PHOTOGRAPHS COURTESY OF PEACH, BLAKE END, BRAINTREE

# GIBSON "CELEBRITY" FIREBIRD

FOR MANY YEARS, manufacturers have created "one-off" and limited edition instruments, in the hope that these will eventually attain the coveted status of a collector's item. Gibson's efforts in this area have been especially shrewd and successful. In 1988, the company's new management team (which had taken over only three years previously) launched a "Showcase" range of short-run guitars (a different one was produced each month) with EMG pickups and other unique features. This was followed, in 1991, by the "Celebrity Series," which, like the "Showcase" category, was made up of familiar, but distinctively customized limited edition "guitars of the month," marked with a special decal (see close-up), and supplied with a certificate of authenticity. The reverse-bodied Firebird in our photographs is one of these "Celebrity" guitars, all of which featured black finishes and gold hardware. It is based on the Firebird V, but does not include the Vibrola unit that was fitted to the original version of this model made between 1963 and 1965.

*Right:* This decal was used on all Gibson "Celebrity" models.

*Below:* Like the Firebird V from which it is derived, the Celebrity Firebird has two humbucking pickups.

*This black finish is found on all Celebrity models.*

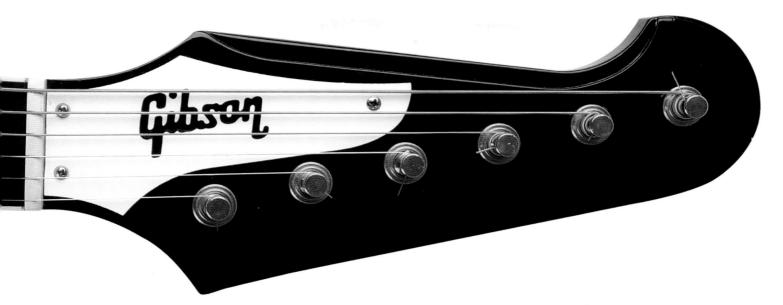

*Above and left:* The guitar's tuners, pickup covers, bridge and "stop" tailpiece are all gold-plated.

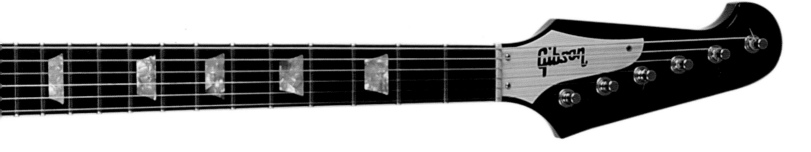

*Above:* The Firebird sports an ebony fretboard, with mother-of-pearl position markers.

Good-condition Celebrity Firebirds continue to attract fairly high resale prices, though the second-hand guitar market is notoriously fickle, and prices can fluctuate considerably from year to year. Later Gibson limited editions are also highly sought after, and the "Centennial" project, inaugurated in 1994 to mark the 100th anniversary of the firm's foundation, has seen its biggest single release of special models to date. These were issued monthly throughout the year, in editions of 101, and came with a number of extras, including a Gibson Centennial gold signet ring!

# GIBSON BOB MARLEY LES PAUL

BOB MARLEY (1945-1981), the first reggae artist to attain international superstardom, was frequently seen on stage with a heavily modified Gibson Les Paul Special, and in 2002, the company's Custom, Art and Heritage division produced a run of limited edition replicas of this instrument, one of which is shown here. The Special first appeared in 1955, and later went through a number of changes to its specification and shape; the type Marley played was the earliest, single-cutaway incarnation, produced at Gibson's Kalamazoo headquarters until 1958. This had twin P-90 pickups, an all-mahogany body with a pickguard screwed directly onto it, and a combined bridge/tailpiece. At first, the guitar was available only in a "limed" finish, but Marley's Special was a later, cherry-colored one.

Like many performers, Bob Marley customized his instrument, replacing the original bridge/tailpiece with separate units, substituting an aluminum pickguard for

*Below: The "aging" process developed by Tom Murphy involves giving the guitar's finish a dulled, slightly checked appearance.*

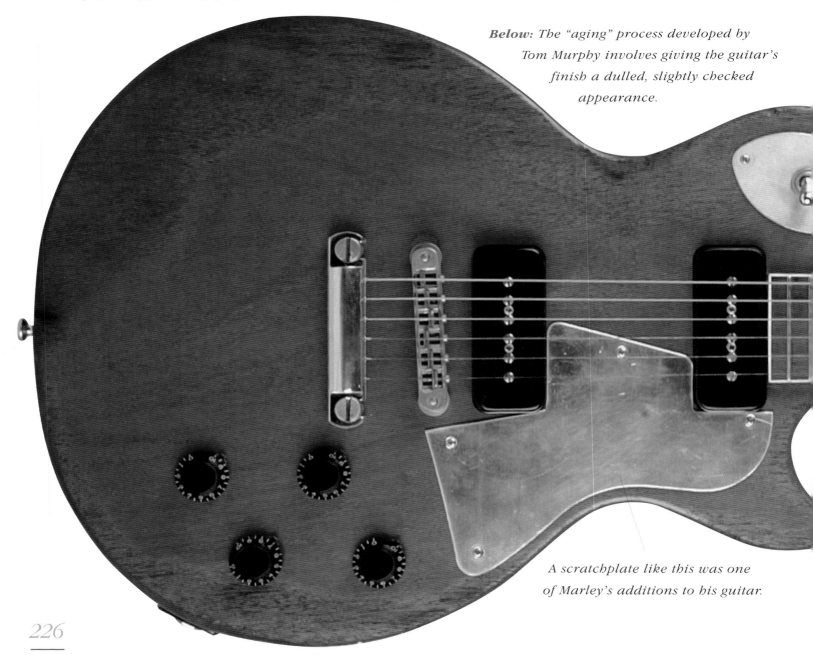

*A scratchplate like this was one of Marley's additions to his guitar.*

*Left:* The Bob Marley Les Paul Special features block inlay fingerboard markers, unlike original Specials, which had dot inlays.

the factory-fitted black plastic one, and adding a second piece of aluminum around the pickup selector switch on the guitar's upper bass bout. All these features have been faithfully reproduced on the Marley Les Paul, which also boasts an skillfully "aged" finish created using a process developed by former Gibson staffer Tom Murphy, who has worked on a number of the company's other Special Edition models.

*Above:* The black volume and tone knobs seen here are regular Les Paul Special components.
*Left:* The headstock, also, is in a standard "Les Paul" shape.

# GIBSON SG SUPREME

THE SG SUPREME was launched, with a considerable flourish, by Gibson in early 1999. A press release proclaimed it to be "a direct descendant of [the company's] original solid guitar, the Les Paul," and, with its maple topped mahogany body, the instrument is certainly an extremely elegant and fascinating hybrid. However, while it is true that the Les Paul name was applied, between 1960 and 1963, to the double-cutaway guitars that we now call SGs (see SG Custom entry on pages 290-1), it is worth noting that no model ever sported the Supreme's unique combination of woods during that period, as original SG-type bodies were made entirely from mahogany.

Despite not being exactly authentic, the Supreme is a fine addition to the SG line, and is every bit as capable as its predecessors when it comes to delivering what Gibson describes as the instrument's "bad boy sound"—beloved by several generations of rockers, including stars as diverse as Pete Townshend of The Who, Tony Iommi of Black Sabbath, Angus Young of AC/DC, and the late Frank Zappa. Most of these players favored SGs with humbucking pickups, which have been fitted to all Supremes since 2001; slightly older examples, including the one in our photographs, have

*AA-grade flame maple is used for the Gibson SG Supreme's top.*

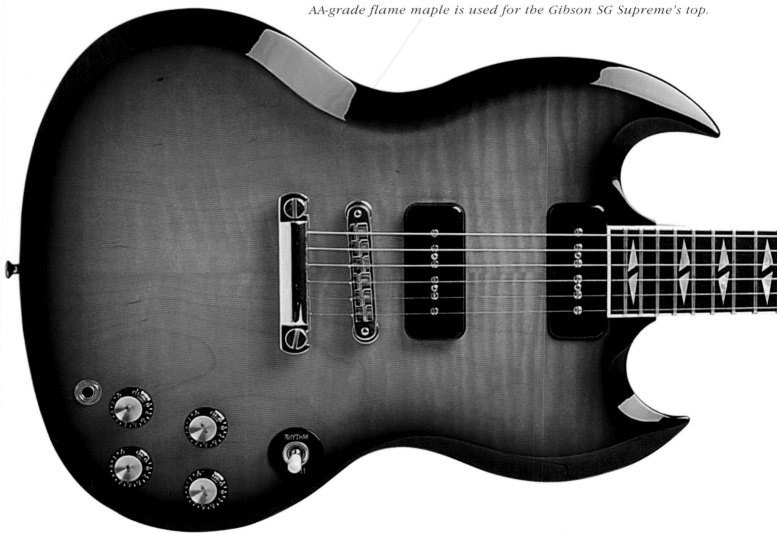

**Bottom:** *The distinctive design on the Supreme fret markers is derived from the pattern on its headstock inlay.*

**Above:** *The Supreme shown here is finished in "Fireburst" (a color no longer offered on this model), and has a gold-plated bridge and tailpiece.*

P-90 single-coil transducers. Other features, such as the model's ultra-slim, 60's-style neck, with its ebony fretboard, "split diamond" fingerboard markers, and kidney shaped tuners, have remained constant since its introduction. The SG Supreme is currently available in four different colors: "Lavaburst," "Emeraldburst," "Midnightburst" and "Trans Black."

# GIBSON L-O

BY THE MID-1920s, Gibson had already established a significant presence in archtop instrument making, but was seemingly less committed to flat-tops, waiting until 1926 to produce its first two examples. These were the L-1 (whose name was borrowed from an previous archtop round-hole model introduced in the early 1900s—although, confusingly, the 1926 L-1 was an entirely different guitar), and L-0. Both new models were plainly finished, inexpensive (according to price lists dating from 1928, the L-1 sold for $50, the L-0 for just $35) and small, measuring only 13 1/2 inches across the widest part of their tops. In contrast, Martin 000 were 15 inches wide, and 00s slightly narrower.

Unlike any other guitars of their type, early L series

*Below: The L-0 has a mahogany top, back and sides. Its body has a white binding, and a dual-stripe soundhole rosette.*

**Right**: *Ebony is used for the L-0's bridge.*

*These white bridge pins are later replacements; the originals would have been black.*

Gibson flat-tops had lower bodies considerably broader and more rounded than their upper halves. This characteristic shape can be seen not only on the pre-1928 L-0 featured here, but in many photographs of the original L-1's most famous user, bluesman Robert Johnson (1911-1938). The design quirk disappeared in 1929, when the guitars were reshaped, and their bodies were widened to 14³/4 inches. The L-0 was discontinued in 1933, the L-1 four years later.

# GIBSON L-oo

THE GIBSON L-00 is believed to have debuted in 1929, although it made its first appearance in the company's catalog three years later. Offered at a retail price of $25, it displaced the L-0 as Gibson's least expensive flat-top; like later L-0s, it measured 14¾ inches across, and had a mahogany back and sides, though with a spruce top.

The L-0's emergence more or less coincided with the Wall Street Crash, and its low cost and high quality helped keep it in production throughout the Great Depression—a period when Gibson was obliged to combine lutherie with non-musical ventures such as toy-making to make ends meet. It had a particular appeal to bluesmen (Georgia-born Eugene "Buddy" Moss, who recorded and performed extensively throughout the early 1930s, often working alongside Blind Willie McTell and other luminaries, is known to have played an L-00); and in 1937, a more buoyant economic climate enabled Gibson to introduce a Hawaiian version of the instrument, named the HG-00.

*Below: Like earlier models, this recent L-00 has a spruce top, mahoagany back, sides and neck, and a rosewood fingerboard and bridge.*

*"Vintage Sunburst" (as here) or "Antique Walnut" finishes are available.*

*Above: Miniature tuners made by Grover are fitted to the L-00's headstock.*

The L-00, dubbed the "poor man's Cadillac" in Eldon Whitford, David Vinopal and Dan Erlewine's comprehensive history of Gibson flat-tops, was dropped at the end of World War II. However, it has retained a considerable following—the late John Fahey was among its most prominent users in the 1970s and 80s—and has recently been reissued by Gibson.

One of these new L-00s, produced at the firm's factory in Bozeman, Montana, and now also known as the "Blues King," is featured in our photographs. Welcoming its introduction, Gibson Chairman and CEO Henry Juszkiewicz commented: "The L-series flat-tops have been favorites of blues guitarists from the very beginning, and we believe the Blues King will inspire a new generation of artists to carry on a great American art form."

# GIBSON ADVANCED JUMBO

IN 1931, THE FIRST Martin-branded Dreadnought acoustics appeared. They were wider (measuring 15⅜ inches across their lower bouts) and more powerful sounding than any other flat-top guitar, and were soon attracting customers away from competitors such as Gibson. The bosses at Kalamazoo responded to the Dreadnought challenge by unveiling their "Jumbo" model in 1934. It had a characteristic "round-shouldered" look, and its 16-inch-wide mahogany body provided reserves of volume quite sufficient to match its rivals. However, its $60 price tag proved to be too high, and it was discontinued in 1936.

That same year, Gibson introduced two new Jumbos, sized similarly to their predecessors. One, the "Jumbo 35," sold for just $35 and had a mahogany body; the other, the high-end "Advanced Jumbo," cost $80 and sported a rosewood back and sides. The former enjoyed considerable success, but the prohibitively

*Below: The Advanced Jumbo's top is made from premium sitka spruce.*

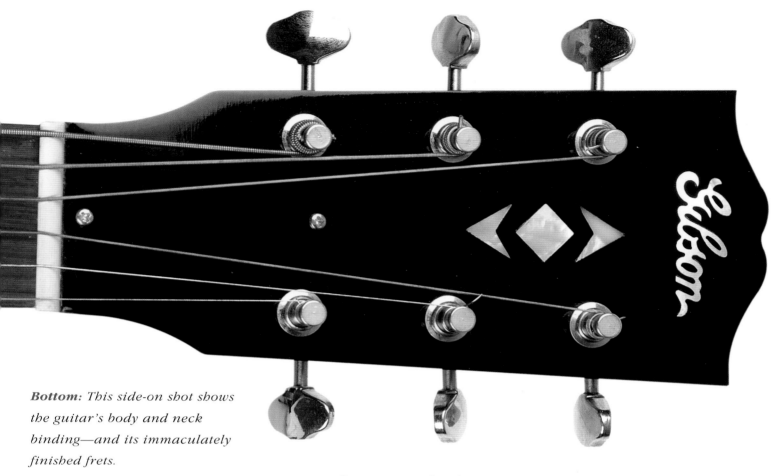

**Bottom:** *This side-on shot shows the guitar's body and neck binding—and its immaculately finished frets.*

**Above:** *"Arrow-head" mother-of-pearl inlays grace the AJ's headstock and rosewood fingerboard.*

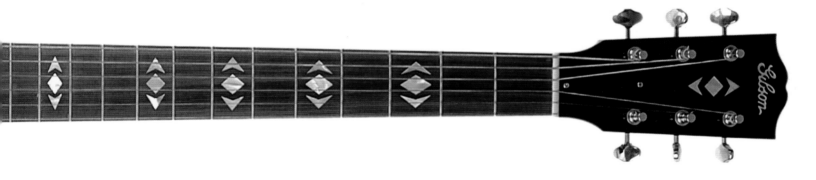

expensive "AJ" only remained available until 1940, and did not receive the recognition it deserved until it was reissued in the 1990s—though since then, leading players from many different musical genres have waxed lyrical over the subtlety and richness of its tone, and a reviewer from the influential ***Vintage Guitar*** magazine has described it as "a little piece of heaven on earth." A recently-made Advanced Jumbo is shown here.

# GIBSON SJ-200

BY THE LATE 1930s, Ray Whitley (1901-1979) was famous as a singer, and for his many "sidekick" roles in cowboy movies; he was also a successful songwriter, soon to make his name as the co-composer of "Back In the Saddle Again," the number later adopted by his fellow film cowboy Gene Autry. With a shrewd eye for publicity, Gibson used Whitley to promote its latest acoustic guitar—a handsome jumbo with a top just under 17 inches wide (it would later be resized to a full 17 inches), a strikingly ornamented scratchplate, and a pearl-inlaid, mustache-shaped ebony bridge. This first and most distinguished member of the company's Super Jumbo range went on the market in 1938; it sold for $200 and was therefore named the SJ-200. Quickly adopted by other major Hollywood names (including Autry and Ray "Crash" Corrigan), the new model was described by Gibson in the 1940s as the "king of the flat top guitars...especially created for those professional entertainers who want an instrument...with a beauty and distinction that projects itself to the audience."

*These "crest" fingerboard markers have been a distinctive feature of the SJ-200 since its introduction in the 1930s.*

**Above:** *One of the SJ-200's 'trademarks' is its pearl-decorated bridge.*
**Left:** *This recently made model has a spruce top, and flamed maple back, sides and neck.*

The guitar's undeniable "star quality" has proved timeless and for decades leading performers, including Elvis Presley, Johnny Cash, Ricky Nelson, and Emmylou Harris have been seen and heard with J-200s. The instrument's "S" prefix was dropped by Gibson in the late 1940s, but has now reappeared.

# GIBSON SOUTHERNER JUMBO

THE SAGA OF GIBSON'S Southerner Jumbo, which began, according to the company's publicity, when "a salesman for the southern territory brought home requests for a sturdy, versatile and attractive round-shoulder dreadnought," is a somewhat confusing one. Though the instrument's name is often abbreviated to "SJ," it is unrelated to the "Super Jumbo" SJ-200 shown on the last two pages. The Southerner's closest sibling in the Gibson line is, in fact, the J-45—a slightly plainer, but similarly round-shouldered jumbo that made its debut alongside the SJ in 1942. (See separate entry.) There are also anomalies in the Southerner's specification: the very first models to come out of Kalamazoo had rosewood backs and sides, but later SJs were made from mahogany (with spruce tops). And its subsequent history abounds in further twists and turns

*Below: Like the original SJs, this Southern Jumbo has a spruce top, a 16 inch body width, and back and sides of mahogany.*

*This "pointed" scratchplate first appeared on 1950s SJs.*

PHOTOGRAPHS COURTESY OF GUITAR CLASSICS, LONDON

…culminating in its recent reissue under the name of "Southern" rather than "Southerner" Jumbo!

Supplies of early SJs were limited due to wartime restrictions, but the new guitar quickly attracted a considerable following: prominent 1940s users included singer and political activist Woody Guthrie, who famously stuck a "This Machine Kills Fascists" label to the body of his Southerner. For a while, the headstock of all SJs carried a slogan of Gibson's own— "Only A Gibson Is Good Enough;" however, this was quickly removed in 1946 after the company's rival, Epiphone, launched an ad campaign based around the words "When Good Enough Isn't Good Enough."

During the 1950s, SJ sales grew, prompting Gibson to produce it in a new, natural-finish version; in 1956, this was given a separate identity as the "Country-Western," and details of it are provided overleaf. The Southerner itself remained in the catalog until the late 1970s, and is now available once more as the "Southern Jumbo:" a newly made example of it is featured here.

# GIBSON SJN COUNTRY WESTERN

AS PREVIOUSLY EXPLAINED, Gibson "Country-Western" flat-tops were simply Southerner Jumbos with natural finishes. The Country-Western name was retained only until 1960, when it was altered to SJN (Southerner Jumbo Natural). This relatively unimportant change was followed by a more significant modification to both the SJN and the original sunburst-finish Southerner Jumbo, as their "traditional," non-adjustable bridges were replaced with units sporting a saddle that could be raised or lowered by two screws.

(The substitution was controversial: quite a number of players felt that the new bridges had an adverse effect on the instruments' tone, and by the end of the decade, Gibson had reverted to the earlier type.)

In 1962, the natural SJN received yet another new name, the SJN Country Western, and that year's Gibson catalog extolled the model's "deep resonance, powerful tone and deluxe appearance." However, the familiar, round-shouldered shape of the SJN and Southerner was about to disappear: a year later, the

*Below: This 1964 SJN Country Western has a spruce top, and mahogany back and sides.*

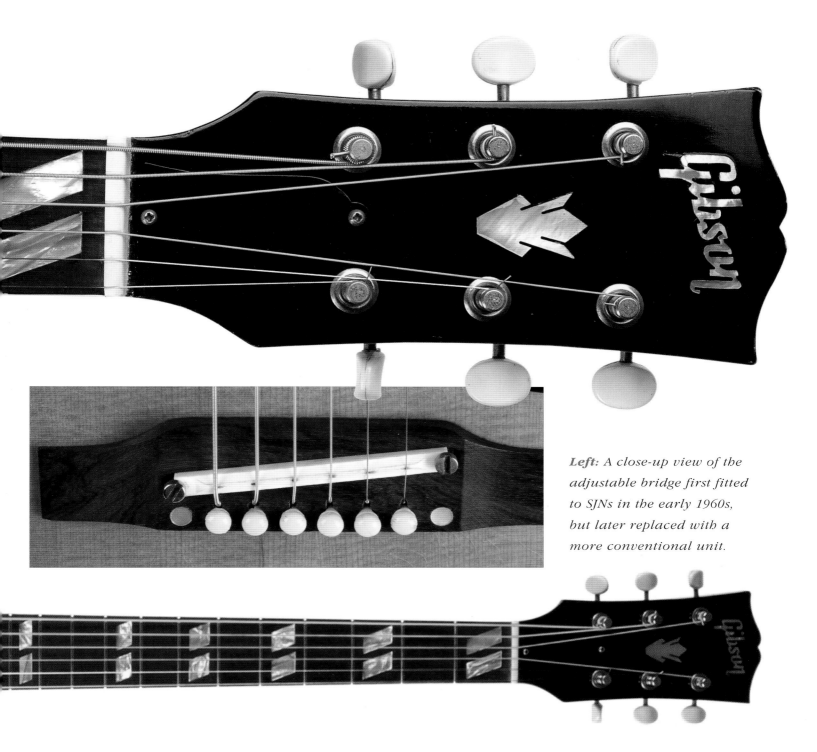

*Left:* A close-up view of the
adjustable bridge first fitted
to SJNs in the early 1960s,
but later replaced with a
more conventional unit.

guitars received new, squarer body stylings similar to those on the highly successful Hummingbird (see separate entry) and Dove flat-tops. The Country Western in our photos dates from 1964, and features the different outline, which the CW and Southerner both kept until they were discontinued in 1978.

Despite the drawbacks caused by its adjustable bridge, the "squared-off" SJN Country Western is a striking instrument, both sonically and visually. Among its many devotees is singer-songwriter Sheryl Crow, who bought one in the 1960s, and has used it onstage and in the studio for many years. In 2000, Gibson launched a "Sheryl Crow Signature Model" closely based on the star's guitar; more recently, the company has produced a "Country Western 1958 Reissue" that replicates the pre-1962 version of the acoustic.

# J-45

# GIBSON J-45

THE JAPANESE ATTACK on Pearl Harbor took place on December 8, 1941. The USA declared war on Japan the following day, and was soon devoting most of its industrial capacity to defence-related projects—a move that inevitably restricted the production of non-essential goods such as guitars. During the war years, Gibson saw the majority of its staff redeployed onto war work (music historians Eldon Whitford, David Vinopal and Dan Erlewine state that only 10% of its craftsmen were available to make instruments between 1942 to 1945), while shortages of wood and other materials led to inevitable variations in the specifications of the models that were actually built. With steel at a premium, some of these lacked truss-rods, while others had to be constructed with non-standard timbers and surplus parts.

America's first full year of conflict was scarcely an auspicious time to launch new flat-tops, but in summer 1942, the company's latest acoustics, the J-45 and the Southerner (featured on pages 330-1), began shipping

*Below: The J-45 is no longer available in this square-shouldered form, but has been reissued in its original, rounder body shape.*

from its Michigan headquarters. Both were 16 inches wide, round-shouldered, spruce-topped jumbos that initially carried an "Only A Gibson Is Good Enough" slogan on their headstocks—although the J-45, unlike the earliest, rosewood-bodied batch of Southerners, had a mahogany back and sides. Its appearance was somewhat spartan, but its gutsy tone quickly endeared it to customers, and, in spite of the uncertainties of wartime manufacturing, it went on to become a best seller.

Post-1945, the J-45 succeeded in retaining its status as a popular "workhorse" instrument, despite several changes in design. The most important of these occurred in 1969, when it acquired the square-shoulder body outline already sported by the Southerner and SJN. The J-45 in our photos dates from this time, and originally had a standard sunburst finish; however, in the 1970s, its then owner had this replaced with its current, "natural" coloring.

*Below: Rosewood is used for the J-45's 20-fret fingerboard, which has mother-of-pearl dot inlays.*

*Left: Though different in appearance to the adjustable bridge on the SJN Country Western (see previous pages), this unit operates similarly.*

# GIBSON J-50

THE GIBSON J-50 shared the same basic specification as the J-45, but had a natural finish instead of the latter's normal sunburst one. It was officially introduced in 1947, although research in the company's factory ledgers by guitar expert Walter Carter suggests that a small quantity of J-50s may have been supplied to dealers as early as July 1942—about a month before the J-45 made its debut.

Initially priced at $100 ($10 more than a J-45), the J-50 enjoyed a wide appeal, especially among folk, country and blues players. One of the first major names to be associated with it was Tammy Wynette, who is said to have chosen it because its tone matched her characteristic singing style; and in the early 1960s, the young Bob Dylan, a former Martin user, bought one and was pictured with it on the cover of his debut

*Below: The J-50 has a spruce top with white ivoroid binding. Its back and sides are mahogany.*

album (**Bob Dylan**, released in 1962). Dylan's instrument must have been purchased second-hand, as it sported a "teardrop"-shaped scratchplate of a kind that Gibson had stopped fitting to J-50s in about 1955; models made between that date and 1969 have wider, pointed pickguards like the one on the 1964 guitar in our photo.

Following a decline in sales in the late 1960s, the J-50, like the J-45, was relaunched in a new, square-shouldered form in 1969, but was eventually dropped

*Top: Though this J-50 no longer has an adjustable bridge, this stamp inside its body indicates that one was originally fitted to it.*

from the Gibson catalog in 1982. However, it has continued to attract high profile musicians (current devotees include singer-songwriters Elvis Costello and Gillian Welch), and is now being made again in its original, round-shouldered version.

# GIBSON LG-O

The first Gibson LG flat-top (the initials stand for "little guitar") was the LG-2, which debuted in 1943. Like the L-00 (which was introduced in 1929 and remained in production until 1945), it had a $14\frac{3}{4}$-inch wide spruce top, and a back and sides of mahogany. After the war, it was joined by three other models: the LG-1 and LG-3, and the three-quarter size LG-$2\frac{3}{4}$; but there were no more additions to the range until the LF-0 debuted in 1958. Unlike its sisters, the LG-0 was made entirely from mahogany.

Its $85 price tag made it the cheapest instruments in the LG range, and it enjoyed immense popularity and impressive sales. It remained in production until 1974 and was among the last "budget" Gibsons.

# GIBSON HUMMINGBIRD

The first Hummingbird, launched in 1960, was the first of Gibson's square-shouldered acoustic guitars. It had an exquisite pickguard inlay, designed by staffer Hartford Synder. The company promoted the guitar as being the "big, round, and full…with the deep rumbly bass so prized by guitar players." It had been specially tailored for vocal accompaniment, and promised prospective buyers that the Hummingbird could be relied upon to provide a combination of "resonant tone, carrying power and striking beauty." The instrument lived up to expectations: folk and country pickers admired its mellow, rich timbre; pop and rock performers found it ideal for creating hard-driving rhythm.

*The exquisite pickguard inlay designed by Gibson staffer Hartford Synder makes the Hummingbird the fanciest flat-top to come out of Kalamazoo since the late 1930s.*

# GIBSON J-180 (EVERLY BROTHERS)

DON AND PHIL EVERLY enjoyed their first US chart success with "Bye Bye, Love" in 1957, and over the years, their music has delighted both pop fans and devotees of the traditional numbers they featured on albums like *Songs Our Daddy Taught Us* (1958). Even a period of personal friction between them, culminating in a 10-year break from joint appearances between 1973 and 1983, failed to diminish the regard and affection felt for them by audiences, and, after five decades in the music business, they are still touring and recording.

In the brothers' early performing days, Don played a Gibson Southern Jumbo (see separate entry). When interviewed for Eldon Whitford, David Vinopal and Dan Erlewine's *Gibson's Fabulous Flat-Top Guitars* (1994), he revealed that this was his "first brand-new guitar," and that he used it on the recording sessions for both "Bye Bye, Love" and "Wake Up, Little Suzie." Later, both Everlys were pictured with SJ-200s; before long, these had been embellished by Gibson with custom-made, oversized pickguards cut to the brothers' own design, which were to became a key visual feature of the "Everly Brothers" jumbo introduced by the company in 1962. It also boasted star-shaped inlays on its headstock and fingerboard, and was finished in black; Everly models with natural tops were made in 1963 and .from 1968 onwards.

Though undeniably striking, the original Everlys guitar, which was discontinued in the early 1970s, is not without its critics. Dealer and expert George Gruhn has pointed out that the mirror-image pickguards had a restrictive effect on the solid spruce top's vibrations, and also observes that its pinless bridge, which was replaced when the Everlys jumbo was relaunched as the J-180 in 1986, "[did] not help with the sound either." The new model, seen here, is made at Gibson's factory in Bozeman, Montana, and undeniably performs better than its predecessor. Nevertheless, 1960s Everlys jumbos retain a special cachet, and currently change hands for high prices.

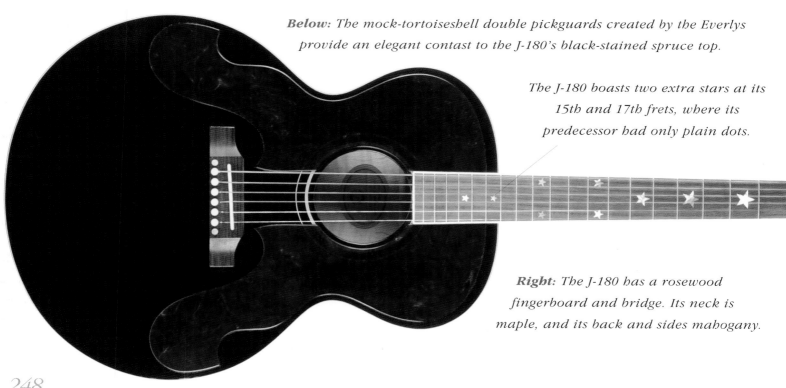

*Below: The mock-tortoiseshell double pickguards created by the Everlys provide an elegant contast to the J-180's black-stained spruce top.*

*The J-180 boasts two extra stars at its 15th and 17th frets, where its predecessor had only plain dots.*

*Right: The J-180 has a rosewood fingerboard and bridge. Its neck is maple, and its back and sides mahogany.*

# GIBSON J-100 Xtra

A CHANGE OF OWNERSHIP at Gibson in the mid-1980s, marked by the arrival of Henry Juszkiewicz as its CEO, reinvigorated the company (whose fortunes and reputation had been at a low ebb in the preceding years), and led to the introduction of a number of exciting new products.

One of the first guitars launched by Juszkiewicz's team, the J-100 jumbo, was actually based on the pre-war SJ-100, which had appeared in 1939 as a slightly plainer, cheaper version of the SJ-200 (see separate entry). Popular with both blues and country artists, the original 100 was discontinued in 1942; its revived version sold moderately well, but in the early 1990s, it was decided to replace it with an upgraded model, the J-100 Xtra, an example of which is shown here.

While the 1985 J-100 had a conventional bridge and a "teardrop" pickguard, the Xtra has reverted to the somewhat fancier stylings found on its 1930s ancestor

*Below: The J-100 Xtra has a sitka spruce top; its back and sides are made from Honduras mahogany.*

*Above: The guitar's top has elegant, multiple binding.*
*Left: This rosewood bridge lacks the mother-of-pearl decorations found on the much more expensive SJ-200 model.*

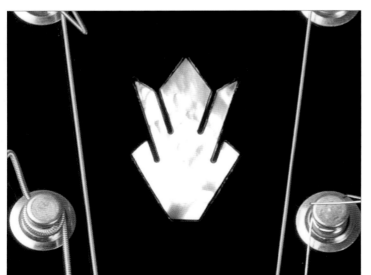

(and, of course, the SJ-200). Consequently, its bridge is in the classic curled, "mustache" shape, and its enlarged scratchplate sports a pointed edge. The guitar has a 17-inch top, a 25½ inch scale, and an "Antique Natural Lacquer" finish.

*Left: The "crown" marker is one of Gibson's most distinctive "trademark" inlays.*

# GIBSON JOHN LENNON J-160E "PEACE"

THE GIBSON J-160E was introduced in 1954. Featuring a discreetly positioned single-coil pickup, it was primarily aimed at players seeking both the practicality of an electric guitar and the conventional elegance of an acoustic jumbo—though there were inevitable compromises in its design, the most significant being its laminated, ladder-braced top, which was rigid enough to repel feedback, but delivered a less than ideal "unplugged" sound. Originally aimed at country and western players, it found its greatest fame when it was adopted by John Lennon and George Harrison of The Beatles; both switched to standard electrics for most of their later work with the band, but Lennon retained a soft spot for his J-160E, replacing its original sunburst coloring with a psychedelic paint job in 1967, then giving it a

*Below: Like John Lennon's 1962 J-160E electric, the "Peace" model has a plywood spruce top, and mahogany back and sides.*

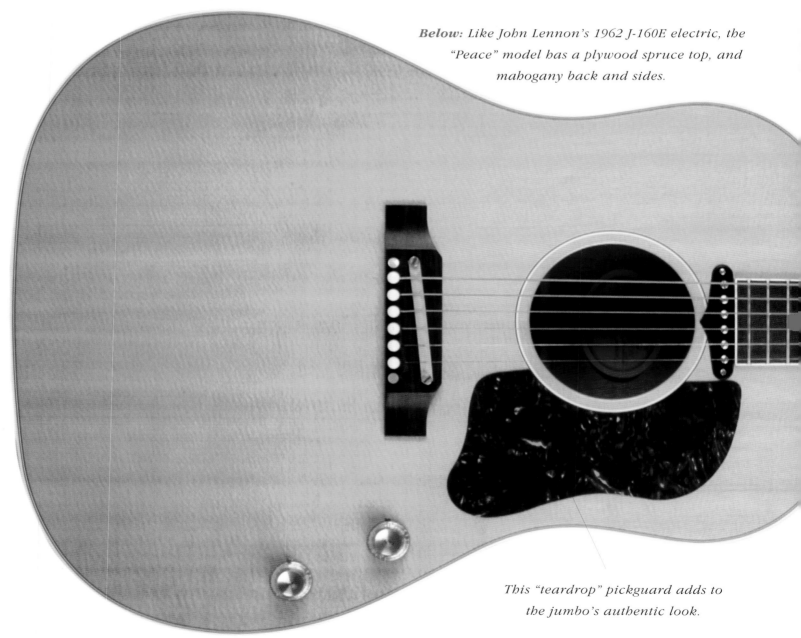

*This "teardrop" pickguard adds to the jumbo's authentic look.*

*The truss-rod cover carries John Lennon's signature.*

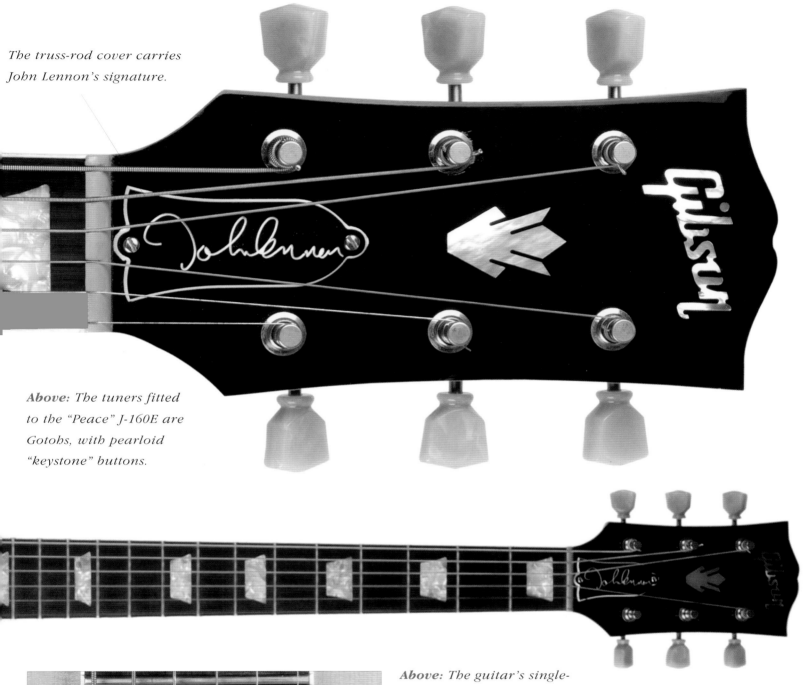

**Above:** *The tuners fitted to the "Peace" J-160E are Gotohs, with pearloid "keystone" buttons.*

**Above:** *The guitar's single-ply bound neck has a rosewood fingerboard and "trapezoid" position markers.*

natural finish prior to using it for his "Bed-In" peace protests with Yoko Ono in 1969.

This limited edition "Peace" model replicates the look of Lennon's own instrument during the "Bed-In" period. It was built at Gibson's plant in Bozeman, Montana, and launched in 2002.

*Right: Top and body are made from maple and poplar laminate, and finished in "Western Orange."*

The Country Gentleman has a master volume control—a feature often fitted to Chet Atkins' guitars.

# GIBSON COUNTRY GENTLEMAN

AFTER THE INTRODUCTION of his nylon-strung acoustic by Gibson in 1982 (see previous pages), Chet Atkins went on to collaborate with the company on updated versions of two instruments bearing his name that had first been produced by Gretsch in the late 1950s. One of these was the Country Gentleman electric archtop, which appeared in its new

Gibson form in 1986. Gretsch Country Gentlemen made between 1957 and 1972 had boasted feedback-reducing sealed tops and fake, painted-on f-holes (a Gretsch-made Chet Atkins electric featuring these is shown later in this book), but for the Gibson model, this striking example of *trompe l'oeil* was

abandoned, and the guitar was given a Gibson 335-style solid center block to improve its performance at higher volume levels, and to boost sustain. Other changes included the replacement of Gretsch's "Filter'Tron" pickups with a pair of Gibson humbuckers, and the provision of a banjo-type armrest on the edge of the body.

This 2003 "CG" differs slightly from the 1986 original: block fretboard markers have replaced the "thumbprint" inlays seen on earlier Gentlemen, and a non-vibrato tailpiece has been fitted.

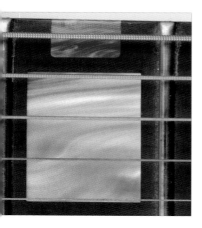

*Left: A close-up of the distinctive double position markers on the instrument's ebony fingerboard.*

*Right: The endorsee's name is inlaid on the guitar's truss-rod cover in "pearl holly."*

*255*

*Below: The CE has a solid-body with a spruce top, though its mahogany back features "acoustic chambering." Mahogany is also used for its neck, and its fingerboard is ebony. Note Chet Akins' signature on the soundhole cover.*

*Right: Both the CE and its wider-necked companion, the CEC, boast gold-plated, classical-style tuners specially made for Gibson by Schaller.*

# GIBSON CHET ATKINS CE

THE CLASSICAL ELECTRIC (CE)—AN ELECTRIC NYLON-STRUNG guitar with a solid body that would make feedback problems (always potentially troublesome when amplifying an inherently soft-voiced instrument) a thing of the past—represented the first fruits of the collaboration between Gibson and Chet Atkins that began in the early 1980s. Chet had been searching for an effective electric classic for years, and had already commissioned a prototype solid-body model from Kentucky-based luthier Hascal "Hack" Haile (1906-1986); this was shown to Gibson, and served as the basis for the "CE" that the company started producing in 1982. The guitar in our photographs was made the same year.

Unlike some later electric classics, the CE retains the look of its more traditional counterpart. However, it has a thinline construction (incorporating "tone chambers," which, as Gibson puts it,"enhance [its] acoustic performance") and a sealed soundhole, and the vibrations from its spruce top are converted to electricity by a Gibson-designed piezo transducer in the bridge. Volume and tone

controls are mounted on the instrument's upper rim, and output levels from each string can be adjusted from inside the body..

The Chet Atkins CE seen here was made in Nashville, but both it and the CEC (a second model with a slightly wider fingerboard) are now crafted at Gibson's acoustic guitar plant in Bozeman, Montana.

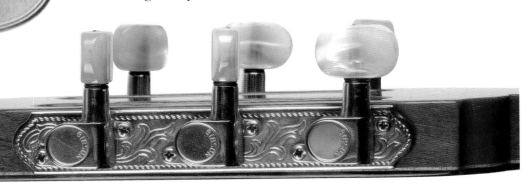

# GODIN MULTIAC STEEL DUET

Canadian designer and musician Robert Godin has been the driving force behind a number of successful and innovative acoustic brands, such as Art & Lutherie, and Norman. However, it is the product line bearing its own name, established in 1987, that features his most cutting-edge instruments, electrics and electro-acoustics. These instruments combine traditional craftsmanship and high technology in ingenious ways. Godin's Multiac series includes both nylon- and steel-strung models.

This Multiac is a steel duet. This instrument has a mahogany body with two acoustic chambers, but is intended to be heard through an amplifier or a PA system, and has two blendable transducers, hence "Duet."

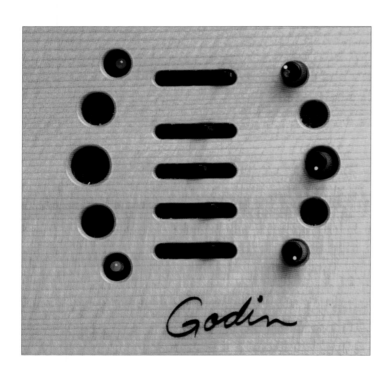

*A detail of the Godin's knobs and slider controls, which adjust to blend the instrument's pickups.*

# GODIN XTSA

The Godin xtSA offers players three separate "voices," which can be deployed separately or combines. Its "standard" electric guitar tones are produced via three magnetic pickups: a single single-coil unit, and two humbuckers at the neck and bridge positions. For realistic "acoustic guitar" sounds, the xtSA has transducers imbedded in each of its bridge saddles. The xtSA's third output is a "hexaphonic" one, via which signals from each of the guitar's six strings can be used to trigger a synthesizer and create and create an almost unlimited range of sounds.

The xtSA's body is made from silver leaf maple and poplar. It has a mahogany neck and an ebony fingerboard. They are built in Berlin, New Hampshire.

*The Godin's silver leaf maple body has four slider controls in the upper bass bout that adjust volume, treble, midrange and bass, levels on the transducers buried in the bridge saddles.*

# GRETSCH "SYNCHROMATIC" ARCHTOP

THE FRED GRETSCH COMPANY was set up in Brooklyn, New York, in 1883. Its founder, Friedrich Gretsch, was a German immigrant; he died in 1895, and was succeeded by his son, later known as Fred Sr. The family firm was both a manufacturer and distributor, handling a wide variety of musical instruments: its first acoustic archtop guitars appeared in 1933, and six years later, it began using the "Synchromatic" name on some of the headstocks. Curiously, it made little attempt to break into the burgeoning pre-war electric archtop market, which was then dominated by two of its principal competitors, Gibson and Epiphone.

For most of the period immediately following Fred Sr.'s retirement in 1942, his son Bill ran Gretsch; on Bill's death in 1948, control passed to another son,

*Below: The lacquer finish on models such as this would have been hand polished to give it an impressive sheen.*

*This distinctively shaped "stairstep" bridge had been a feature on Gretsch archtops since well before World War II.*

*Above: In 1939, the first Gretsch "Synchromatic" archtops were exhibited, to considerable acclaim, at New York's World's Fair.*

*Right: The slight discoloration on these inlays is largely caused by wear and tear.*

Fred Jr., who remained in charge for almost two decades. By the 1950s, he and his subordinates were energetically developing Gretsch's range of electrics (see overleaf), although its "Synchromatic" acoustics were to retain a favored place in the company's catalogs for several years to come. The one shown here is a Super Auditorium model dating from 1952; its features include a slim, fast-playing "Miracle Neck," as well as a 16-inch top made from what Gretsch describes as "fine, straight grained spruce."

**Below:** *The 17-inch-wide Country Club has a body depth of 2²/₃ inches, and its rosewood fretboard is inlaid with "hump-back" position markers.*

*This Country Club is finished in "Tobacco sunburst," Gretsch also offered "Natural"-color and (later) "Cadillac Green."*

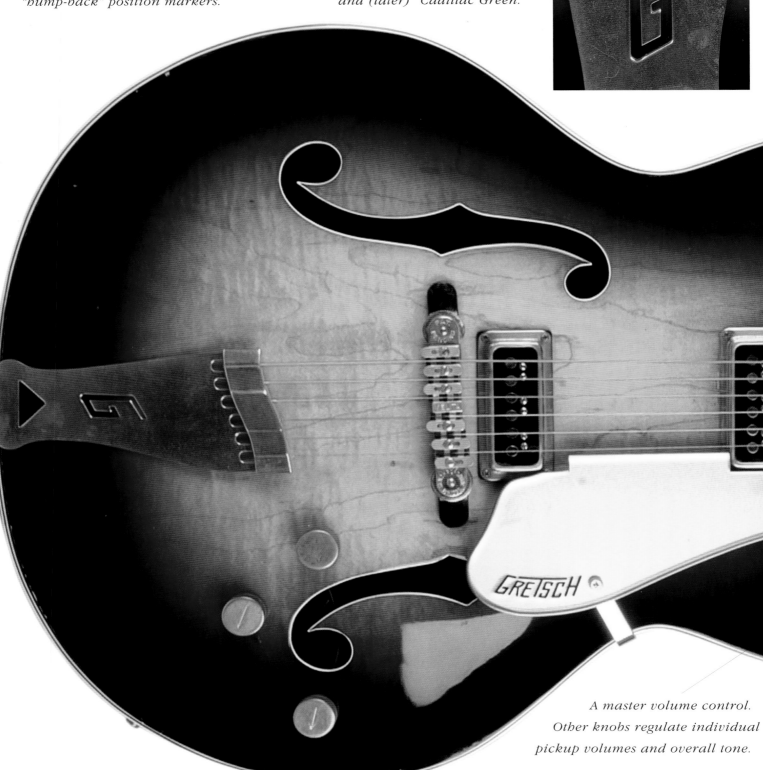

*A master volume control. Other knobs regulate individual pickup volumes and overall tone.*

262

# GRETSCH COUNTRY CLUB

G RETSCH LAUNCHED its first archtop electric guitar, the single-pickup, maple-bodied Electromatic Spanish, in 1940. Only sketchy details of its specification are known, and, in the words of Tony Bacon and Paul Day's history of the firm, *The Gretsch Book*, "it certainly does not seem to have made much impact on the market—if indeed it was made in any quantity at all." Gretsch enjoyed more success with its post-war electrics, and its popular Country Club model, which debuted in 1954, was actually an updated version of the Electro II that had appeared three years before.

The Country Club illustrated here was made in 1956: it has a spruce top and maple back and sides, its twin pickups are single-coil "Dynasonics" created by an early pioneer of transducer design, Harry DeArmond manufactured in Toledo, Ohio, and it is fitted with a "Melita" bridge—introduced in 1952, and the first such Gretsch unit to allow precise intonation adjustment for individual strings.

*Bottom: On this "Melita" bridge, designed by Gretsch contractor Sebastiano Melita, each string rests on its own adjustable bakelite saddle.*

# GRETSCH 6121 CHET ATKINS

**B**Y THE MID-1950s, Chet Atkins (1924-2001) was already one of Nashville's most respected guitarists, with several best-selling records and many high-profile TV and radio appearances to his name. He became a Gretsch endorsee in 1954, and the company quickly introduced two new electric models bearing

his signature: they were somewhat unimaginatively named the Chet Atkins Hollow Body (serial number 6120—see next two pages for a later example of one of these), and the Chet Atkins Solid Body (6121). The latter model is shown here.

While these instruments are described in the firm's

*Below: Though nominally a "solid", the 6121 has extensive internal routings.*

*This model's mahogany and maple body is 13¹/2 inches wide.*

1955 catalog as "a blend of Chet Atkins' own ideas...with Gretsch 'know-how,'" some aspects of their design were not to the musician's liking—notably the "Western-style" decorations on their headstocks and fret markers, and the carved saddle-leather body binding on the 6121. These were subsequently removed, but the 1956 example in our photographs boasts the original cattle and cacti inlays

*Below: These designs were cut out with a panograph tool and then colored in.*

*Right: An embellished Atkins signature graces the 6121's pickguard.*

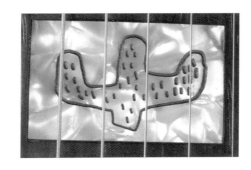

that Atkins scornfully rejected as "junk," but are now among the model's most sought-after features.

Other aspects of the 6121 are comparatively conservative. Its body shape resembles that of the company's Duo Jet, and the two pickups are DeArmond single-coils; Gretsch's own humbucking "Filter'Trons" were not fitted to 6120s and 6121s until 1958. The aluminum bridge offers less scope for string adjustment than the Melita unit on the Country Club (see previous pages); and the instrument has a Bigsby vibrato, named for its creator, engineer Paul Bigsby.

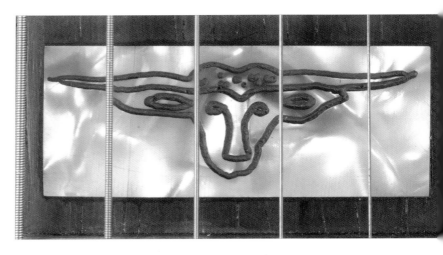

# GRETSCH 6120 (NASHVILLE)

THE GRETSCH 6120 Chet Atkins Hollow Body debuted in 1954, and, like the Solid Body 6121 (see previous pages), initially featured Western-style decorations, and a large black "G" on its top. After Chet voiced his disapproval, such fripperies were quickly dropped from the Hollow Body (though not the Solid Body), and the version lower treble bout, and selector and tone switches (the latter providing "normal," "bass boost" and "treble boost" settings) on the upper bass bout. Near the twin volume knobs are a lever that activates a built-in string mute—not a device likely to appeal to experienced players capable of creating a "damped" effect with their picking hands—and a "standby" switch that cuts the output from the pickups. Like all 6120s made from 1961 onwards, this Hollow Body/Nashville has a double cutaway; it also boasts the painted-on f-holes introduced the same year, following Gretsch's decision to seal the top as a feedback-reducing measure.

shown here, renamed Nashville and dating from 1967, is comparatively staid in its appearance.

Over the years since its introduction, Gretsch had also made some modifications to the original 1954 design, and these can be seen on this later model. The DeArmond pickups fitted to earlier 6120s have now given way to humbucking "Filter'Trons," which are controlled by a master volume on the upper treble bout, two individual volume knobs on the

*Right: The 6120's sober-looking metal nameplate was more to Chet Atkins' taste than the steer's head that appeared on the original Hollow Body's headstock.*

*Opposite page: This picture clearly displays the "trompe l'oeil" f-holes which appeared on the 6120 between 1961 and the early 1970s.*

**Right:** *This "comfort cushioning," with its leather covering, was patented by Gretsch in 1963.*

**Below:** *Like the Corvette from which it derives, the Princess has an unbound, 13¹/₂-inch mahogany body and a rosewood fingerboard.*

*See the "Daisy Rock" section of this book for some other guitars intended for women.*

PHOTOGRAPHS COURTESY OF GUITAR VILLAGE, FARNHAM

# GRETSCH PRINCESS

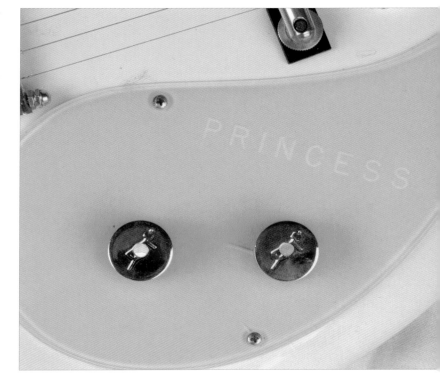

KEEN TO CAPITALIZE on the growing market for solid-body electric guitars that was already being exploited by Fender and Gibson, Gretsch introduced its double-cutaway Corvette solid in 1961. A year later, the firm unveiled a restyled variant of the Corvette; named the Princess, and priced at $169, it was probably the first-ever electric specifically aimed at women players, who, it was hoped, would be attracted by the instrument's "feminine" color scheme, including pink and white and blue and white options. The Princess also featured a "Tone Twister" that attached to the strings between the bridge and the tailpiece, and was intended to provide a vibrato effect when activated by the palm of the performer's hand. However, the device was never very effective, and has been removed from the 1962 Princess shown in our photographs.

The other principal differences between the Princess and the Corvette were the former's slightly shorter scale length and beveled sides (the original Corvette had a flat body, though it later gained contours similar to the Princess's), as well as the padded back that was intended to make the Princess

*Above: The volume and tone controls on this Princess are not the original ones, and the instrument has also lost its 'Tone Twister' palm vibrato.*

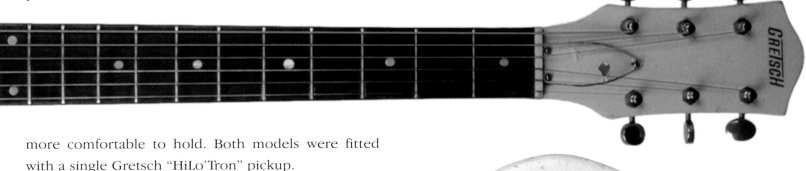

more comfortable to hold. Both models were fitted with a single Gretsch "HiLo'Tron" pickup.

The Princess was not a success, and had been dropped by 1964; Gretsch also failed to attract many customers with another Corvette-based model, the garishly finished Twist, although the Corvette itself remained in the catalog in various incarnations until the 1970s.

# GRETSCH ELLIOT EASTON DUO JET

THE 6128 GRETSCH DUO JET debuted in 1953. Though nominally a solid, it concealed a substantial degree of chambering beneath its mahogany top—a design quirk that ended in about 1970, when the instrument acquired a truly solid body. Within a few years, the Duo Jet had been joined by the closely related Round-Up, Silver Jet, and Jet Fire Bird models, and was being acclaimed in Gretsch's promotional literature for its "solid tone projection, wonderful sustain, [and] infinite variety of tonal coloring." In 1958, its DeArmond pickups were replaced with "Filter'Tron" humbuckers.

The Duo Jet's impressive performance, as well as its association with Beatle George Harrison and other leading players ensured its survival in Gretsch's regular electric roster until the early 70s. By then, the company, which had been sold by the Gretsch family to Baldwin Manufacturing in 1967, had launched a new generation of Jets, starting with the Roc Jet in 1969, and before long, the Duo was withdrawn from regular production. However, it made a comeback when Gretsch itself, which had been shut down in 1980, re-

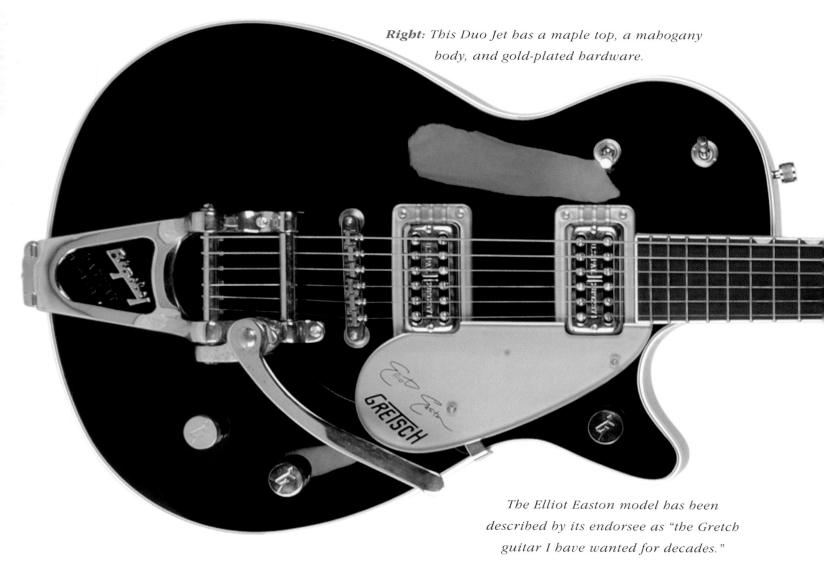

*Right: This Duo Jet has a maple top, a mahogany body, and gold-plated hardware.*

*The Elliot Easton model has been described by its endorsee as "the Gretch guitar I have wanted for decades."*

*Right:* Elliot Easton's signature appears on his guitar's pickguard. The edge of its bridge, set into the body to help provide stable intonation, can also be seen.

*Bottom:* The Duo Jet seen here is fitted with a Bigsby B7 vibrato; however, an alternative model is also available with a non-vibrato, "G-Stop" tailpiece.

emerged with a Japanese-made line of instruments in 1989; and 11 years later, a Signature Jet model, endorsed by former Cars and Creedence Clearwater Revisted guitarist Elliot Easton, was announced. Like the original, it has a semi-hollow mahogany body, but its 25-inch scale is slightly longer than those on 50s and 60s Jets. Locking Sperzel machine heads are fitted to improve tuning stability, and the pickups are "Filter'Trons."

# GRETSCH G6120 BRIAN SETZER

**B**RIAN SETZER shot to prominence in the 1980s with his trio, the Stray Cats, and, since 1992, has been serving up his distinctive brand of big band rockabilly with the Brian Setzer Orchestra. A longtime fan of Gretschs, he purchased a 1959 "6120 Nashville" electric in New York in 1999, and has used it extensively on stage ever since. Gretsch's "Artist Signature Model" range currently contains a pair of

6120s closely resembling this prized guitar. Named the G6120SSU and G6120SSL, these have identical specifications, but slightly different finishes; the SSL is seen here. Like the company's other Setzer-endorsed instruments, they feature pickups designed by TV Jones, who has worked on the star's personal guitar collection since the 1990s…as well as "white dice" control knobs like those on Setzer's own Gretsch!

*Below: The bracing on this model matches that used on Brian Setzer's own 6120, providing (in Gretsch's words) "a more solid feel with tons of sustain."*

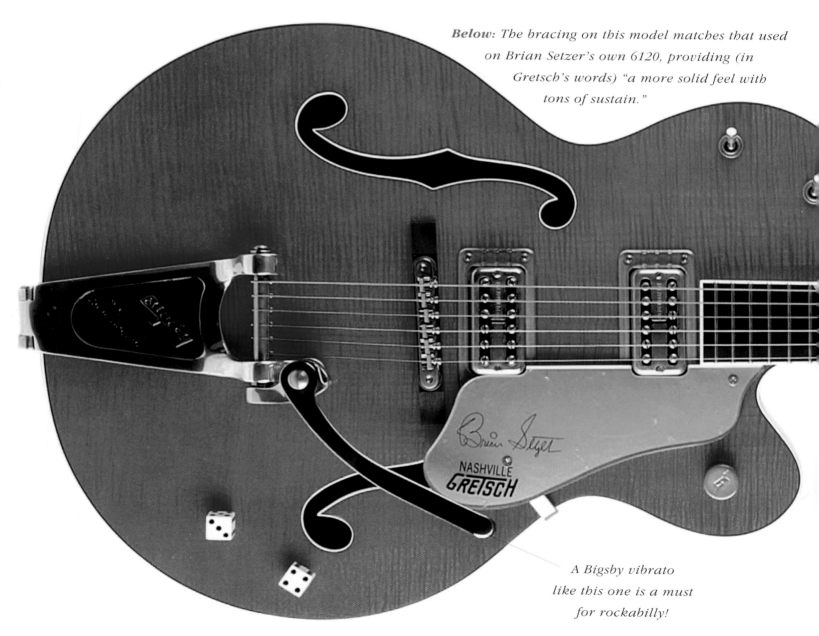

*A Bigsby vibrato like this one is a must for rockabilly!*

*Above:* The inclusion of these "dice" on the Setzer Gretsch may be inspired by a line mentioning them in his classic song "Drive Like Lightning (Crash Like Thunder)."

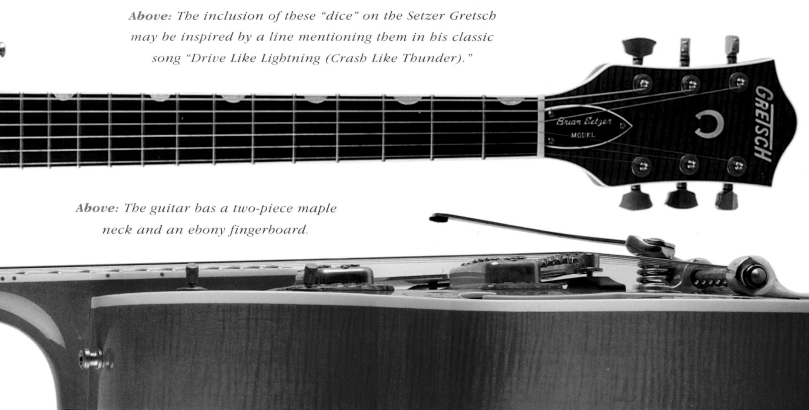

*Above:* The guitar has a two-piece maple neck and an ebony fingerboard.

# GRETSCH SILVER FALCON

THE JAPANESE-MADE SILVER FALCON seen here is a direct descendant of the famous #6136 White Falcon—Gretsch's top-of-the-range model, introduced in 1955 at what was then the astronomical price of $600. Featuring gold-plated hardware, sparkly inlays and "wing"-decorated fret markers (later replaced by "thumbnail"-style ones), it was, even by Gretsch's less-than-restrained design standards, an extraordinarily glamorous guitar. At its launch, the company declared that it was intended as "an instrument for the artist-player whose calibre justifies and demands the utmost in striking beauty, luxurious styling, and peak tonal

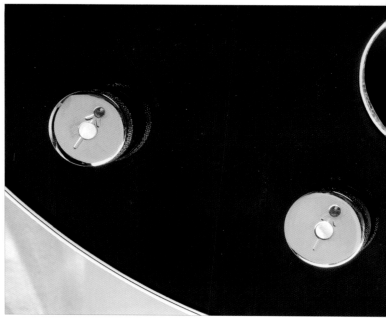

*Right: The Silver Falcon's stylish control knobs closely resemble those on late 1950s Gretsch electrics.*

*Below: The Silver Falcon has a 17-inch wide, 2³/₄-inch deep hollow body made from laminated maple.*

*The Falcon's ebony fingerboard boasts suitably avian inlays!*

performance, and who is willing to pay [for this]."

Over the next few years, the Falcon—whose name, according to Tony Bacon and Paul Day's **The Gretsch Book** (1996) may have been inspired by a World War II US services newspaper also called the **White Falcon**—was graced (or, perhaps, cursed) with a succession of specification changes and gimmicky add-ons. One beneficial upgrade was the substitution of "Filter'Tron" humbuckers for its original DeArmond pickups in 1957. Among the less successful innovations was the "Project-o-Sonic" option introduced in 1958. This provided a twin-channel effect that sent the output from the top three strings to one amplifier, and signals from their lower-pitched neighbors to another; an even more elaborate (and bewilderingly complex) "stereo" Falcon appeared in the mid-1960s.

The Falcon disappeared from regular production in the early 1980s, but was revived in 1990, and has subsequently been joined in the Gretsch catalog by Black and Silver Falcons (these made their debuts, respectively, in 1992 and 1995).

With its dual "Filter'Trons" and single-cutaway body (Falcons sported a double cutaway from 1962 to the

early '70s), the "silver bird" in our pictures has many similarities to a late '50s White Falcon; and although its Bigsby vibrato is a slight anachronism (Bigsbys were not fitted as standard to Falcons until 1962), its construction and inlays all closely match those found on its distinguished forbear.

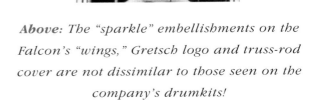

*Above: The "sparkle" embellishments on the Falcon's "wings," Gretsch logo and truss-rod cover are not dissimilar to those seen on the company's drumkits!*

# GUILD ARTIST AWARD ARCHTOP

THE GUILD COMPANY was founded in New York in 1952 by Polish-born store proprietor and musician Alfred Dronge (1911-1972) and his business partner George Mann, who had formerly worked for Epiphone (see separate entries). Mann's involvement with the new firm was relatively brief, but, as a result of Dronge's energy and enterprise, Guild soon managed to establish an extremely impressive reputation for its guitars, which were especially highly regarded by some of the Big Apple's leading jazz players.

In 1955, one of this elite group of musicians, Johnny Smith (who had achieved international recognition as a result of his recording of "Moonlight in Vermont" with saxophonist Stan Getz three years previously), agreed to collaborate with Dronge on the development of a Guild archtop, to be named the Johnny Smith Artist Award. The instrument appeared a year later, by which time the firm had relocated to Hoboken, New

*Below: The Artist Award has a carved solid spruce top, maple back and sides, and a maple and walnut neck.*

These inlays are mother-of-pearl; the same material is used for the headstock decoration.

**Top:** *The guitar has a 17-inch wide body, and is just over 3 inches deep.*

Jersey; however, due to a disagreement between Smith and Guild over its specification, the musician never actually used it in public or in the studio. It continued to bear his name until 1960, after which it became known simply as the Artist Award Model. It remained in production for decades, and is now regarded as a design classic. This example dates from the 1990s.

# GUILD B-302F FRETLESS BASS

GUILD'S FIRST bass guitar, the solid-body Jet-Star, debuted in 1964; like nearly all the company's basses, it was closely modeled on an existing 6-string design—in this case, the Thunderbird electric that had appeared the previous year. Its single pickup was supplied by the Swedish Hagström guitar company, which was to provide transducers and bridges for all Guild basses until about 1972.

1965 saw the launch of the Starfire bass. It was quickly adopted by up-and-coming players such as Jack Casady of the Jefferson Airplane, and in an article for

*Bass Player* magazine in 2005, Dave Pomeroy observes that the "beefy, resonant, and wonderfully dirty tone" Casady obtained from his customized Starfire paved the way for the bolder bass modifications subsequently undertaken by electronics experts such as Ron Wickersham of Alembic (see separate entries).

Guild continued to come up with distinctive basses throughout the late 1960s and 70s: the semi-solid, dual pickup M-85 was introduced in 1967 and recreated as a solid-body five years later; while in 1976 and 1977, the firm unveiled the B-301 and B-302. These were,

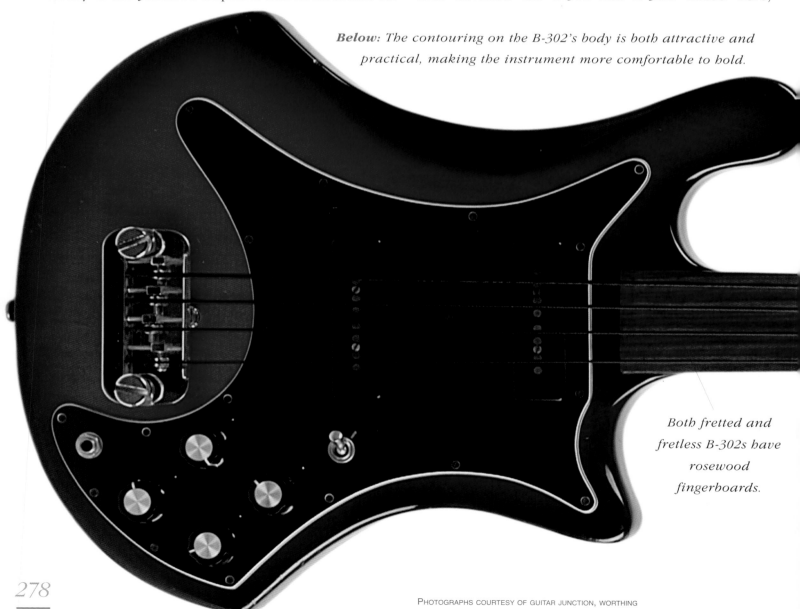

*Below: The contouring on the B-302's body is both attractive and practical, making the instrument more comfortable to hold.*

*Both fretted and fretless B-302s have rosewood fingerboards.*

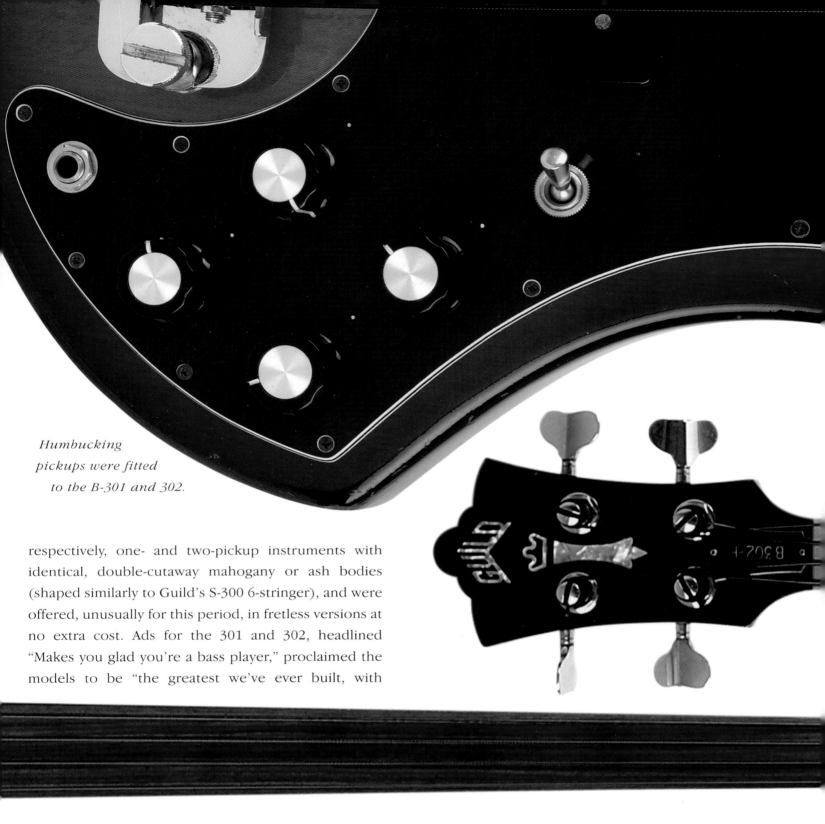

*Humbucking
pickups were fitted
to the B-301 and 302.*

respectively, one- and two-pickup instruments with identical, double-cutaway mahogany or ash bodies (shaped similarly to Guild's S-300 6-stringer), and were offered, unusually for this period, in fretless versions at no extra cost. Ads for the 301 and 302, headlined "Makes you glad you're a bass player," proclaimed the models to be "the greatest we've ever built, with

***Left:*** *According to Guild expert Hans Moust, this type of inlay is known as a "Chesterfield," as it resembles the logo on a Chesterfield cigarette packet.*

everything you want for the way you play today," and with their long-scale fretboards, optional stereo wiring, and striking looks, they lived up to their publicity, and proved to be steady, though not spectacular sellers.

A fretless Guild B-302 dating from 1978 is shown in our photographs; the 301 and 302 were both discontinued in 1981.

# GUILD D-40

Guild began producing flat-top acoustics in 1954. Its early models had both prosaic catalog numbers and more evocative, Spanish-inspired, names. So the F-30, F-40, and F-50, were also known as the Aragon, Valencia, and Navarre. The Aragon was just over 15 inches wide, and had a spruce top and maple back and side (later changed to mahogany). The 16-inch Valencia and jumbo-sized Navarre were also maple-bodied, and unlike the Aragon, were available in a choice of sunburst and blonde finishes.

Two years later, the Troubador F-20 augmented the line. This guitar was smaller and cheaper than its sisters. It was intended, in Guild's words, for both "solo playing and ballad accompaniment."

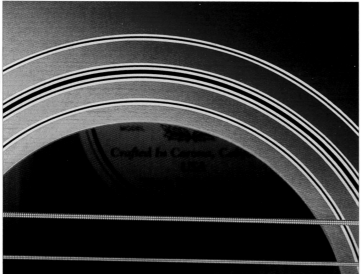

*The reference to Corona, California on the label inside the body indicates that our D-40 was manufactured after 1995, when Fender took over Guild.*

# GUILD D-50

The D-50 was the second of the Guild "dreadnaughts" (Guild's own spelling) to be launched in 1963. Subsequently named the "Bluegrass Special" the guitar endeared itself to many folk and blues performers and singer-songwriters. Major artists seen with these models during the 1960s and 70s included Richie Havens, Carolyn Hester, and Bonnie Raitt. While both guitars shared the same body dimensions (15¾ inches wide, and 5 inches deep), the D-50's back and sides were of rosewood instead of the mahogany used on the D-40. It also had an ebony fingerboard and bridge. This instrument was made in the mid-1970s at Guild's factory in Westerly, Rhode Island. The company moved there in 1969.

# GUILD F-122 12-STRING

1963 saw not only the launch of Guild's dreadnought range, but also, that December, the introduction of its first two 12-string flat-tops: the 16-inch F-212 and the slightly narrower F-312. In 1966, an even smaller companion, the 15½-inch wide F-112, which is shown here, joined these. Several other models followed. The new range, which in the tradition of Guild, was competitively priced, found its way into the hands of many up-and-coming performers. 12-string Guilds were soon a familiar sight at folk clubs and festivals. They were later to win even wider fame, thanks to their association with high-profile users such as singer-songwriter John Denver, Steve Miller, and Slash from Guns N' Roses.

*The Guild symbol inlaid into its headstock is known as a "Chesterfield," as it resembles the logo on a Chesterfield cigarette packet.*

# GUILD G-37

On May 3rd 1972, Guild founder Alfred Dronge was killed in an air crash, en route to the company's factory in Rhode Island from his home in New York. The plane he was piloting was caught in bad weather, and made several abortive attempts to land before crashing. Although morale was greatly affected by his loss, the company continued, and among the products launched the following year was a new dreadnought, the G-37.

Its body shared the same dimensions as the D-40 and D-50. All three guitars are 15¾ inches wide and 5 inches deep. The G-37 had an arched back, made from maple, and a spruce top. Its neck was mahogany, and its fingerboard and bridge made from rosewood. It had no decorative headstock inlay.

*The label inside the sound hole carries details of the Guild G-37's guarantee*

# GUILD T-100D

Guild's electric models, like its acoustics, sometime had names with a faintly exotic, European flavor. Its mid-1950s archtops included the Granada and Capri, both were 16⅜ inches wide, and just under 3 inches deep. But when Guild introduced a shallower version of the Capri in 1958, it chose a more informal label, the "Slim Jim." The instrument was described as "light in weight and easy to handle."

Two versions were available. T-100 had a single pickup, while the T-100D had two transducers and a fancier, "harp"-style tailpiece. Both models had a Florentine cutaway, and were made from laminated maple. The T-100D has been described as having "that lovely Rockabilly sound" of the 50s.

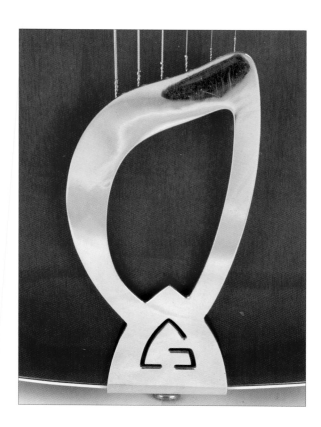

*The fancy "harp"-style tailpiece was available on the two-transducer T-100D. The cheaper T-100 model had only a single pickup.*

# GUILD X-175

The X-175 "Manhattan" was one of Guild's earliest instruments. A companion to the one-pickup X-150 "Savoy," the Manhattan had a spruce top, with maple back and sides, and was initially fitted with two single-coil transducers.

These were later replaced with humbuckers. The guitar was aimed principally at the jazz musicians who were Guild's earliest supporters. In its original form, the guitar had some similarities to 1940s and 50s Epiphones, and many Guild employees had worked for that company. It was designed to provide "professional tone quality [and] distortion free performance," but it can also supply a rich, fruity timbre ideal for rock and blues. This X-175 was made in the early 1980s.

*This wooden bridge is adjustable for height, but, unlike more sophisticated units, has only preset positions for individual string intonation.*

# X-170

# GUILD X-170

ALTHOUGH THE ORIGINAL X-175 Manhattan (see previous pages) was dropped from the Guild catalog in 1984 after two decades in production, the company soon introduced a substitute for it. Named the X-170 "Mini-Manhattan," it was slightly narrower and thinner than its distinguished predecessor, and, with its internal soundpost and more rigid, laminated maple top (the old Manhattan's had been made from spruce), was better able to resist feedback in noisy onstage conditions. The guitar was also given a glamorous new look, with gold plating on its pickups, machine heads, and "harp" tailpiece.

By now, Guild's instrument output had diversified considerably. A glance at one of its mid-1980s catalogs reveals old favorites such as the Artist Award and the Starfire rubbing shoulders with boldly styled solids—including, most strikingly, the angular, cut-out body X100 Blade Runner, designed by a third-party, David Andrews Guitar Research, and used by Eddie Ojeda of the heavy metal band Twisted Sister. Despite such courageous innovations, however, times were not easy for the firm in the 1980s, a period that saw two changes of ownership, and various financial problems.

In 1995, Guild was purchased by Fender, a development that prompted one delighted long-time staffer to comment "We finally hit a home run." For a while, its guitars continued to be built at its Rhode Island factory, but this closed in August 2001, and Guild is now based alongside its parent in Corona, California.

*Above:* Sealed Grover Rotomatic tuners are fitted to the X-170, which also sports the classic Guild "Chesterfield" headstock inlay (see pages 380-1).

*Left:* The X-170's top is 16⅝ inches wide; its pickups are Guild HB-1 humbuckers with adjustable pole pieces.

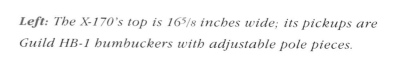

*This instrument was made in 1997; the X-170 was discontinued in 2002.*

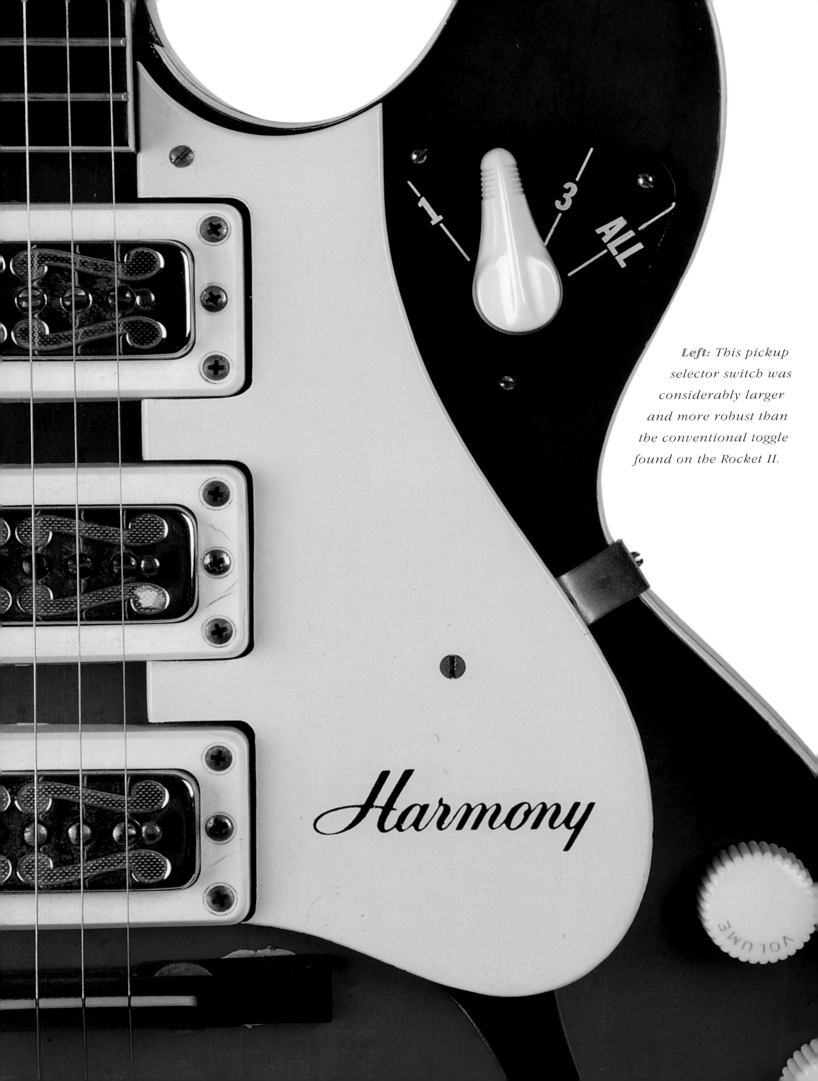

*Left: This pickup selector switch was considerably larger and more robust than the conventional toggle found on the Rocket II.*

Harmony

# HARMONY ROCKET III

HARMONY, FOUNDED IN CHICAGO in 1892, became a major supplier of inexpensive stringed instruments to retailers and catalog houses, including Sears, Roebuck & Company, which purchased it in 1916. A subsequent endorsement deal with vaudeville, movie and radio star Roy Smeck, who excelled on guitar, banjo and ukulele, brought Harmony even greater prosperity, and in the post-war era it skillfully adjusted its product range to match new musical trends by offering attractive, if basic, electrics alongside its longer-established lines.

The Harmony Rocket range of electric guitars debuted in 1958. The name seems to have been chosen in response to the "space-age" overtones of Fender's Stratocaster; significantly, other Harmonys launched during this period included the Stratotone Mercury and Stratotone Jupiter. The firm's 1960 catalog lists three Rockets, boasting (respectively) one, two and three pickups; all had single cutaways and ultra-thin bodies. This Rocket III dates from 1962; by the late 1960s, the Rocket models had been revamped, and double cutaways introduced.

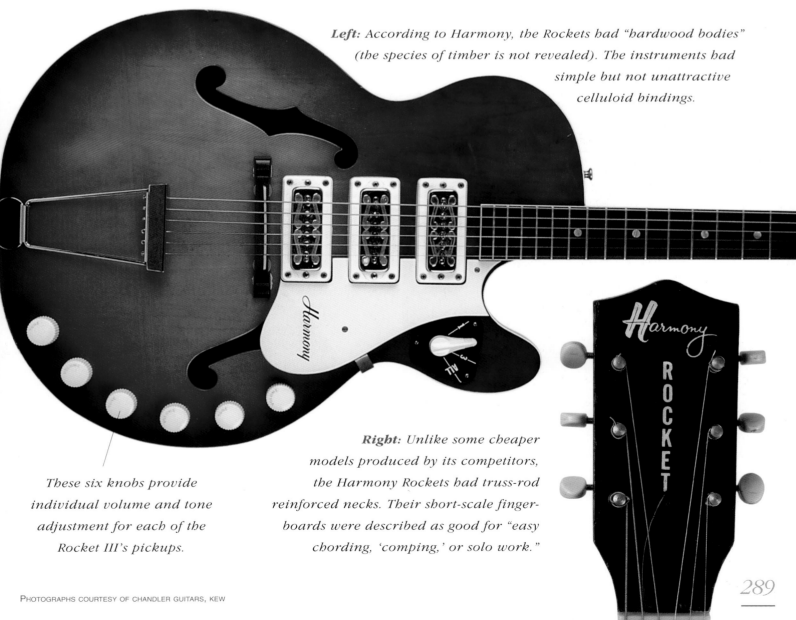

*Left:* According to Harmony, the Rockets had "hardwood bodies" (the species of timber is not revealed). The instruments had simple but not unattractive celluloid bindings.

*These six knobs provide individual volume and tone adjustment for each of the Rocket III's pickups.*

*Right:* Unlike some cheaper models produced by its competitors, the Harmony Rockets had truss-rod reinforced necks. Their short-scale fingerboards were described as good for "easy chording, 'comping,' or solo work."

*289*

# HARMONY H22 BASS

Harmony's H22 "Hi-Value" electric bass is often referred to as a "Rocket" bass, perhaps it sometimes shared a catalog page with the company's Rocket 6-strings. Introduced in 1961, it had a cutaway body, white pickguard, and a wooden finger rest (both of these have been removed from this example). It was fitted with a single pickup, designed, like those on the Rockets, in conjunction with DeArmond.

The white switch above its volume control altered the tonal response of its electronics, giving a choice of "full bass" or "lighter baritone registers." It remained in production until 1968. The H22 is especially associated with British musician Ronnie Lane of the British group the Small Faces.

*The H22's "Torque-Lok" neck is bolted to its laminated maple body.*

# HARMONY FOLK FLAT TOP

Harmony's flat-top acoustics were inexpensive enough for almost any would-be picker to afford, and the company promoted its cut-price instruments assiduously. Its motto was "music self-played is happiness self-made." For decades, Stella was to be Harmony's budget brand, and Sovereign was kept for the more upmarket guitars.

The Folk range occupied the middle ground between Sovereign and Stella. This Folk flat-top model is from the mid- to late-1960s. It is made from mahogany, a ladder-braced spruce top, a rosewood fingerboard, and a bridge with a bone saddle. At a price of $50, its makers correctly described it as a "value stand-out." This guitar has an attractive "eggshell lacquer" finish.

*The Folk model had a basic stop tailpiece in rosewood.*

The H-550
is 3 inches
deep, and its
top is 17 inches
wide. Its
pickups, tuners,
bridge and
tailpiece are
nickel-
plated.

The company's
headstock logo,
"The Heritage," is
an echo of "The
Gibson"—a marque
that once appeared
on that company's
Kalamazoo-
made guitars.

# HERITAGE H-550

WHEN, IN 1984, GIBSON left its base in Kalamazoo, Michigan, having built guitars there for the previous 67 years, it seemed as though the town's great tradition of lutherie might be coming to an end. Thankfully, this turned out not to be the case, as the Gibson factory was almost immediately taken over by a brand new firm, Heritage Guitars. Its co-founders, Jim Deurloo, Marvin Lamb, and J.P. Moats, were all ex-Gibson employees, and its staff was comprised mainly of former Gibson craftsmen who had decided against relocating to their old firm's new headquarters in Nashville, Tennessee.

Heritage's first instrument, a solid-body electric guitar, debuted in 1985, and since then, the company has won numerous plaudits for the superb quality of its instruments; satisfied customers have included jazz giant Kenny Burrell, British rocker Gary Moore, and the late Clarence "Gatemouth" Brown.

The Heritage H-550 model shown here is a full-depth semi-acoustic, perfect for jazz and blues. It boasts a maple body, two humbucking pickups, and mother-of-pearl inlays and bindings.

*Below: The laminated curly maple used for the H-550's top and body (and as a veneer on its pickguard) gives the instrument an elegant, sophisticated look.*

# HÖFNER SENATOR

IN 1887, KARL HÖFNER founded the stringed instrument making business that bears his name in Schönbach, a town in the European Sudeten region (see Framus entry). As Gordon Giltrap and Neville Marten explain in their definitive history of the firm, Karl's sons, Josef and Walter, took over as its managers when he retired after World War I; and it was they who supervised its eventual relocation to the German state of Bavaria in the mid-1940s. By the early 50s, Höfner had become Germany's best known and most prolific guitar producers, and its fortunes received a further boost in 1958, when Höfner acoustics, electrics and basses were made available in Britain by the London-based Henri Selmer.

Among the first Höfners sold in the United Kingdom was the Senator: an inexpensive but serviceable non-cutaway archtop, issued in acoustic or electric versions (the latter is shown in our pictures), and in blonde or

*Below: This Senator has been restored by Tom Anfield, who has installed a Kent Armstrong magnetic pickup, and an Al Jones transducer.*

*The Senator has a 16¹/₂-inch wide top.*

*Left and right: New, locking Spertzel tuners have been fitted here.*

*This once severely warped neck has been extensively recarved.*

*Left: The vibrato fitted to our Senator was salvaged from a box of spare parts in a luthiers' workshop!*

brunette finishes. Selmer described it as "dimensioned for playing comfort and tonal brilliance," and, during its 15 years in the catalog, it went on to find its way into the hands of thousands of budding jazzmen and rockers, including the young John Lennon.

# HÖFNER 500/1 BASS

THE HÖFNER 500/1 BASS was the brainchild of Walter Höfner, son of the firm's founder, Karl. Its shape betrays Walter's background as a violinmaker, and its relatively small, hollow body gives it a pleasingly lightweight feel very different from most modern bass guitars. The 500/1 first appeared in Germany in 1956, and two years later, the Selmer company began distributing it in the UK, along with a variety of other Höfner models. However, the little bass's most famous player, Paul McCartney, acquired his 500/1 not in Britain but in Hamburg, during one of the Beatles' residencies at the city's Star-Club prior to their first chart success. When interviewed about what was soon to be known as the "Beatle bass" in Gordon Giltrap and Neville Marten's book *The Höfner Guitar—A History* (1993), McCartney revealed that, for him, one of its principal selling points was its symmetrical outline, which allowed him to play it left-handed without it

"looking quite as stupid as some other [instruments] did." He soon came to appreciate the 500/1's solid, resonant tone as well—even though its intonation was less than perfect, especially higher up its fingerboard. Surprisingly, McCartney never had a formal

*Below: Despite its lack of tone controls, the 500/1 can produce a surprising range of timbres, although the pickup switching takes a little getting used to.*

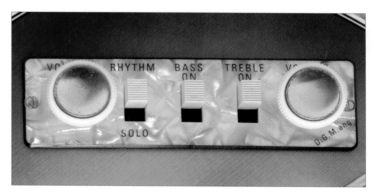

*Below: One of the 500/1's cruder features, retained on this reissue, are its bridge saddles, which are made from pieces of fret wire.*

*The bass's two Höfner-designed single-coil pickups are largely responsible for its characteristic sound.*

PHOTOGRAPHS COURTESY OF PEACH, BLAKE END, BRAINTREE

*Above: Like the original, this bass has paired, open-geared machine heads.*

*Above: The 500/1's spruce topped, maple-backed body is only 18 inches long, and 11 inches across at its widest point. It is just over 2 inches deep.*

*This zero fret removes some of the "ring" from openstrings, and helps the instrument stay in tune for longer.*

endorsement deal with Höfner, although for many years new 500/1s were sold with a label carrying his face and signature, plus a personal message wishing new purchasers "every success with this guitar."

The "Beatle bass" seen here is a modern, reissue instrument, produced by Höfner's factory in Hagenau, Germany. It retains all the distinctive features of the original 500/1, including a zero fret and somewhat quaint control panel, and despite its 50-year old design, still has considerable appeal to today's bassists.

# HÖFNER 172 SOLID-BODY

BY THE EARLY 1960S, the traditional, violin-inspired appearance of Höfner's archtops was beginning to seem somewhat staid and dated, especially in comparison with the slim, solid-bodied electrics being produced by Fender in the USA. The German company responded by introducing solid guitars of its own: but confusingly, the names given to these (and Höfner's other products) by its British distributors, Selmer, were quite different from those used in other countries. Hence, the "Model 172" shown here, which was marketed in mainland Europe, would have been labeled a "Super Solid" in the United Kingdom. The 172 in our picture dates from about 1963, and, while it has only two pickups (other 172s

*Below: The 172 has a bolted-on neck, whose "strip" fret markers replaced the dots seen on earlier models.*

*On later models, this basic bridge was upgraded to a fully adjustable one.*

PHOTOGRAPHS COURTESY OF CHANDLER GUITARS, KEW

*Above:* All Höfner electrics of this type had smart, slimline headstocks with six-a-side tuners—some were finished in "Black," others left "Natural."

*Bottom:* This chunky pickup switch is built to withstand years of rough treatment!

had three), is clearly influenced by the Fender Stratocaster. Its controls are basic and its finish relatively plain; later Höfner solids were equipped with a plethora of additional circuits and switches, and, by 1968, a few were even sporting ostentatious colored vinyl body coverings! These instruments all sold well, though it is likely that many of their users would have preferred an American electric, had one been obtainable at an affordable price.

# HOHNER B2A BASS

THE HOHNER COMPANY was founded by Matthias Hohner in Trossingen, south of the German city of Stuttgart, in 1857. Its first product was the harmonica, which had been invented (by a German clockmaker) in 1821, but never previously made in quantity. The little instrument proved to be an international best seller, and, within a few decades, Hohner had also established itself as one of Europe's leading accordion builders.

The firm has gone on to enjoy many more recent musical successes: in the 1960s, it developed the Pianet and Clavinet electric keyboards (the latter was featured memorably on Stevie Wonder's classic 1972 song "Superstition"), and in 1990, its American division became the first major manufacturer to license and produce its own version of Ned Steinberger's revolutionary headless bass guitar.

The Steinberger (whose full history is explored on pages 664-7) sprang from the notion that conventional basses, with their bulky headstocks, were uncomfortable to hold and poorly balanced. Ned Steinberger remedied these perceived problems by moving the tuners from the necks of his instruments to their bridge ends, and radically reshaping and lightening their bodies. He also constructed his guitars from epoxy resin, reinforced with graphite, but this aspect of his design remained the sole property of his own firm, the Steinberger Sound Corporation, and Hohner's headless models, including the B2A seen here, have always been made of wood.

Unlike the substantial quantities of shoddy "pirate"

*Above: Steinberger Sound is now part of Gibson.*

*Below: The B2A has two humbucking pickups and active electronics.*

*The headless bass is made from maple, and has a through-body design.*

**Above:** *This instrument's rosewood fretboard has a metal nut; to the right of it is the fixing that holds the string ball-ends in place.*

*The key features of Ned Steinberger's headless bass design were patented by him in 1980.*

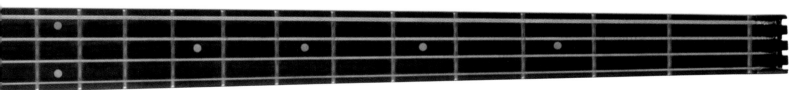

copies of Steinberger basses that were polluting the market in the 1990s, the Hohners were well made—and also, of course, substantially cheaper than the graphite originals. Unsurprisingly, they proved highly successful, and Hohner was soon augmenting its headless range with a fretless bass and a five-stringer. It has continued to produce high quality Steinberger-licensed instruments: its current catalog contains no less than four of these: three basses, and a 6-string guitar with a locking tremolo.

*301*

# IBANEZ RG2620-CBL

Since they debuted in 1987, Ibanez's RG (Rock Guitar) electrics have been the "weapon of choice" for musicians seeking to "visit sonic mayhem on the metal masses." The RGs' many fans include high profile players like Terry Balsamo of Evanescence. A number of RGs, including the RG 2620 featured here, are equipped with Edge Pro tremolos, whose sliding strike holders (which move when the unit's "whammy bar" is oFperated) are built into the main bridge assembly for maximum stability and sustain.

The 2620's striking looks complement its high performance, and its "cubed pewter" finish (available in blue or black) is hand-stamped onto its double-cutaway, basswood body.

*This rear view of the RG2620 shows part of the mechanism for its Edge Pro vibrato.*

# IBANEZ GB10
# GEORGE BENSON

Many years before he achieved success as a pop singer, George Benson (b. 1943) had already been recognized as one of the finest jazz guitarists of his generation. For his recordings, Benson plays archtop Gibsons, but found these instruments had a tendency to feed back at high sound levels during live appearances.

Before long, he was in discussions with Ibanez over the development of a new electric guitar, tailor-made to his requirements, and bearing his name. The result was the Ibanez GB10, a 2½ inch deep hollow-body, which was launched at the National Association of Music Merchants Association (NAMM) trade show in Chicago in 1977, and has remained in production ever since.

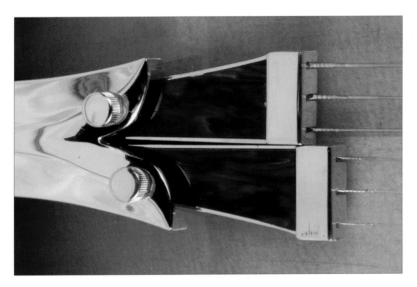

*This handsome tailpiece (covered with gold like the rest of the GB10's hardware) features twin knobs that vary the tension of the upper and lower groups of strings.*

303

# JACKSON KVX10 KING V

Wayne Charvel set up Charvel's Guitar Repair in southern California in 1974. His shop undertook refinishing work for Fender, while catering to the needs of rock star clients such as The Who, Deep Purple, and Eddie Van Halen. In 1978, Wayne Charvel sold his business to a member of his staff, Grover Jackson, who continued to trade under the Charvel name. He worked with many stars, including Ozzy Osbourne band member Randy Rhoads, and built a "Flying V"-like electric to his specification in 1980. Jackson was reluctant to use the Charvel name on this wild-looking axe, and signed his own last name on the headstock. The first Jackson guitar was born. This is the current production model, the KVX10.

# JACKSON DK2 DINKY

One of Jackson's most popular design categories is the so-called "Superstrat." The first production Superstrat named the Soloist, was launched in 1983-4. It featured a "neck-through-body" configuration, rather than the Fender-type bolt-on neck. It was soon joined by the Dinky, a "bolt-on" Superstrat that was otherwise very similar to its "neck-thru" cousin. Both are now recognized as Jackson classics.

The 2005 DK2 Dinky in our pictures remains faithful to the Superstrat tradition. The company's custom department has long been renowned for its ability to produce "anything from life-like figures to off-the-wall abstract concoctions." Grover Jackson left Jackson in 1989, which is now owned by Fender.

*This Dinky has an alder body and a maple bolt-on neck; it boasts two Seymour Duncan humbucking pickups, a rosewood fingerboard, and shark fin inlays. It is finished in transparent black.*

# KAY VALUE LEADER

Kay has been manufacturing musical instruments for both students and professional musicians since 1890, in its various incarnations. The company got its name from Henry Kuhrmeyer (1894-1956), whose nickname was "Kay." Kuhrmeyer and his wife moved to Chicago in 1920, and invested in the Stromberg-Voisinet Instrument Company. He attracted several talented luthiers to the company, and it thrived.

He gradually assumed control of Stromberg-Voisinet, and it became the Kay Musical Company in 1935. Sidney Katz bought Kuhrmeyer out in 1955. At this time, Kay's ambition was to dominate the "value" market, and the Value Leader range spearheaded this. Jazzman Lonnie Johnson played the instrument.

*The Kay Value Leader parallelogram pickguard always had a slightly "homemade" look to it as did the controls and bridge.*

# LAKLAND SKYLINE JOE OSBORN BASS

In 1994, Dan Lakin began manufacturing bass guitars in partnership with instrument technician Hugh McFarland. They christened the business Lakland. The company manufactured meticulously crafted basses started to attract leading players including the late Rick Danko, formerly of The Band. More recent customers have included US's Adam Clayton, Booker T, and the MGs and Blues Brothers stalwart Donald "Duck" Dunn, and Daryl Jones, who plays with the Rolling Stones. Today, Lakland is based in Chicago's Goose Island.

The Lakland model is shown here is a Skyline Joe Osborn is a celebrated session player. It represents a Fender Jazz bass, but incorporates updated pickups and other updates.

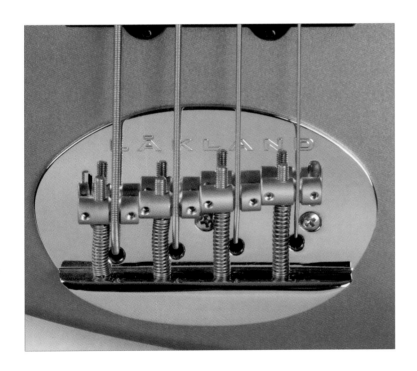

*This neat bridge design allows the strings to pass either through the body (as here) or through the unit itself.*

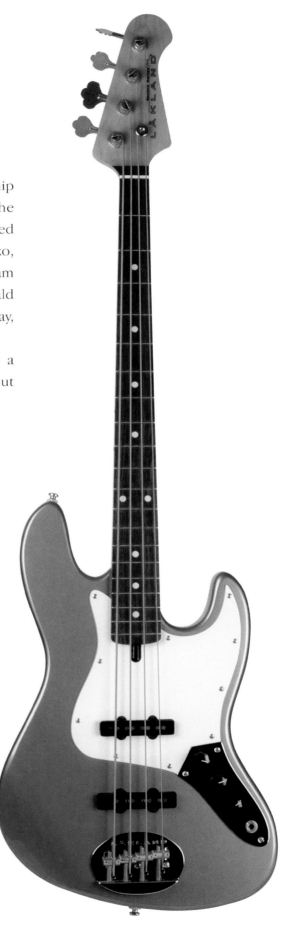

# LINE 6 VARIAX 700

LINE 6, BASED IN AGOURA HILLS, west of Los Angeles, is renowned for its pioneering work in developing digital devices that provide realistic recreations of classic amplifier sounds and effects. In 2003, it made a significant addition to its range of so-called "modeling" products when it launched the Variax, the first-ever guitar to offer simulations of a variety of instruments—from acoustic flat-tops to solid electrics—at the turn of a switch. Reviewers gave the revolutionary new axe a warm reception, although a number of them commented that some of its emulations inevitably lacked the last degree of tonal

magic provided by the originals, and the Variax technology has since been built into several differently specified types of Line 6 guitars. The one featured in our photographs is a tremolo-equipped model from the company's 700 series.

Unlike a MIDI controller, which merely triggers samples or synthesizer waveforms, the Variax uses its strings as the starting point for its sounds. Their vibrations are converted to electrical currents by its onboard piezo pickups; to quote Line 6's publicity literature, a "patented [digital] process [then] shapes the raw string signal to replicate the [tones] of the

*Below: This Variax 700 has an ash and mahogany body, a one-pice maple neck, and a 22-fret rosewood fingerboard.*

*The model shown here is finished in translucent "Amber;" Variax 700s are also available in "Blue," "Red", "Gold," "Sunburst" and "Black."*

recreate a 6- or 12-string Rickenbacker). All the named settings can be modified by the Variax's volume and tone controls, and also via a 5-position selector that switches between different sounds associated with the simulated guitar models.

*Above: The right-hand socket connects the Variax to standard amplifiers; the one on the left interfaces with other Line 6 modeling equipment, and can also be used to transfer the guitars' sounds to and from a computer for editing.*

modeled instruments." These imitations are selected via a rotary switch carrying one-word descriptions of them (see photo): trademark restrictions obviously forbid any direct mention of, say, a Fender Telecaster or Gibson Les Paul on this knob, which uses suggestive terms such as "T-Model" and "Lester" instead. Other emulations include "R-Billy" (based on the timbres of 1950s Gretsches), and "Chime" (for players seeking to

*Left: This knob allows Variax players to access what Line 6 describes as "the sounds of an entire guitar collection."*

# ANDY MANSON CUSTOM 7-STRING

LUTHIER ANDY MANSON is based in Credition, in the English West Country, and has been designing, building and repairing fretted instruments for over thirty-five years. He specializes in exotic and unusual creations, such as the triple neck he made for Led Zeppelin bassist John Paul Jones; as Manson explains in his book *Talking Wood: A Guitar Maker's Diary* (1998), the idea for this came about after he saw Jones switching between mandolin, 6-string guitar, and 12-string guitar during a single song, and thought, "Pity you can't hang 'em all around your neck at once." When he presented the finished model to Jones, the star was delighted, and told Manson that he "couldn't wait to see [Zeppelin guitarist] Jimmy Page's face when I walk on stage with it." Other famous Manson clients include Ian Anderson and Martin Barre of Jethro Tull, Andy Summers, and Mike Oldfield.

The Manson guitar seen here is a 7-string Magpie I flat-top, custom built for British jazz guitarist Andy Robinson. Some years ago, this instrument was

*Below: The Manson 7-string Magpie has a spruce top, and Indian rosewood back and sides.*

*The signal from this pickup can be combined with the guitar's bridge transducer.*

*Right: Guitarists are always in danger of losing their flatpicks in the heat of a gig: this magnetized post is a safe place to keep a spare one!*

featured in one of the author's previous books, ***The Acoustic Guitar***: since then, it has been fitted with a soundhole pickup and some other additions by its owner, and has suffered a little inevitable wear and tear; however, it remains a fine example of Andy Manson's work. Andy's brother, Hugh Manson, is also a notable guitar maker, some of whose models can be seen on the following pages.

*311*

# HUGH MANSON SOLID-BODY

LIKE HIS ACOUSTIC GUITAR-MAKING brother Andy (see previous pages), luthier Hugh Manson is based in the English West Country. His professional career began in the late 1970s (though he built his first-ever guitar at the age of only 14), and today, his small workshop, located near the city of Exeter, produces some of the United Kingdom's finest custom-built electric instruments. Among his long list of distinguished clients are Martin Barre of Jethro Tull, ex-Led Zeppelin bassist John Paul Jones (who has been known to take up to fifteen Hugh Manson instruments on tour with him), Kelly Jones of The Stereophonics, and Matt Bellamy of Muse, who owns no less than seven custom Mansons.

Hugh is famous for instruments that he himself rather modestly describes as "a little revolutionary;" these have included two-, three- and even four-necked models, custom-built lap steels, mandolas and electric sitars, as well as guitars and basses with special finishes and other unique touches. However, the example of his work shown here is somewhat more conventional, though equally distinguished. Made in 2003, it has a

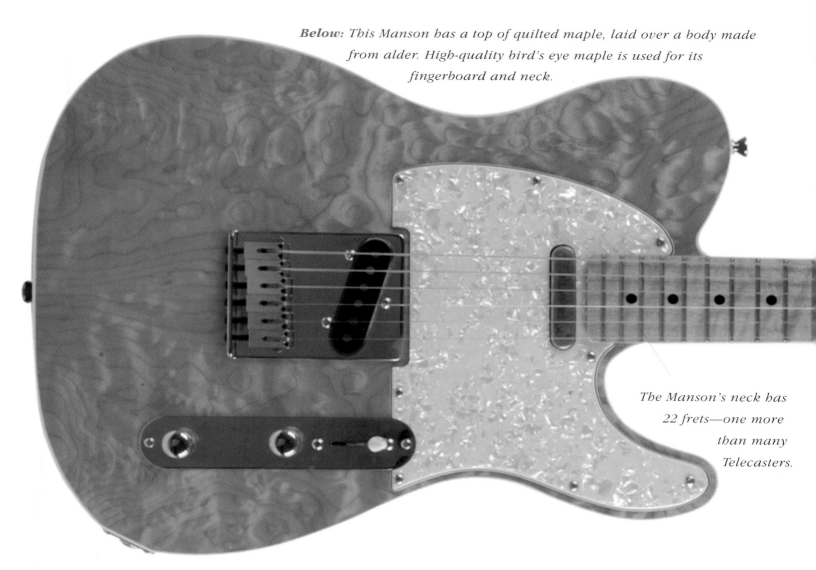

*Below:* *This Manson has a top of quilted maple, laid over a body made from alder. High-quality bird's eye maple is used for its fingerboard and neck.*

*The Manson's neck has 22 frets—one more than many Telecasters.*

Telecaster-style body and neck, but features superb tonewoods and high quality electronics (its pickups, like those on all Mansons, are wound to Hugh's exacting specifications) which combine to provide outstanding tone and overall playability. It was recently sold by a British guitar dealer for just over $2,600.

*Above: A closeup showing the Manson's bound, pearloid pickguard and high performance neck pickup.*
*Bottom: These metal collars help to hold the strings' ball-ends in place at the back of the guitar's body.*

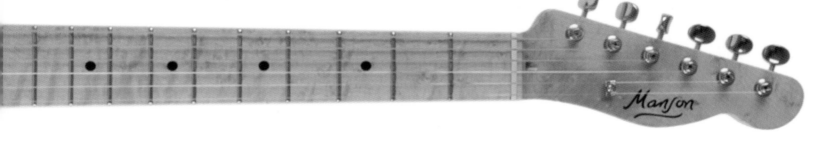

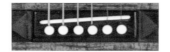

# MARTIN 0-28K

IN NAZARETH, PENNSYLVANIA, C.F. Martin's guitar business flourished, though, as Walter Carter has commented in *The Martin Book* (Balafon, 1995), he was obliged to adapt his elaborate European designs "to a rougher-edged, simpler American society" by making them "plainer [and] more utilitarian." Gradually, Martins lost their scrolled headstocks and abalone body inlays, and started to acquire outlines closer to those of a 20th century flat-top instrument; while in the 1850s, the firm began applying X-bracing to its tops (Stauffer-style Martins had mostly horizontal strutting)—a key element of modern acoustic guitar construction, widely copied by other makers.

As Martin's catalog expanded over the following

*Pyramid bridge embellishments like this are a distinctive feature on early Martin flat-tops.*

**Above:** *Rectangular, open headstocks such as this take standard, easily available tuners—unlike the 6-a-size peghead fitted to the Stauffer Martin on the previous two pages.*

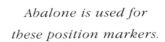

*Abalone is used for these position markers.*

*The koa from which this instrument is made comes from Hawaii; musicians on the islands were among the earliest users of steel-strung guitars.*

decades, it developed its now familiar system for naming instruments with a prefix denoting body size, followed by a code number identifying decorative style and woods. "0" sizes, such as the 1927 guitar seen here, are 13½ inches wide; and while a "Style 28" like this one would normally have a rosewood back and sides, the K suffix indicates that koa has been used. The 0-28K's steel strings were, at the time of its introduction, a comparative novelty: steel had only replaced gut as standard on Martins in 1922.

# MARTIN OM-18GE

THE GROWING POPULARITY of steel-strung guitars, whose bright, powerful tone made them far more suitable for many kinds of onstage performance than their gut-strung counterparts, was not universally welcomed. Some players simply disliked the sound made by metal strings, while many banjoists feared that the louder new instruments would usurp their once dominant role in dance bands.

Perry Bechtel (1902-1982) belonged to the latter category of concerned musicians. A star banjoist and bandleader, he was being asked to play more and more guitar on shows and broadcasts. After failing to find one that satisfied him, he approached Martin in 1929, and asked the company to make him a flat-top that would retain such banjo-like characteristics as a narrower neck and better access to the upper frets. The outcome of his request was the "Orchestra Model" (OM)—the first-ever Martin to have 14 frets to the body (only 12 frets had been easily reachable on earlier guitars), and a solid, unslotted headstock.

*Below: Adirondack spruce is used for the OM-18GE's top; its back and sides are mahogany, and it has a bridge made from ebony.*

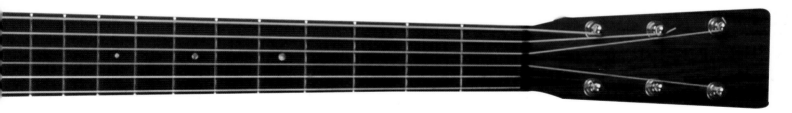

*Above: OM fingerboards are 1³/₄ inches wide at the nut; previous models measured 1⁷/₈ inches.*
*Right: Banjo-type tuners like these were a distinctive features of the early OMs.*

The OM went into full production in 1930; the example seen here is a recent replica of an OM-18 from this period, issued as part of Martin's "Golden Era" series.

# MARTIN 0-15, 1942

A T THE TIME of their introduction, by C.F. Martin I himself in 1854, Martin "size 0" guitars, with a maximum body width of 13½ inches, were the company's largest models. They remained so until the advent of the 14⅛ inch "00" in 1877, but eventually came to be seen as relatively small instruments, following the introduction of OMs and Ds (measuring, respectively, 15 and 15⅝ inches) in the 1930s. Inevitably, the 0s' modest dimensions restricted their ability to produce a big sound, but their sweet timbre and comfortable feel kept them in steady demand, especially among singers.

*Above: This internal stamp gives the instrument's model designation and individual serial number.*

The earliest Martin 0s all had rosewood bodies; mahogany was first used on an 0 size guitar in 1906, for the back and sides of the spruce-topped 0-17. This model was reissued in 1929 as an entirely mahogany instrument, probably in response to the earlier, overwhelming success of the all-mahogany 2-17. According to figures given in **Acoustic Guitar** magazine by Marshall Newman, over 6,000 2-17s were sold between 1922 and 1928; its early purchasers included the "Singing Brakeman," Jimmie Rodgers (1897-1933, often termed the "Father of Country Music").

The unique tonal quality of guitars made from this wood has been succinctly described by luthier Bob Taylor, who comments, in Newman's **Acoustic Guitar** article, "A mahogany soundboard on a mahogany body creates warm, full tone with a character all its own"—and Martin was keen to capitalize further on the market for them. The firm therefore launched a new mahogany instrument, the 0-15, in 1940; a somewhat spartan-looking flat-top, it nevertheless sold well, and remained available until the early 1960s. The example in our photographs dates from 1942.

**Left:** *Like all Style 15 Martins, the 0-15 seen here has no body binding, and fretboard markers of plastic rather than pearl.*

**Right:** *This instrument had a single owner for nearly all its life—a fact that helps to account for its superb condition!*

*Below*: Like all modern era Style 15 Martins, this model has a spruce top, mahogany back and sides, and a rosewood bridge and fingerboard.

*Right and far right*: The instrument's tuners and other fittings are all original.

# MARTIN 000-18, 1948

*This guitar left the Martin factory on November 23 1948.*

T HE MARTIN 000-18 debuted, in its original, gut-strung version, in 1911, but came into its own in the 1930s and 40s, by which time it was sporting steel strings and a neck with 14 frets to the body, as the 1948 example in our pictures does. Thanks to its 15-inch body width, it delivered a good deal more volume than smaller Martin flat-tops such as the 0-15 (see previous pages), and over the following decades, it was to prove its worth in a wide range of musical settings.

Its famous users included singer, writer and political activist Woody Guthrie (1912-1967), and influential folk-style picker and vocalist Elizabeth Cotten (1895-1987). Elvis Presley also briefly owned a 000-18 in the mid-1950s (he later switched to a Martin D-18 Dreadnought), and among the instrument's current devotees is Martin Carthy, one of the UK's leading folk singers—in whose honor the Martin Company recently produced a Signature Model that has inevitably been nicknamed "Carthy's Martin"!

*Vintage Martins like the one here are highly sought after by both musicians and collectors.*

# MARTIN 000C-16GTE

OPINIONS ARE DIVIDED over the best way of amplifying high-end flat-tops such as Martins. Bridge-saddle piezo systems are favored by many manufacturers and players, and are efficient and unobtrusive; however, they can sound somewhat glassy, and do not always succeed in conveying the full, rich timbre of a fine acoustic. The two commonly used alternatives to them also have their advantages and drawbacks: fitting a standard magnetic pickup to a flat-top provides a strong signal, but can result in feedback, and may impart an unwanted "electric" quality to the tone; while simply placing a microphone in front of the guitar confines the player to a single position onstage, and can be less than ideal if other, louder instruments are in close proximity.

Martin's 000C-16GTE offers an ingenuous solution to these problems. Its Fishman Prefix Premium preamp system can blend together (or select separately) the outputs of an under-saddle transducer and an internally mounted microphone, allowing guitarists—in the words of a review of the 000C-16GTE published in *Guitar Player* magazine in May 2003—to "combine

*Below: Like all 000s, this model has a 15-inch wide body.*

*This faux-tortoiseshell pickguard
complements the guitar's sitka spruce top.*

**Bottom:** *The "blend" slider on the Fishman
preamp mixes the microphone and piezo
signals. Comprehensive EQ controls are also
provided.*

**Above:** *The 000C-16GTE's microphone is
mounted on an adjustable gooseneck inside
its body; it is not visible from this angle.*

the clarity and definition of a piezo pickup with the airy
dimensionality that only a mic can provide." The
instrument's outstanding unamplified sound is worth
taking trouble to preserve: its spruce top and
mahogany body deliver all the mellow sweetness
traditionally associated with 000 Martins, and its
cutaway and Micarta (ebony substitute) fingerboard
make it easy as well as rewarding to play.

# MARTIN D-18

THE OLIVER DITSON company had its origins in a music publishing firm started by a Boston bookstore, Batelle's, in 1783. Later, the business expanded into instrument sales, and by the early 20th century, Ditson had branches in the cities of Philadelphia and New York—with the latter describing itself proudly on its letterhead as retailers of "Everything in Music and Musical Merchandise."

In 1916, the firm's New York division commissioned Martin to produce a line of Ditson-branded guitars, including a model with a wider body (measuring 15⅝ inches) than the luthiers at Nazareth had ever made before. According to Martin historian Mike Longworth, these instruments were supplied to Ditson until 1921, and again between 1923 and 1930. After they were finally discontinued, Martin decided to make the 15⅝-inch model part of its own regular range, and created a new size category—"D"—for it. Appropriately, the

*Below: This D-18 is in fine condition, though, like many older guitars, it has suffered slight cracking (now repaired) to its top and back.*

**Bottom:** *Early D-18s had 12 frets to the body; 14-fret models like the one here first appeared in 1934.*

**Above:** *The honey colored spruce top on this D-18 shows only slight signs of wear.*

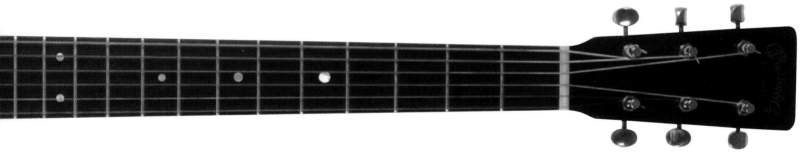

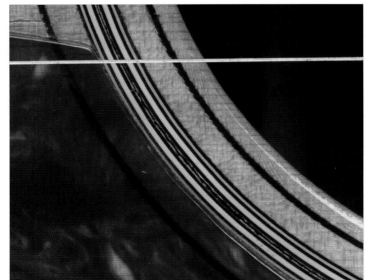

initial stood for "Dreadnought," a name borrowed from the British navy vessel HMS *Dreadnought*, one of the biggest battleships of its kind.

The first Style 18 (spruce top, and mahogany body) Martin Dreadnought, designated a D-18, appeared in 1931. It proved highly popular with musicians seeking powerful volume and booming bass, and has remained in the catalog ever since. The example seen in our photos dates from the early 1950s.

*Like standard Style 28 models, the HD-28 has a spruce top and rosewood back and sides*

# MARTIN HD-28

Guitars produced in Martin's Style 28 incorporate an especially famous feature: the "herringbone" marquetry that embellishes their tops. First used in the 19th century, herringbone trim is made from strips of intricately cut wood, originally bought in from European suppliers, but later sourced domestically. The first Style 28 Dreadnoughts appeared in the early 1930s; they and other "28s" continued to include herringbone decoration until 1946, when it was dropped from the Style 28 specification because it had become so hard to obtain.

The lack of herringbone was a major disappointment to customers, and in 1976, Martin reintroduced it—not on Style 28 itself, but as a key feature of a new "Herringbone Dreadnought" category. The HD-28 was the first model to sport the revived trim, and has been a perennial best-seller.

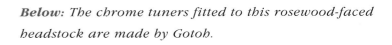

*Below: The chrome tuners fitted to this rosewood-faced headstock are made by Gotoh.*

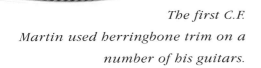

*The first C.F. Martin used herringbone trim on a number of his guitars.*

*The OMC-16E's backstripe and binding contrast elegantly with its koa back.*

# MARTIN OMC-16E

LIKE THE 000C-16GTE shown on pages 498-9, this 21st century version of Martin's classic Orchestra Model features a high-specification Fishman preamp system, utilizing both a gooseneck-mounted microphone and a bridge-saddle pickup. The most striking difference between the two sets of electronics lies in the way they are installed and adjusted; while the 000-16 sports a conventional preamp panel on its side, the OM's remarkably unobtrusive "Ellipse" unit is positioned beneath the instrument's top, and its blend, volume, phase and microphone trim controls are all accessible via the soundhole.

The guitar itself is available with three different body woods. The example in our photographs has a back and sides of figured koa; maple and sapele are substituted for this on other OMC-16Es, although all the models have a sitka spruce top, and an ebony fingerboard and bridge.

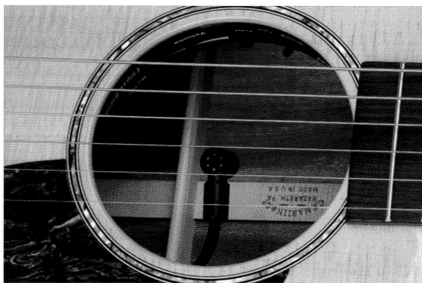

*Above right: This tiny microphone can be moved within the body to create the sound the player wants.*
*Above left: The Fishman's ingenious mounting conceals its presence from audiences.*

*Left: The guitar's soundhole rosette features a ring of abalone shell, surrounded with fiber.*

# CFM (MARTIN) EM-18

THE LATE 1970s were difficult times for acoustic guitar makers, as the cost of raw materials and labor rose, while the use of synthesizers and other—mostly Far Eastern-made—electronics continued to grow. Martin responded to these problems by attempting to break into the solid electric guitar market, and the company introduced its CFM range, with a fanfare of publicity, in 1979. The CFMs initially comprised two 6-stringers and a bass, and were glowingly described by Martin's promotional literature as "a new energy source...quality handcrafted instruments incorporating custom electronics and hardware as factory installed standard equipment." An additional guitar and bass appeared in 1981.

Despite giving the range a high-profile launch, Martin had a somewhat ambivalent attitude about it; significantly, it was decided not to use the full company name on the new guitars' headstocks, and, according to guitar expert Walter Carter's *Martin Book*, there was considerable disagreement within the firm over some aspects of the instruments' design. None of them sold especially well, but the model shown here, the EM-18, which featured twin humbucking pickups with coil-taps and phase reverse switches, did rather better than its sisters: official Martin figures published by the late Mike Longworth show that a total of 1,375 EM-18s were produced between 1979 and 1983, when all five CFM solid electrics were discontinued.

*Left: The CFM range all sported contoured maple and walnut bodies, and mahogany necks with rosewood fingerboards.*

*Left: The EM-18's pickups are powerful, high quality humbuckers.*
*Right: The scrolled CFM headstock is reminiscent of 19th century Martin designs like the one on pages 486-7.*

# MARTIN ALTERNATIVE XT

MARTIN INTRODUCED the first-ever instrument in its "ALternative" range, the 00-size "X" model, in 2001. The capitalization of the L in its name is deliberate: AL is the scientific symbol for aluminum, and ALternatives all sport tops made from this ultra-light metal. Thanks to its exceptional strength, it requires much less internal bracing than a conventional wooden top, and many reviewers and players have commented favorably on the clear, responsive tone it produces on the X and its numerous successors—both when played acoustically, and when the guitars' built-in electronics are plugged in.

The Martin ALternative XT shown here debuted the following year. Constructed similarly to other models in the series (whose aluminum tops are combined with backs and sides made from high pressure laminates (HPL), and necks of Stratabond wood veneer), its most striking feature is its Bigsby vibrato—a heavy-duty unit that would be impossible to install on a conventional acoustic without dire structural consequences! The XT also boasts a DiMarzio Fast Track 2 pickup, which can be used in both humbucking and single-coil modes.

*Below: The XT's aluminum top is decorated in what Martin terms a "graffiti pattern."*

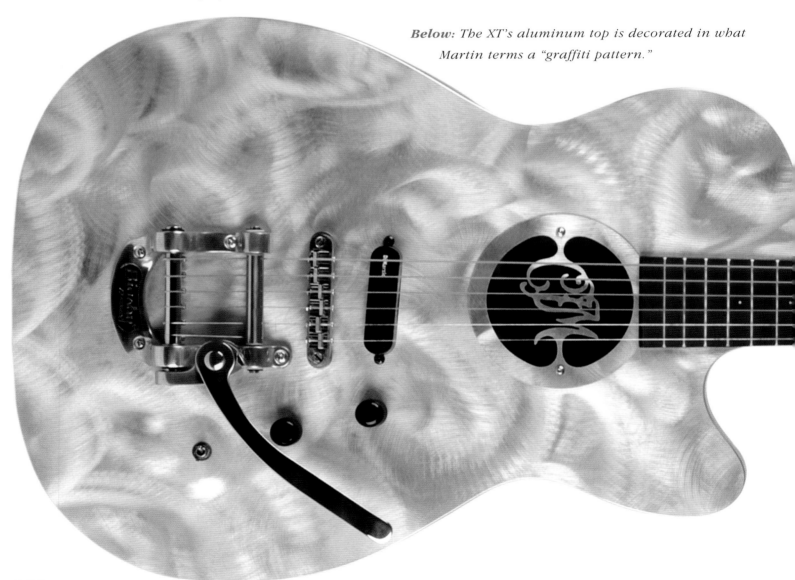

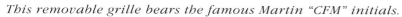
This removable grille bears the famous Martin "CFM" initials.

**Above:** The XT's black fingerboard.is made from Micarta, a synthetic ebony substitute.
**Left:** A "Tune-O-Matic"-type bridge like this is not often seen on a Martin!

# MARTIN CF-1 ARCHTOP

DALE UNGER (b. 1954) grew up in the area around the C.F. Martin guitar company's headquarters in Nazareth, Pennsylvania. As a budding luthier, he was profoundly influenced by the firm's dedicated and painstaking approach to flat-top design; however, he chose to specialize in building archtop guitars. In the 1990s he went on to study and develop his craft with one of the greatest living makers of such instruments, Robert Benedetto—a New Yorker who was then based in the little Pennsylvanian town of East Stroudsburg.

After three years' work with Benedetto, Dale Unger set up American Archtop Guitars in 1995, and started producing his own models, some of which were built using Benedetto's patterns and molds (though Unger tended to use laminated tops instead of the solid woods found on Benedetto archtops). The next stage of Unger's career began in 2001, when he approached Martin with a proposal for a new range of f-hole guitars

*Below: The CF-1 has a 3-inch deep body, with a 3-ply spruce/obeche/spruce top; its back and sides are made from maple.*

*Below: The label inside the CF-1's f-hole is signed by Dale Under and Christian Frederick Martin IV, Martin's Chairman and CEO*

*Above: The CF-1 and CF-2 represent Martin's first venture into archtop guitar production since the 1960s.*

*This "American Archtop" logo was co-designed by Dale Unger and Martin's Dick Boak.*

that would, as he put it in an article written for the company's **Sounding Board** newsletter, "blend Martin's extraordinary craftsmanship and process with my particular archtop designs." The idea found favor with Martin's bosses, and two Unger/Martin instruments, the CF-1 (seen here) and the thinline CF-2, were launched in 2004. Both are made from premium tonewoods, and are fitted with Seymour Duncan pickups.

# MARTIN BC-15E ACOUSTIC BASS

I T IS EASY TO FORGET that Martin's first-ever basses were the EB-18 and EB-28 electrics, launched, respectively, in 1979 and 1980. These were never big sellers, but recently, the company has enjoyed much more success with its acoustic bass guitars. The BC-15E in our photos is part of the relatively plainly appointed 15 series; this style was first introduced at Nazareth in 1935, and has traditionally featured unbound mahogany bodies and a natural finish. Today, Martin also uses sapele for some of its 15s, and describes the instruments in the series as "among our most affordable solid wood guitars."

The BC-15E debuted in 2000; it is produced in both mahogany and sapele versions, and is a sister model to the Dreadnought 6-string DC-15E. Its 16-inch wide body supplies a rich, mellow timbre; one satisfied customer, bassist Eddie Foronda, has also referred, in an online review, to the pleasant "forest fragrance"

*Below: "Herringbone" decoration surrounds the BC-15E's soundhole, but the guitar's overall finish is pleasingly spartan.*

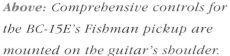

*Above: Comprehensive controls for the BC-15E's Fishman pickup are mounted on the guitar's shoulder.*

*Above: The bass has a rosewood headstock; the same wood is used for its 34$^{1}$/$_{8}$-inch fingerboard.*

exuded by its woods, though this (unlike the instrument's sonic qualities) proved to be short-lived! A built-in pickup system is provided, whose onboard equalizer allows players to "sculpt" the tonal response of the BC-15E, and "dial out" troublesome frequencies using its notch control. Pickup and preamp are supplied to Martin by Fishman Transducers—a Massachusetts-based firm, founded by Larry Fishman (himself a bass player) in 1981, which has been a pioneer in the development of electronics for acoustic instruments. The guitar also features a Venetian-type cutaway to facilitate access to its 23-fret fingerboard.

*Above: This close-up shows the substantial, robust bridge saddle (made from Tusq) and pins required for the instrument's thick strings.*

# MARTIN 000-28LD LONNIE DONEGAN

SCOTSMAN LONNIE DONEGAN (1931-2002) introduced audiences throughout the world to Skiffle—a viscerally exciting musical genre, infused with elements of blues, folk and country, that began sweeping Great Britain in the mid-1950s, and inspired future stars such as John Lennon and Paul McCartney of The Beatles to start playing guitar. Donegan's first major hit, "Rock Island Line" (released in 1956) was a UK Number 1 that also reached the American Top Ten, and in a career that spanned five decades, he went on to sell millions of records, as well as enjoying massive success as a live performer.

Lonnie was a long-time devotee of Martin guitars, and in early 2002, the company announced plans to honor him by producing a limited edition series of acoustics based on his own favorite Martin model, the 000-28 he had played since 1967. He took an active role in developing these "signature" instruments, and they now stand as a fitting memorial to his life and work.

Two Lonnie Donegan flat-tops were eventually issued, differing only in the provenance of the wood used for their backs, sides and headstock facings. These are made from East Indian rosewood on the 000-28LD shown here, whereas Brazilian rosewood was chosen for the 000-28LDB. Both Donegan guitars have sitka spruce tops, and feature identical "personalized" decorations, including a crown at the 3rd fret of their black ebony fingerboards (acknowledging Lonnie

*Below: Inlays on the guitar's fretboard spell out Lonnie Donegan's name and his chosen genre of music.*

*The 000-28LD has a gloss laquer finish, and blue paua shell inlays around its soundhole.*

*Above: Each of the 72 limited edition 000-28LDs carries the signatures of Lonnie Donegan and Martin's Chairman and CEO Chris Martin IV.*

Donegan's status as the "King of Skiffle"), and the inlaid "water rat" emblem and "G.O.W.R." lettering on their headstocks—a reference to the Grand Order of Water Rats, a British showbusiness charity, supported by the star, that receives part of the proceeds from the sale of each of the guitars. The 000-28LD and LDB also boast built-in, Martin-designed Gold Plus Natural II electronic pickups.

*Below: Solid black ebony is used for the 000-EC's bridge, as well as for its fingerboard.*

*Herringbone inlays are among Martin's most distinctive decorations.*

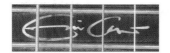

# MARTIN 000-28EC ERIC CLAPTON

*A pickup system for the 000-28EC is available as an optional extra.*

A LONG-TIME DEVOTEE OF MARTIN GUITARS, rock legend Eric Clapton first collaborated with the company on a limited edition model in 1995. This was the 000-42EC, whose design was partly based on Clapton's much-prized pre-Second World War 000-42; only 461 of the new acoustics were made (the number is a reference to "Slowhand's" classic *461 Ocean Boulevard* album), and they were sold out within 24 hours of being released. The following year saw the launch of a production "Signature Model" 000-28EC; this has become a best seller, and a recently-made example of it is featured here. It has a spruce top with Indian rosewood back and sides, boasts fine herringbone inlays, and carries an inlaid autograph of the great guitarist at its 20th fret. There have been two subsequent limited edition "EC" instruments: the 000-42ECB in 2000, and, two years later, the 000-28ECB; these were restricted to runs of (respectively) 200 and 500.

*Below: Chris Martin has been active in promoting his company's "signature series" models.*

# MARTIN HD-35SJC JUDY COLLINS

JUDY COLLINS MADE HER NAME in the late 1960s as an unrivalled interpreter of classic songs such as Joni Mitchell's "Chelsea Morning" and "Both Sides Now;" her version of the former, released as a single in 1969, is said to have led Bill and Hillary Clinton to christen their own daughter Chelsea, and Mr. Clinton has subsequently credited Collins with "inspiring a whole generation who had the same kind of dreams [as her]." Over the following decades she has remained perennially popular as a singer, actress and author, and in 2002, Martin saluted her achievements—and her long-standing use of its instruments in the studio and onstage—with the release of two "signature edition" Judy Collins guitars: a 6-string (seen here) and a 12-string (featured overleaf).

They are D-35 type models with Sitka spruce tops and Collins' "trademark" wildflower inlaid on their headstocks: her *Wildflowers* album, released in 1967,

*Below: The striking inlays on this Judy Collins model's soundhole are created with green abalone.*

*Top: Abalone "snow-flake" markers adorn the HD-35SJC's black ebony fingerboard.*

*Right: Ebony is also used for the knobs of the guitar's chromed Schaller tuners.*

was the first of her records to include her own compositions, and her current record company and other personal projects also carry the Wildflower name. Each of the instruments (just 50 6-strings and 33 12-strings were made) carry the star's signature on their inside labels, alongside that of Martin CEO Chris Martin IV, and proceeds from their sale have been donated, at Collins' request, to the United Nations Children's Fund.

# MARTIN HD12-35SJC JUDY COLLINS

OF THE TWO MARTIN JUDY COLLINS "signature edition" guitars, the 12-string model shown here is perhaps the most personal to her, as its basic design is similar to the D12-35 Martin Dreadnought that she has performed with for many years. Like many folk-influenced singers of her generation, she was almost certainly inspired to take up the 12-string, whose rich, jangling sound is ideal for vocal accompaniment, after seeing and hearing it being used by Pete Seeger, and before him Leadbelly; she has also frequently recorded with former Byrd Roger McGuinn, perhaps the most distinctive of all the instrument's exponents.

The Collins guitar combines sonic excellence with fine woods and outstanding decoration. Like its 6-string sister, it boasts a three-piece back with a center section of Pacific Big Leaf maple, set between "wings" and sides of Indian rosewood. Its herringbone and abalone inlays are equally exquisite, and (unlike some 12-strings from lesser manufacturers) it is also very easy to play, with a comfortable string action and a low

*Below: The HD12-35SJC has a bridge of African ebony, and a beveled black pickguard to match.*

**Below:** *The heel perfectly matches the elegantly bordered central maple section of the instrument's back.*

profile, as well as a solid mahogany neck.

Martin's program of special instrument production has paid tribute to some of the most distinguished names in acoustic music. However, the company has also recently created a guitar to commemorate one of its own longtime staff, the late Mike Longworrth: it appears on the next two pages.

**Left:** *The "wildflower" on headstocks of both the Collins guitars is a columbine.*

# MARTIN D-45 MIKE LONGWORTH

MIKE LONGWORTH WAS BORN in 1938, and grew up in Chattanooga, Tennessee. While still in high school, he had developed a reputation for creating elaborate inlays on guitars and other fretted instruments, and by the mid-1950s, his skills were being called upon by a succession of music stars. Among them was bluegrass great Lester Flatt, to the fingerboard of whose Martin D-28 Dreadnought the teenage Longworth added a number of embellishments, including a mother-of-pearl "Lester."

Later, he developed another ingenious sideline—providing D-28s with pearl inlays that made them correspond visually to the company's fancier D-45 model, which had been out of production since 1942.

Word of Longworth's talents eventually reached Martin headquarters in Nazareth, Pennsylvania, and in 1968, the firm took him on as an employee; one of his first jobs there was the creation of inlays for the relaunched D-45, which proved to be a substantial seller. Subsequently, his encyclopedic knowledge of

*Below: Adirondack spruce is used for the top of this special Dreadnought; its back and sides are Indian rosewood.*

Martin instruments, and his ability to handle the most arcane of queries from players and collectors, led to his appointment as Customer Relations Manager; and in 1975, the first edition of his definitive history of the company was published.

Mike Longworth retired in 1995, and died in 2003. His unique contribution to Martin has since been marked by the release of a "Commemorative Edition"

*Top: The "torch" inlaid on the headstock is a feature "borrowed" from earlier Martin Style 45 instruments.*

D-45. Only 91 of these guitars have been made: the number corresponds to the total of D-45s produced between 1933 (when "Singing Cowboy" Gene Autry ordered the first one) and 1942.

# MARTIN LITTLE MARTIN LX1E

THE LITTLE MARTIN, which was introduced in 2003, is a robust, compact, "go-anywhere" flat-top acoustic equally suitable for adults and children. Unlike some other instruments of similar size, it is designed to be played at standard pitch, and, remarkably, its 23-inch scale length is only $2^2/_5$ inches shorter than a Martin Dreadnought's.

Several alternative types of Little Martin are available. Some, including the original LXM and LXME versions, have bodies made entirely from high pressure laminates, but the model seen in our photographs, the LX1E, boasts a solid sitka spruce top, with a back and sides of "mahogany pattern" HPL. It is fitted with a Fishman-designed "Mini Q" under-saddle transducer system that delivers impressive "plugged-in" results when recording or playing through an amplifier…though it seems unlikely that such facilities were available to mountaineers Vernon Tejas and Dolly Aliverzatos when they carried a Little Martin up America's highest peak, Denali (Mount McKinley) in

*Below: This model has a fiber-inlaid soundhole rosette. Its bridge is made from Micarta, and its saddle from Tusq.*

Bottom: *Despite its small size, the guitar has 14 frets clear of its body.*

Above: *This shot shows the layers of wood veneer making up the Little Martin's neck.*

Alaska, shortly after the guitar's launch. Their exploits were subsequently documented in Martin's online journal, **The Sounding Board**: it reports that the guitar, which was entirely unaffected by cold or altitude during the expedition, has since been taken by Tejas (a skilled player whose repertoire includes a tune called "Frostbite Blues") to mountain tops on three other continents!

# MARTIN COWBOY III

MARTIN HAS A PROUD history, and a long-standing dedication to the highest standards of flat-top lutherie—but, as the pictures on the next four pages demonstrate—the firm also possesses a sense of humor. Among the more unusual new products it launched at the National Association of Music Merchants' Nashville show in 2000 was the "Cowboy X," a limited edition model decorated with a colorful "campfire scene" painting by artist Robert Armstrong, whose illustrations and cartoons (showcasing characters such as Mickey Rat and the Couch Potato) have graced magazines and books since the 1970s. Collaborating with Martin was especially enjoyable for Armstrong, as he is himself an accomplished guitarist and accordionist, who has appeared as a sideman with fellow cartoonist R. Crumb's Cheap Suit Serenaders, and is also famous for playing the musical saw solo featured on the soundtrack to the movie *One Flew Over the Cuckoo's Nest*!

The Cowboy X sold well, and was followed by several

*Idyllic mountain scenery forms the backdrop for the antics at the corral.*

**Above:** The dog in Robert Armstrong's picture seems to be howling along to the tune being picked by the cowboy guitarist!

**Right:** Stratabond, a laminate containing resin, is used for the Cowboy III's neck.

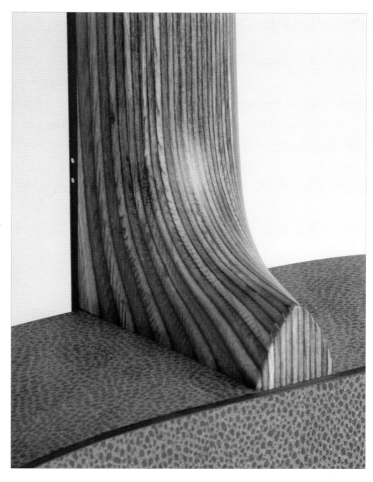

The guitar's fingerboard is fashioned from black Micarta, instead of wood.

subsequent Martin/Armstrong instruments: the Cowboy II debuted in 2001, and the Cowboy III (shown here) a year later. Like its predecessors, the III boasts artwork full of subtle touches and allusions that will delight Martin aficionados. The guitar being played by the figure on the instrument's lower bout is unmistakably one of the company's OM-28s, while the character on the bucking bronco in the corral behind him is Martin CEO Chris Martin IV! Robert Armstrong's picture has been applied to the Cowboy III's top using a high pressure decorative laminating (HPL) technique that ensures vivid colors as well as high scratch resistance.

Only 750 Martin Cowboy IIIs were produced, but the range has continued in recent years with the Cowboy IV and the Hawaiian X.

# MARTIN "FELIX" LIMITED EDITION

THE CARTOON CHARACTER Felix The Cat made his debut in a movie short in 1919; it was produced by the New York-based Pat Sullivan studio, and Felix himself was created and originally drawn by Otto Messmer, who directed the picture. Other film appearances helped to establish Felix as a star, and in 1928 he was used as a testcard image for RCA's pioneering television transmissions; he also featured in newspaper cartoon strips and comics, acquiring a restyled look when Joe Oriolo took over the production of "Felix" artwork from Messmer.

The lovable feline has proved perennially popular in a variety of different media, and in 2004, it was announced that Joe Oriolo's son Don (who collaborated with his father on Felix projects for many years, and has been exclusively responsible for them since Joe's death in 1985) had teamed up with the Martin company to produce a "Felix" guitar. The limited edition instrument (only 756 were produced, one of which is seen here) has a travel-size body made

*Below: Micarta, also seen on the Martin Cowboy guitar, is used for this model's fingerboard.*

*Don Oriolo has helped bring Felix to a new generation of fans.*

***Above:*** *Martin's publicity describes this instrument as "the ideal guitar for very hip cats!"*

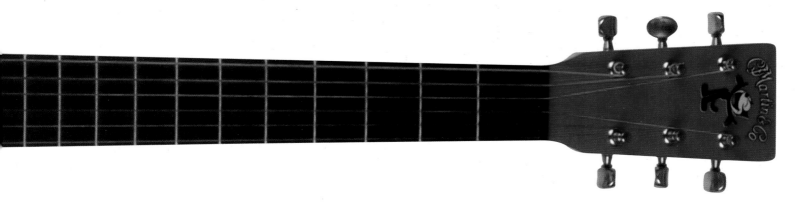

from high pressure laminates. Its back and sides are black, and its spruce-braced top is adorned with multiple Felix heads, as well as a "Felix The Cat" logo and Don Oriolo's signature. A miniature, full-length Felix appears on the headstock.

Unsurprisingly, this first Felix guitar quickly sold out, and in 2006, a second limited-run model appeared. Based, like the original, on a Little Martin acoustic, it boasts a new set of graphics, created by Don Oriolo and his colleague Jen Henning, on its top: these show more than one hundred miniature Felix figures—just one of whom is clutching a plectrum! Among the additional goodies supplied with the guitar are a comic book, and a "laughing Felix" flatpick.

A total of 625 "Felix IIs" has been made, and they have proved every bit as popular as their predecessors.

# MARTIN BACKPACKER

THE MARTIN BACKPACKER'S uniquely compact design allows it to be taken to places that would be strictly out of bounds to regular-sized acoustics. Since the first of these endearing little guitars—built for Martin in Mexico, and based on an instrument originally created by luthier Robert McNally—rolled off the production line in 1991, they have been seen and heard in a string of exotic locations, from the South Pole to the Mount Everest Base Camp in Tibet. Backpackers have also been carried onboard the US Space Shuttle *Columbia*, and are said to be a particular favorite among airline staff: some years ago, Martin's *Sounding Board* magazine published a picture of a pilot strumming one while perched inside the engine cowling of a DC-10!

Despite its small size, the Backpacker's 24-inch scale length and standard fingerboard width make it easy to play; the only serious concession to portability lies in the design of its body, which, because of its narrow dimensions, requires a strap to keep it in position whether the user is sitting or standing. The lack of a truss-rod (as extra-light strings are fitted, the Backpacker does not need one) helps to reduce weight, and a built-in bridge transducer enables owners to plug the guitar into any amplifiers, PA systems or tape machines they may encounter on their travels. While the steel-strung Backpacker remains the best seller of the range, a "classical" model has also proved successful, and recently, Martin has introduced Backpacker mandolins and ukuleles.

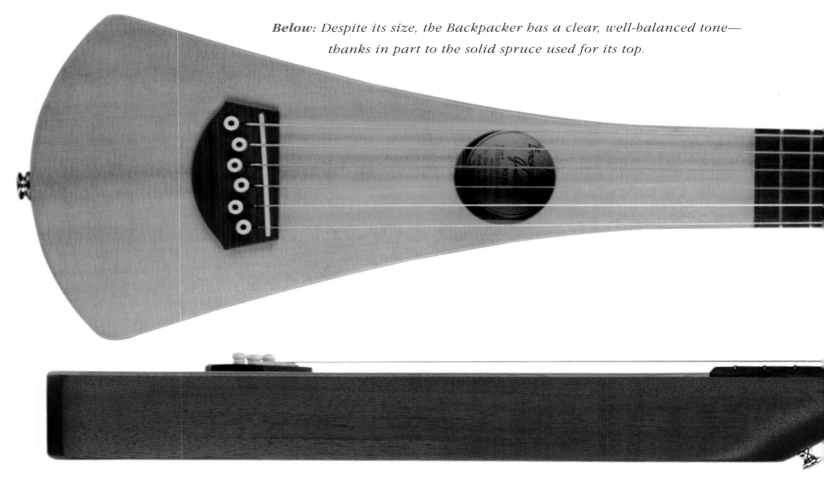

*Below: Despite its size, the Backpacker has a clear, well-balanced tone—thanks in part to the solid spruce used for its top.*

*Above:* Miniature chrome tuners are fitted to the Backpacker's headstock.

*Below:* Thanks to the Backpacker's unusual shape, all fifteen of its frets are easily accessible.

This nut is made from Corian, a solid material developed by DuPont.

# MATON EBG808

ATON, AUSTRALIA'S ONLY sizeable guitar producer, is based in the Box Hill area of the city of Melbourne. The firm was established by musician, craftsman and teacher Bill May, who set up an instrument-making and repair shop in the garage of his home in the Melbourne suburbs in the mid-1940s. He christened the fledging business "Maton" (a blend of his own surname and the word "tone"). With the assistance of his cabinetmaker brother Reg, who began collaborating with him in 1946, he was able to open the first Maton factory at a former soap works in nearby Canterbury by the end of the decade.

Over the next 40 years, Maton's product range and reputation grew steadily; it relocated to larger premises in 1989, and moved into its current Box Hill headquarters—where its highly acclaimed acoustic and electric guitars are made using a combination of state-of-the-art Computer Numeric Control (CNC) technology and traditional craft skills—in December 2002. Sadly, Bill May himself did not live to see this latest expansion; he died in 1993, but the company remains a family-run concern, with Bill's daughter

*Below: Maton's "Bluegrass" models have narrower bodies than Dreadnoughts or Jumbos, and are favored by fingerstyle players.*

*Right:* The EBG808 has a "satin" finish, and herringbone trim around its soundhole.

*Above:* This AP5 pickups gives players precise control over the guitar's amplified sound.

Linda and her husband Neville Kitchen at the helm.

In an international market dominated by American luthiers, Maton has had to struggle to gain the recognition it deserves, but superb instruments such as the EBG808 shown here are attracting increasing numbers of customers. Like all the company's "Bluegrass" (BG) series of flat-tops, it has a 14⁴/₁₀-inch wide body, and features a combination of traditional and Australian tonewoods: on this 808, cedar is used for the top, but the back and sides are made from blackwood (grown in Maton's home state of Victoria), and the neck is Queensland maple. Rosewood is used for the fingerboard and bridge, and the instrument includes a Maton-designed AP5 pickup system.

# BRIAN MAY SIGNATURE

UNLIKE MANY LEADING rock guitarists, Brian May, who made his name with Queen in the 1970s and 80s, and was recently voted one of the world's top five players, has stayed largely faithful to a single instrument throughout his long and distinguished career. Even more unusually, he designed and built his favorite "Red Special" electric himself, with a little initial assistance from his father. The guitar dates from 1964: it was made with wood from a Victorian fireplace, and, in its earliest form, featured movable pickups for extra tonal versatility. Though it has undergone many subsequent modifications, the Red Special's essential character and appearance (its distinctive color comes from the fence varnish used on the body timber!) have remained largely unchanged, and it has been heard on decades of hit records as well as during memorable live performances—including May's unforgettable rendition of the British National Anthem from the roof of London's Buckingham Palace on the occasion of Her Majesty the Queen's Golden Jubilee in 2002!

The first official replica of the Red Special was produced as a limited edition by Guild in 1984. The

*Below: This instrument is signed by Laurie Wisefield, one of the original guitarists in the UK stage show* We Will Rock You, *based around Queen songs.*

*The guitar has an ebony fingerboard with 24 frets, and a maple neck.*

*These knobs are master volume and tone controls.*

*Each of the three pickups has a dedicated on-off switch, and, below it, a phase switch, allowing the creation of a wide variety of sounds.*

same company introduced a second Brian May model nine years later, but it was not until 2001 that a less expensive version appeared. This was the Brian May Signature, launched by Burns London (see separate Burns entries) in 2001. The original Red Special boasts 1960s-vintage Burns Tri-Sonic pickups, and the three transducers on the copy are closely modeled on these, while their associated controls (see caption) are identical to those on May's own instrument. Other aspects of the Special have also been carefully reproduced (though a basswood body has been substituted for the "fireplace" timbers), and the model has proved hugely popular with Brian May's legions of guitar-playing admirers. London's House of Guitars has now taken over its distribution from Burns.

# MOSRITE VENTURES

Semie Moseley started building guitars in his teenage years, including a triple-neck model. He and his brother Andy founded Mosrite of California in 1956. At first, they produced custom guitars, but sales increased dramatically after Nokie Edwards of the Ventures endorsed their instruments. Barbara Mandrell also played Mosrites. But bad business decisions meant that the company went bankrupt in 1968, but they were back in business by 1970. This solid body electric has a Sunburst finish on its carved body. Its neck pocket is dated June 30, 1966. It also boasts a bound rosewood 22-fret fretboard, dot markers, and two pickups with "Mosrite of California" covers. The tailpiece and bridge are Moseleys, and the tuners are Klusons.

*The guitar has two pickups with "Mosrite of California" covers, a Moseley tailpiece with vibrato, and a yellowed pickguard.*

# MUSIC MAN STINGRAY 5 BASS

Leo Fender co-founded Tri-Sonics in 1972, together with two former Fender staffers. The new company was renamed Music Man in February 1973. Music Man started out as a manufacturer of amplifiers, but introduced its first instrument, the StingRay bass, in 1976. The guitar had a particularly distinguished headstock design. Further basses and guitars followed. Like the StingRay, these were built at Leo Fender's own CLF factory (the initials stand for Clarence Leo Fender) in Fullerton, California. Sadly, Music Man's management soon became riven with tensions and personality clashes. By the end of the decade, Leo Fender had effectively ended his involvement with the business, and was planning a new venture, G&L.

*A rear view of the StingRay 5's body: the instrument's neck plate carries its serial number and maker's trademarks.*

# MUSIC MAN SUB 1

THE SUB 1 WAS LAUNCHED in January 2004; a mid-price, though very impressively specified guitar, it was the third instrument in the SUB series, which already featured two electric basses. The range's name is derived from the initials of Sterling Ball, the company's president: his father, Ernie Ball, who acquired the firm in 1984 (see previous entry) passed away in September 2004, at the age of 74.

It is a matter of intense pride within Music Man that the SUBs are built at the firm's headquarters in San Luis Obispo, California, rather than overseas. Sterling Ball has recently commented that "foreign manufacturing, along with current economic woes, have put tremendous pressure on top quality American made instruments and their price points. Many companies have all but given up on domestic manufacturing, but we at Music Man really feel that with clever engineering and alternative materials,

*Below: The distinctive pickguard mounted on the guitar's poplar body is made from aluminum.*

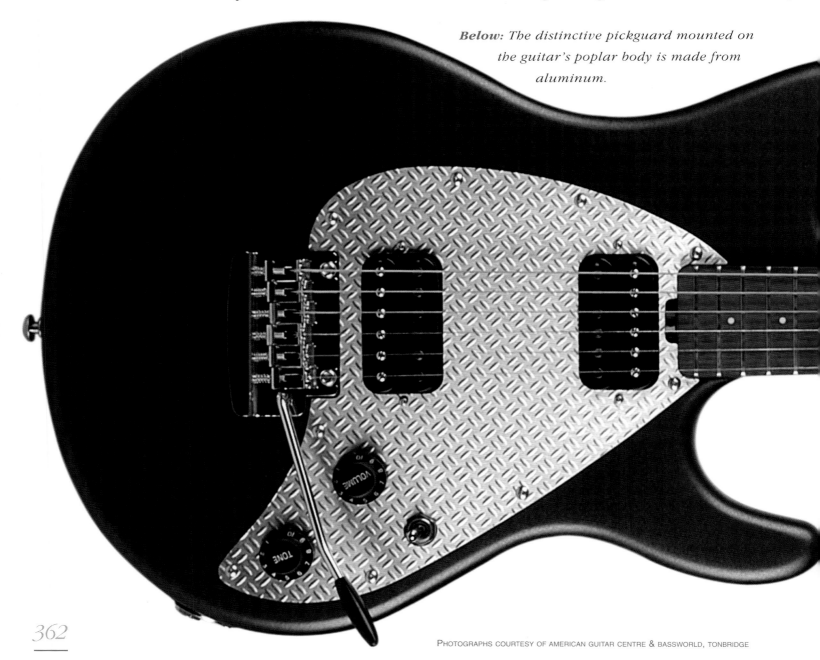

**Above:** *Locking tuners are fitted to this vibrato-equipped Sub 1.*

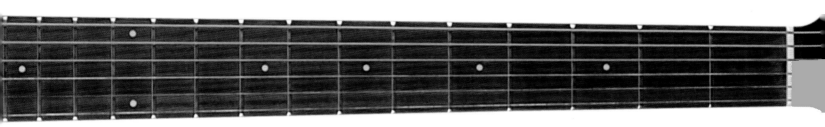

along with more focused manufacturing techniques, we can prosper as a true American manufacturer."

The SUB 1 demonstrates the success of his strategy: available in seven alternative textured colors, and with single or dual humbucking pickups (an example of the latter is seen here), it has been widely admired for its sound, its fast playing action, its looks, and its light weight: the "hardtail" (non-vibrato) version tips the scales at no more than 6 pounds 5 ounces!

**Left:** *The instrument's neck bolt, concealed by this plate, is said by the manufacturers to offer "perfect alignments with no shifting."*

363

# MUSIC MAN ALBERT LEE

**B**RITISH GUITARIST ALBERT LEE (b.1943) began his professional career as a teenager, quickly building an impressive reputation for his country-influenced picking style. He fronted the underrated Head Hands & Feet in the early 1970s, but always enjoyed his greatest success as a sideman and session player, and was soon spending much of his time in the USA, where his performances with the late Buddy Holly's former group, The Crickets, were followed by a stint as lead guitarist for Emmylou Harris's Hot Band from 1976 to 1978; his immediate predecessor in this role was the great James Burton.

Albert has subsequently appeared with a long list of other famous names, including Eric Clapton, the Everly Brothers, and ex-Rolling Stone Bill Wyman's Rhythm Kings. He won a Grammy award in 2002 for his work with country banjo legend Earl Scruggs, has (to date) been voted "Best Country Guitar Picker" five times by *Guitar Player* magazine, and is currently touring and recording with the band Hogan's Heroes.

Albert Lee's "signature" Music Man guitar began life as a prototype in the late 1980s, and has been commercially available since 1994; prior to its introduction, Albert's main instrument had been a

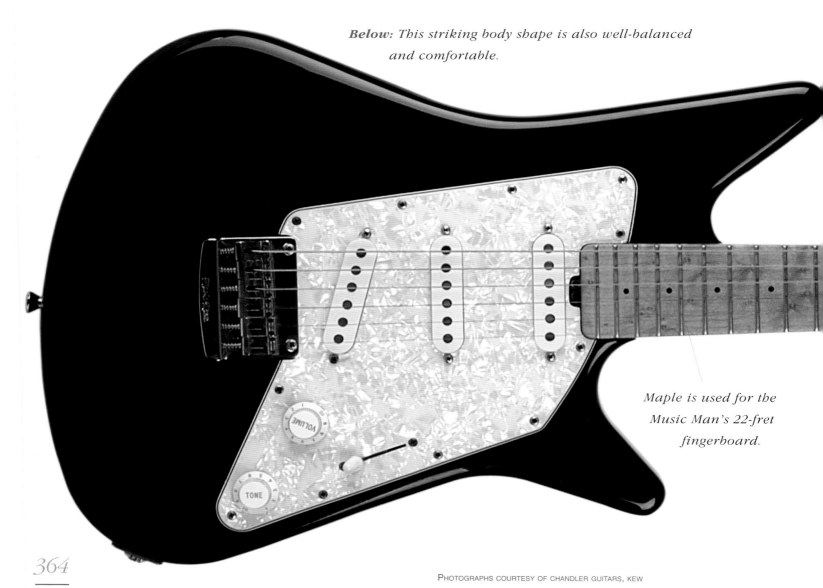

*Below: This striking body shape is also well-balanced and comfortable.*

*Maple is used for the Music Man's 22-fret fingerboard.*

PHOTOGRAPHS COURTESY OF CHANDLER GUITARS, KEW

*Above:* Like the
Fender guitars that partly
inspired it, the Music Man Albert Lee
has a bolted-on neck.

*Bottom:* The single-coil pickups on the Albert
Lee model are supplied by Seymour Duncan.

*This unusual 4/2 tuner
configuration resembles those
found on Music Man basses.*

Fender Telecaster. The Music Man model features a distinctively shaped body made from ash, and three single-coil pickups whose controls resemble those on a Stratocaster, though only single volume and tone knobs are fitted. The example seen in our photographs is a "hard-tail:" there are also versions with vibrato, and with a bridge-mounted piezo transducer.

365

# NATIONAL ROSITA

THOUGH NATIONAL remained financially buoyant in the early 1930s, the company was in considerable turmoil. The principal cause of this was the legal action initiated by John Dopyera and his colleagues (including several of his brothers) at Dobro, who alleged that their rival resonator-making business had been damaged by false statements made by National's General Manager, George Beauchamp. As Bob Brozman reveals in his history of the company, Beauchamp had indeed been visiting instrument dealers and claiming, quite baselessly, that "Dobro [guitars] infringed on National patents and that National had won a lawsuit with Dobro." His behavior eventually undermined his standing at National, and in 1931, he was sacked from his post there.

The dispute with Dobro dragged on for two more years before being settled out of court. Its resolution led to a rapprochement between National and the Dopyera family, who acquired a substantial financial stake in the company, and in July 1935 Dobro and National merged, with John Dopyera's brother Emil becoming the National Dobro Corporation's General

*Below: This Rosita dates from 1936, the year in which National began its move from LA to Chicago.*

*The guitar's body is made from birch plywood.*

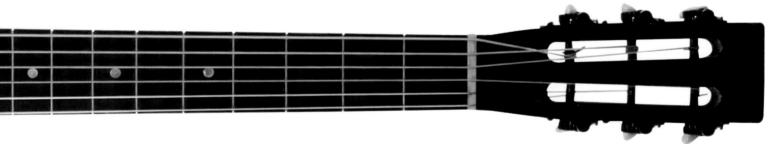

*Above: The Rosita's resonator cover is decorated very differently to those on earlier Nationals.*
*Left: This V-shaped neck profile is a favorite with many players.*

Manager. Under this new regime, National continued, for a while, to make both metal- and wood-body resonator instruments, including the elegant Rosita model illustrated here. However their sales were being increasingly eroded by the rise in demand for electrics, and it was in the latter area that the company chose to stake its future. By the start of World War II, its production of tri-cones and single-cones had ceased.

# NATIONAL COSMOPOLITAN

AMERICANS AFFECTED BY the Great Depression frequently sought better fortune by heading westward. The National guitar company, however, chose to buck this trend by moving its manufacturing base east from its Los Angeles birthplace, establishing a Chicago works in the mid-1930s, and completing its move to the Windy City early in the following decade. Now renamed Valco, the Chicago operation was soon making instruments for third parties such as catalog houses, as well as acoustics and electrics carrying the National brand name.

The National solid-body shown here is a Cosmopolitan with a blond finish; the model first appeared in 1954, two years after a simpler, one-pickup electric National, prosaically christened the Solid Body Electric Spanish, had made its debut. The range was almost certainly inspired by the success of Leo Fender's Telecasters, and, like them, had bolt-on necks, single cutaways and an unpretentious, workmanlike appearance.

National electrics were widely used by blues players—both Memphis Minnie and Memphis Slim

*Below: The Cosmopolitan's pickups are attached to its pickguard; and their wiring is concealed beneath its plastic.*

*This distinctively shaped switch selects either or both of the guitar's pickups.*

*A screw-type bolt attaches the guitar's neck to the body.*

were photographed with them—while the firm's later, flashier axes, including "map-bodied" models whose shapes roughly corresponded to the outline of the USA, were aimed at a younger clientele, and promoted using ads that proclaimed their "versatility, beauty and elegance." Sadly, though, their sales proved insufficient to save Valco from bankruptcy in 1967.

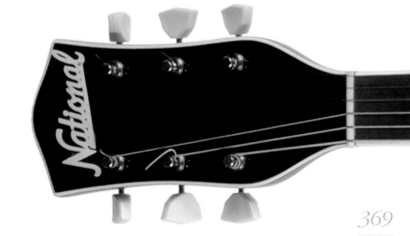

# NATIONAL RESO-PHONIC DELPHI

NATIONAL RESO-PHONIC, based in San Luis Obispo, California, is recognized as the principal "torch-bearer" of the resonator instrument-making traditions associated with the original National company. It was founded in 1988 by Don Young and McGregor Gaines, who had previously worked together at the Dopyera brothers' Original Musical Instruments (OMI) factory. During their first few years in business for themselves, they were unable to afford the tooling needed to build metal guitar bodies, but eventually succeeded in putting their steel-bodied

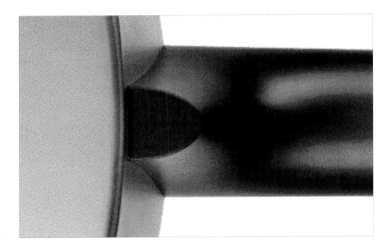

**Above:** *The Delphi's body is 14 inches wide, and just over 3 inches deep.*

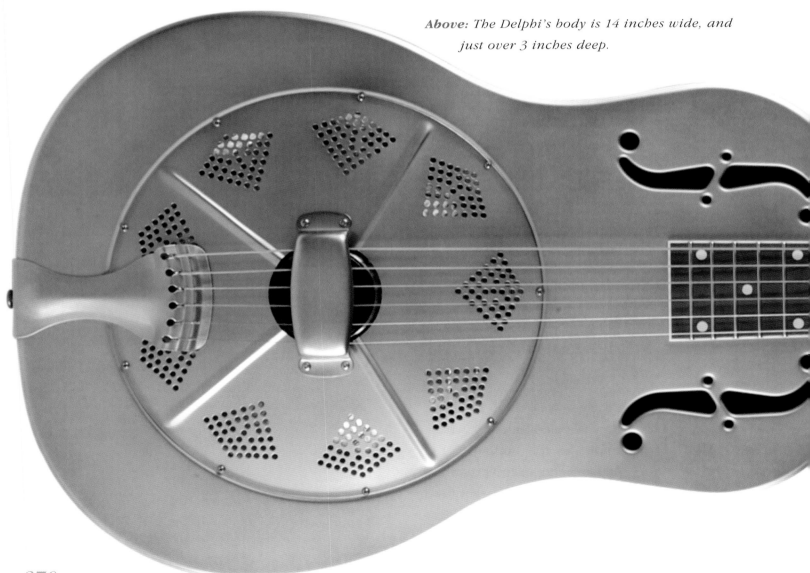

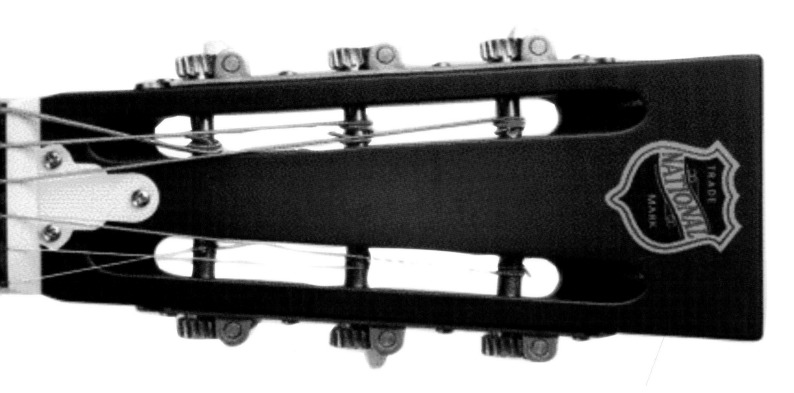

*Below:* Ivoroid binding around the Delphi's neck provides a striking contrast with its steel body.

*Above:* Like many resonator models, the Delphi has a open headstock with "three-on-a-plate" machine heads.

These San Luis Obispo-made instruments carry the original National trademark.

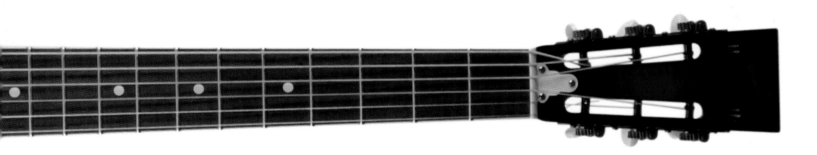

Delphi and brass Style O models into production in 1992; their output now includes an impressive range of resonator guitars, mandolins and ukuleles made in steel, brass and wood, and Don and McGregor share managerial duties with McGregor's wife, Marie, who oversees administration and artist relations.

The Delphi single-cone has been a perennial best-seller for National Reso-Phonic, and is currently available as a "standard" version, in a deluxe reworking with a mahogany neck and mother-of-pearl diamond markers, and as a "Delphi Vintage Steel" model (seen here), which features what National describe as "a satin nickel finish that will age with use and the passage of time." The resonator cover plate is also given a satin nickel finish, and the instrument has a hard rock maple neck, with a rosewood fingerboard.

*Below: The Radio-Tone's single cone resonator and maple "biscuit" bridge deliver a powerful, punchy tone that especailly suits slide guitarists.*

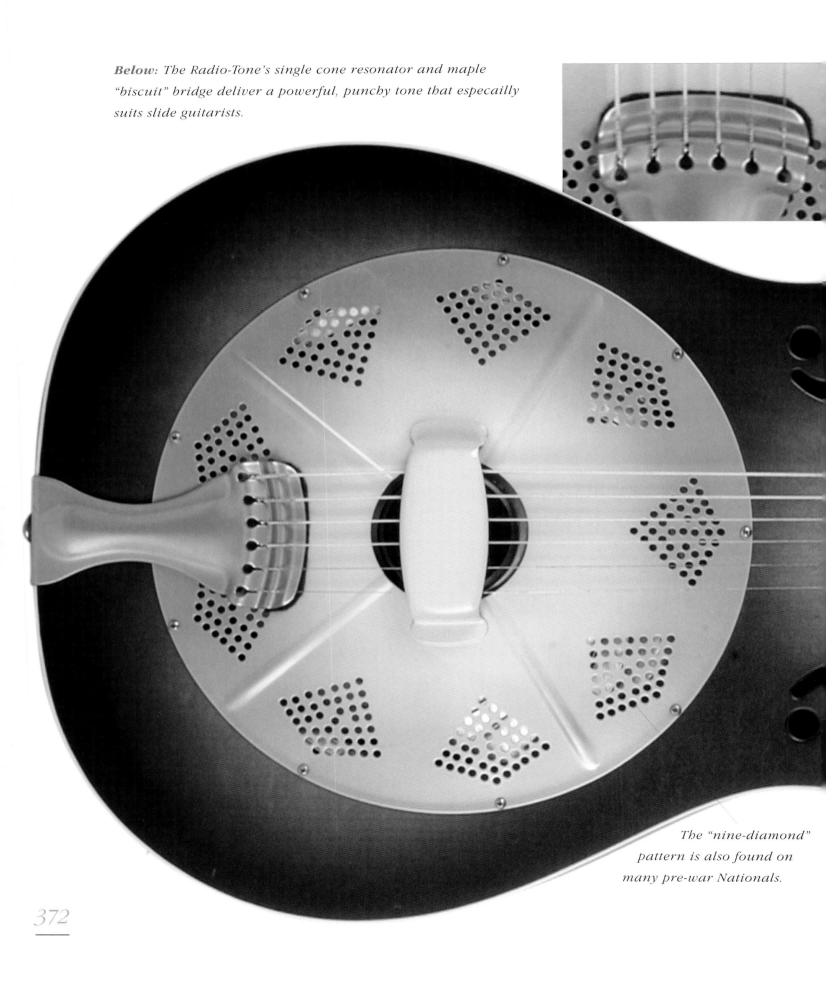

*The "nine-diamond" pattern is also found on many pre-war Nationals.*

# NATIONAL RADIO-TONE

*Below: This model's maple-sided body is just over 3 inches deep.*

THOUGH NATIONAL RESO-PHONIC is rightly celebrated for its metal resonator guitars, the first instruments it produced in the years after its launch in 1988 were single-cone models with wooden bodies. The sonic difference between the two materials is a subtle one: in the opinion of resonator expert and virtuoso player Bob Brozman, "Wood body single-cones have all the snap and punch of any single cone, but the wood does mellow the sound a little, which some players may prefer."

The Radio-Tone, with its maple sides and 12-fret-to-the-body maple neck, draws some inspiration from an "old-time" National model, the 1928 Triolian; but other features, such as the strikingly attractive headstock with its echoes of the glamorous "Radio Days" of the 1920s and 30s, are all its own. Sadly, this model—which, at $1199, was the least expensive guitar in the company's range—is now no longer in production, though its distant cousin, the cutaway-body Radio-Tone Bendaway, continues to draw plaudits from players: Michael Messer recently described it as "probably the most 'multi-purpose' guitar that National currently build."

*Right: The Art Deco-influenced headstock was created by Don Young and McGregon Gaines.*

# NEWTON TEVOLUTION (PROTOTYPE)

EMMA NEWTON is a stringed instrument designer based in the English county of Surrey, just south of London. Her father David, now retired, was a highly regarded violin restorer, and Emma worked alongside him for a number of years before founding her own company, Rainbow Violins, in 1999. As its name suggests, Rainbow produces brightly colored fiddles, violas and cellos that are aimed principally at younger players; Emma Newton had discovered there was a demand for them when, as her website reveals, "visitors to her shop [began] enquiring for violins that looked like electric violins, but were cheaper, didn't need amps, and were available in small sizes." Rainbow's instruments are all made from solid tonewoods, which are sourced from the Far East, and are then individually hand-painted and expertly set up at its Surrey workshop. Both acoustic and amplifiable models are available, and among the firm's customers are both amateur and professional players from all around the world.

*Below and right:* The Newton Tevolution's hardware, including its bridge and machine heads (both made by Gotoh), is all chromed.

**Above:** *The guitar has a 25$^1$/$_2$ inch scale length; its neck and 21-fret fingerboard are made from maple.*

More recently, Emma Newton has established Newton Guitars, which, at the time of writing, is about to unveil its first full range of electrics. The Newton "Tevolution" seen here is a prototype, finished in "Surf Blue," and featuring a cutaway ashwood body and two single-coil pickups. Other pre-production Newtons seen by this author include a black-bodied "Tevolution II" with a similar specification to its namesake, and two higher priced guitars, the TC-24 and ST-24—the former sporting a Union Jack color scheme. The Newtons have been described as "very individual designs, combining aspects of a well tried formula with a dash of spice;" they seem destined for success.

# OAHU LAP STEEL

IN THE 1890s, A YOUNG HAWAIIAN, Joseph Kekuku, pioneered a method of producing notes from the strings of his guitar by pressing and sliding a flat steel implement (such as a bar or a knife blade) against them. To accomplish this most effectively, Kekuku and his successors placed their guitars flat on their laps, raising the height of the strings relative to the neck to prevent unwanted contact with the fingerboard, and retuning from the standard EADGBE to chordal settings like "open G" (DGDGBD). Doing so flattened, and therefore slightly loosened, several of the strings,

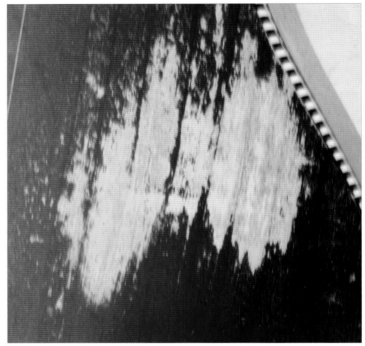

*Right: With no pickguard to protect it, the Tonemaster's body bears the scars of long years' vigorous playing!*

*Below: The Oahu's headstock is finished in mock tortoiseshell, and bears a silkscreened logo.*

*The instrument's mahogany body measures about 10 inches across at its widest point; it is 1³/4 inches deep.*

and the term "slack key guitar" was coined to describe this form of Hawaiian-style playing.

Appearances by guitarists from Hawaii at the 1915 Panana Pacific Exposition in San Francisco helped to popularize the islands' music (and other aspects of their culture), and soon, a craze for all things Hawaiian had taken hold throughout America. This proved to be long lasting, and US manufacturers responded by flooding the market with "lap steel" guitars for slack-key playing. In 1931, Ro-Pat-In, the Californian firm that later developed into Rickenbacker, launched its famous "Frying Pan"—a solid-body lap steel that was the world's first mass-produced electric guitar. Others followed Ro-Pat-In's lead, and by the mid-1930s, the

**Above left**: *This shot shows the extra distance between strings and neck needed for slide playing.*

**Above right**: *There is a hint of Art Deco in the design of the Tonemaster's pickup cover.*

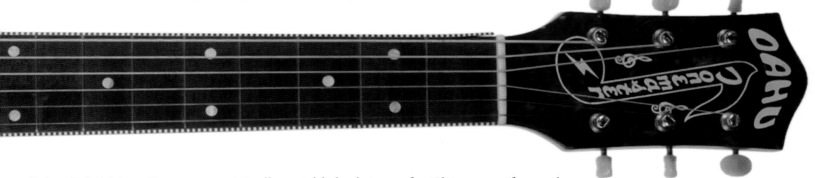

Oahu Publishing Company, originally established in Flint, Michigan, but now based in Cleveland, Ohio, was selling electric lap steels (as well as standard guitars and ukuleles) built for them by third-party makers. The late 1940s Tonemaster lap steel shown here is the work of Oahu's principal electric guitar supplier, Valco

of Chicago (formerly National). A relatively inexpensive, workhorse model, it would have been ideal for beginners, who could also purchase an extensive range of tutor books, sheet music and tablature from Oahu. Tonemasters like this one currently change hands at approximately $400.

# OVATION BALLADEER (NYLON-STRUNG)

CHARLES H. KAMAN'S guitars were named Ovations by jazzman Charlie Byrd (1925-1999), who, after seeing an early model, commented that "it deserved an ovation." Byrd was keen to try one of the revolutionary, Lyrachord-backed acoustics for himself: however, he preferred classicals for his Latin-influenced music (including the best-selling *Jazz Samba* LP, released a few years previously, on which he had partnered saxophonist Stan Getz), and the steel-strung Ovation was not suited to his technique. Kaman quickly solved the problem by developing a nylon-strung version: this debuted in September 1967, and Charlie Byrd went on to adopt "classical-style" Ovations as his main instruments—using them both for solo projects, and when appearing alongside fellow jazz greats Barney Kessel and Herb Ellis in the "Great Guitars" trio, formed in 1973.

Unlike more traditional classicals,

nylon-strung Ovations (a 1970s example is seen here) are easily amplifiable and comparatively robust—qualities that render them particularly attractive to busy touring musicians. Over the years, they have become especially popular with folk and country players, but also have a place in rock: Eddie Van Halen famously featured one on "Spanish Fly," a brief solo track from the *Van Halen II* album (1979).

*Right:* This 1970s Ovation nylon-strung has a built-in pickup whose concentric volume and tone controls are mounted opposite its neck; these have been resited on more recent models

*Far right:* The Ovation's open headstock and wide neck are classically influenced, though a reinforcing truss-rod (never found on standard classics) is fitted.

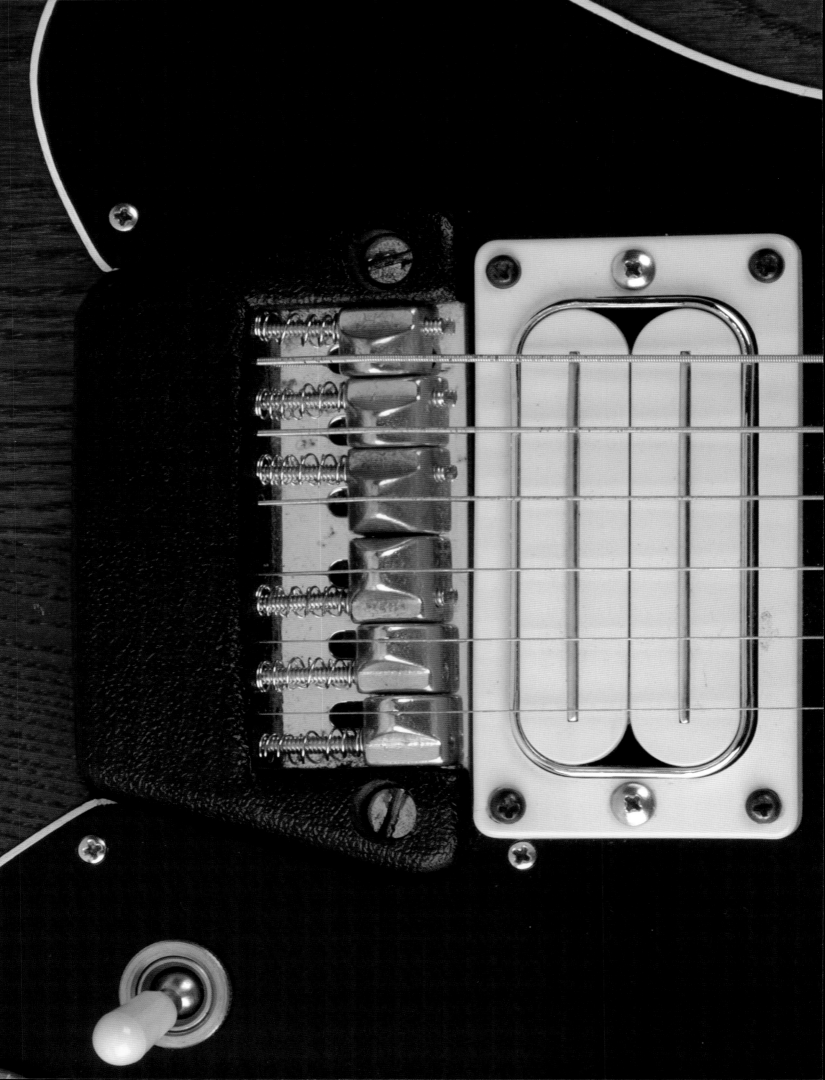

# OVATION VIPER

OVATION ENTERED the conventional electric guitar market in 1968 with its "Electric Storm" range. This comprised seven semi-hollow models, including a 12-string and two basses, all of which were given appropriately "meteorological" names (Thunderhead, Tornado, Hurricane, Typoon). Various additions and changes were made to the line over the next few years, but the instruments were not especially successful, and were eventually dropped.

The company's second generation of electrics was solid-bodied. The Breadwinner and Deacon, launched, respectively, in 1972 and 73, shared a curious, asymmetrical shape, but the Preacher and Viper, dating from 1975, were more conventional-looking. The former sported a double cutaway and stereo circuitry, while the latter (shown here) was a simpler, single-cutaway design. It also had single-coil pickups, which have been replaced with twin-coil units on the instrument in our photos. None of these guitars ever attained the same popularity as Ovation's acoustics, although the Viper and Deacon were the longest lived of the group, remaining in production until the 1980s.

*Below: On its 1970s electrics, Ovation chose to retain the "3-a-side" headstock shape already familar to users of its acoustic models.*

*Above: Unusually, the Viper's maple neck is both glued and bolted to its body.*

# OVATION ADAMAS II 1681-8

OVATION WAS NOT CONTENT to rest on its laurels following the introduction of its innovative acoustics in the mid-1960s. Having replaced wood with Lyrachord on the backs of its guitars, it now turned its attention to the formulation of their tops, and began experimenting with the use of graphite fiber for them. In 1976, after several years of painstaking research, the company unveiled its first Adamas acoustic, whose top comprised three layers: two ultra-thin slices of carbon graphite, and a center made from a slightly wider section of birch. As Ken Achard writes in his book *The History and Development of the American Guitar* (Musical New Services, 1979), the carbon top was "about one third the thickness of a conventional spruce top…and many times stronger." There was no standard soundhole; instead, a total of twenty-two smaller apertures were positioned on the instrument's upper bouts. The model's sound, carefully tailored by the scientists and luthiers who created what Ovation called its "fibronic graphite soundboard," was praised

*Below: The Adamas's bridge, fingerboard and headstock veneer are all made from walnut.*

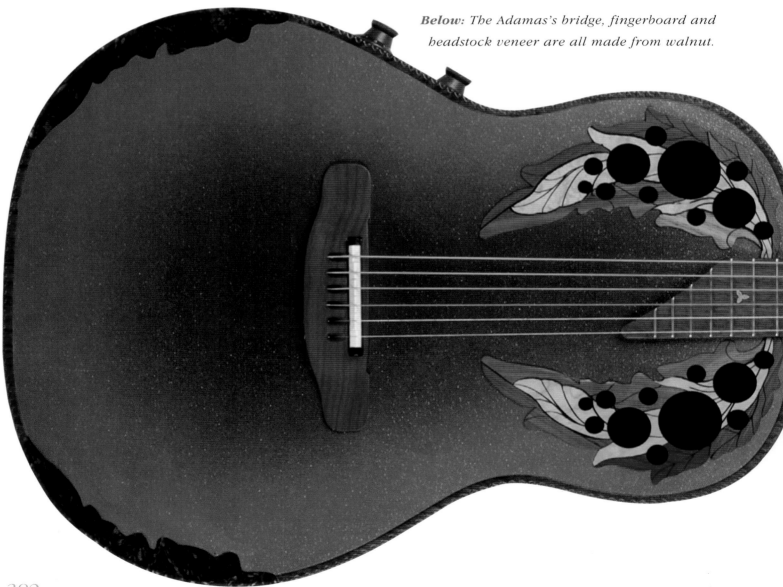

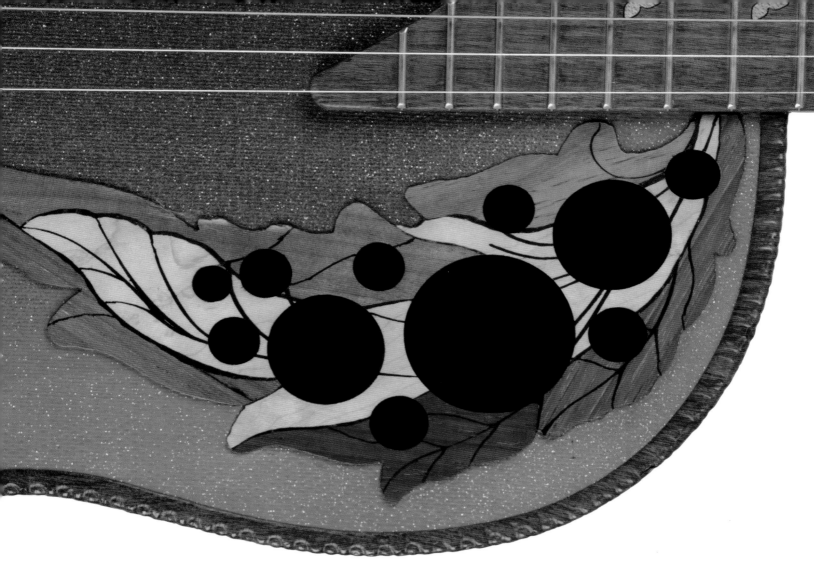

*Bottom: These volume and tone knobs are undoubtedly elegant, but more modern Adamas guitars have more comprehensive controls.*

*Above: The "leaf epaulets" around these mini-soundholes were produced using maple veneer.*

by many (though not all) previously skeptical players, and Adamas flat-tops are now well established in the pantheon of high-end guitars.

The Adamas in our photographs is a top of the range 1681-8, dating from 1982. It has a blue-tinted top, a stereo pickup with individual piezo transducers for each string, and a five-piece neck made from mahogany and laminated maple.

**Right:** Signals from the 6- and 12-string sections of the guitar are routed to the OP24+ preamp via a toggle swtich on the instrument's shoulder.

PHOTOGRAPHS COURTESY OF AMERICAN GUITAR CENTRE & BASSWORLD, TONBRIDGE

# OVATION CSD225-BCB DOUBLENECK

DOUBLE-NECKED GUITARS have a long history: as early as 1902, the Martin company had produced a two-necked harp guitar (though its second neck had no frets, and served only to support the instrument's twelve "drone" strings); and by the 1930s, Gibson was making electric Hawaiian models with twin necks that could each be tuned differently in order to expand the instrument's harmonic capabilities. Leo Fender later took this concept even further, with his mid-1950s three- and four-necked Stringmaster Hawaiians, while pedal steel instruments are also frequently made in paired-neck configurations.

doubleneck acoustics or electrics. Among this brave minority is Ovation, which has recently introduced the production-model Celebrity Deluxe Doubleneck shown in our photos at the comparatively modest price of just over $1,400. Aware of the problems with size and weight that often dog the design of these guitars, the company has developed a scaled-down roundback body (approximately three-quarter size) for it. Care has

*"Dots and diamonds" inlays grace the guitar's twin necks.*

*Gold-plated tuners are fitted to the CSD-225.*

"Spanish-style" doublenecks (i.e. those held upright, rather than placed on the player's lap or on a stand) are most usually 6-/12-stringers (see earlier entry for an electric Gibson SG double), although the additional

**Left:** *The two necks have rosewood fingerboards, and a 25¹/4-inch scale length. The guitar's bridge is walnut.*

neck sometimes carries bass guitar or even mandolin strings, and a few triplenecks, created by specialists like Hugh Manson or the Canadian luthier Linda Manzer, are also in circulation. The more exotic and elaborate of such instruments tend, for obvious reasons, to be custom-built, and only a handful of manufacturers currently supply "off-the-shelf"

also been taken with the central cutaway, which allows easy access to the upper, 12-string neck; and the guitar has been fitted with a modified version of Ovation's OP24+ preamp system that controls the pickup output from either or both of the necks. The top is made from laminated spruce, and the Celebrity Deluxe is finished in "Black Cherryburst."

# OVATION TANGENT M.O.B.

PREMIUM-PRICE OVATIONS, which carry the Ovation and Adamas names, are built at Kaman's Connecticut headquarters; but the corporation's cheapest, Applause-brand guitars are made in China, while its mid-price Pinnacle and Celebrity ranges, as well as Tangent models like the "M.O.B." seen in these photographs, originate from Korea. The M.O.B. initials stand for "My Other Board," and Ovation's publicity

*Below: The M.O.B.'s rosewood bridge is wave-shaped, while its soundholes and fret markers resemble surfboards!*

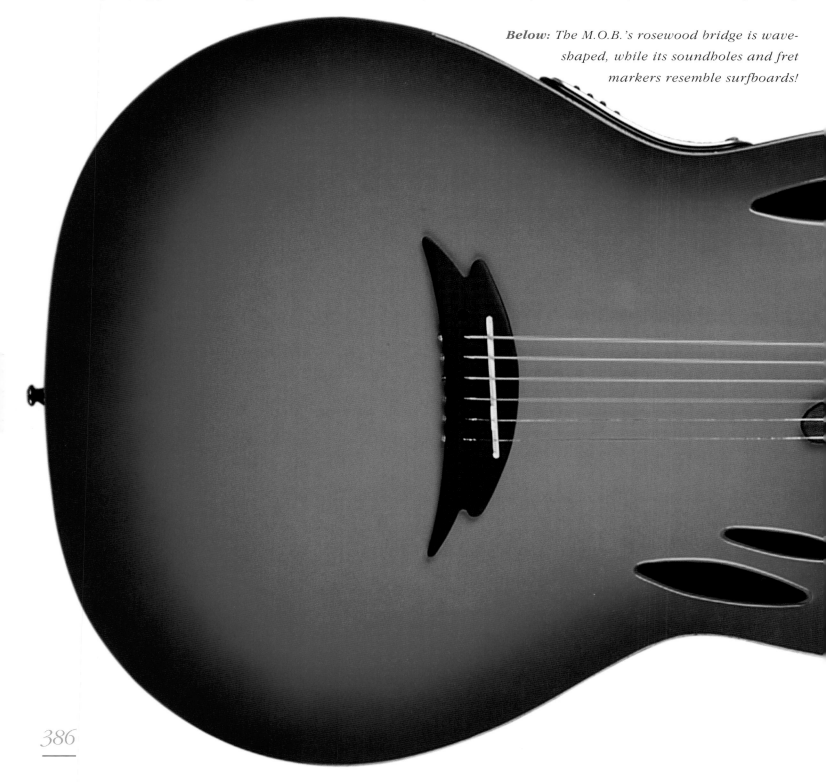

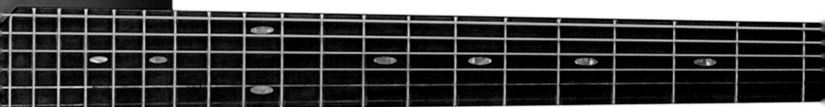

**Above:** *The guitar's preamp offers switchable three-band EQ, plus a "pre-shape" setting that boosts bass and treble, while reducing unwanting low frequencies. There is also an onboard chromatic tuner.*

**Right:** *The M.O.B. has an unusually configured headstock, with four of its six gray gun-metal tuners mounted on the treble side.*

describes it as "a rugged axe [that] can stand up to the stage, the beach and the street better than any other pro-quality acoustic."

The guitar's "Blue Surf Burst" finish and board-shaped soundholes contribute to its informal, fun-looking image, but it is unquestionably a serious instrument, with no shortage of bright, powerful tone—especially when plugged into an amp or PA that can do justice to its impressively specified internal pickup system and OP30 preamp. Like most

Ovations, it boasts a slimline neck (made from a single piece of nato—also known as eastern mahogany) that will please players accustomed to the easy feel of electric guitars, and its laminated spruce top is braced in Ovation's unique "Quintad" pattern, which uses nine internal lengthwise struts rather than the X-bracing more commonly found on acoustics.

The M.O.B. is available in two different Lyrachord bowlback sizes: "mid-depth" (providing optimum acoustic sound) or "super-shallow."

The Progress III Deluxe bass seen here has two output
sockets mounted on the right edge of its body: a standard
jack and a 3-pin XLR.

This rear shot shows the instrument's "neck-
through-body" construction, with two "wings" on
either side of the central neck section.

# OVERWATER PROGRESS III

FOUNDED BY DESIGNER, MUSICIAN and craftsman Chris May in 1979, Overwater operates from a converted Victorian mill in the Cumbrian city of Carlisle, near the English/Scottish border. Over the last quarter of a century the company has produced more than three thousand basses, and specializes in high-end models, aimed principally at professionals and serious amateurs. Overwater makes a wide variety of instruments, including bolt-on neck and semi-acoustic models. The bass in our photographs, however, comes from the firm's Progress range, described by Chris May as his "flagship series" of through-neck designs. These are produced in 4-, 5-, 6- and 7-string versions; the "deluxe" 5-stringer seen here is tuned (bottom to top) BEADG. It has an Indian mahogany body, with a top facing of figured jarrah, and a five-piece maple and walnut neck section. Its electronics include low-noise twin-coil pickups and a 3-band onboard EQ.

*Right: The instrument's solid brass bridge is set into its body to maximize sustain.*

*The 24-fret neck has a 36-inch scale length; its fingerboard is made from Indian rosewood.*

# PARKER FLY DELUXE

KEN PARKER made his first guitar, from timber and cardboard, aged 13. He went on to study various aspects of woodworking and toolmaking, and, while working in the New York area in the 1970s, gained valuable insights into instrument design from established experts such as lute builder Robert Meadow and archtop luthier Jimmy D'Aquisto. These eclectic influences all contributed to the birth, in 1992, of the Parker Fly—named thus because it has an "exoskeleton" (like an insect's) of carbon and glass fiber over its wooden neck and body. As Parker has put it, "this structure allows us to sculpt a beautiful lightweight guitar, optimized for its ability to respond to the strings' vibrations." The Fly, featuring both piezo and standard pickups, offers a vast range of sounds and has proved hugely successful.

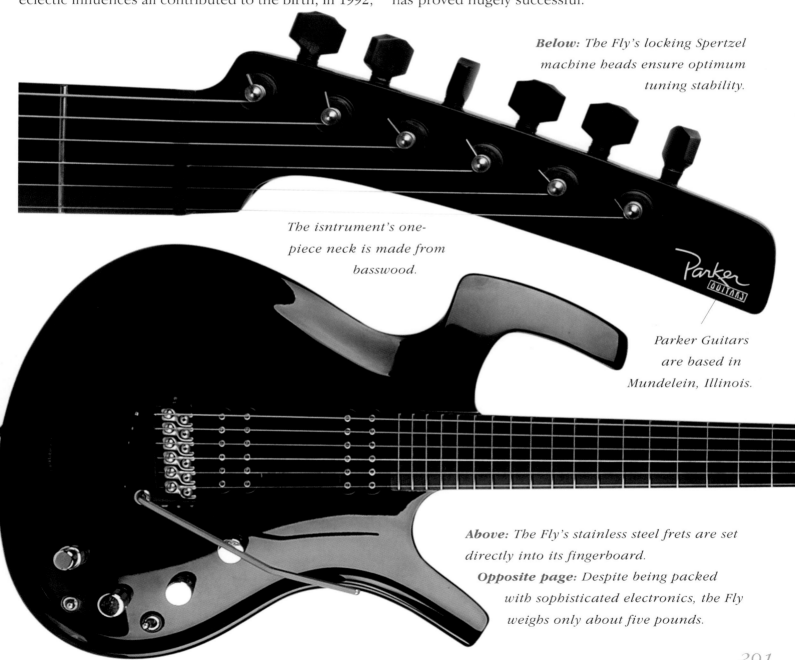

*Below: The Fly's locking Spertzel machine heads ensure optimum tuning stability.*

*The isntrument's one-piece neck is made from basswood.*

*Parker Guitars are based in Mundelein, Illinois.*

*Above: The Fly's stainless steel frets are set directly into its fingerboard.*
*Opposite page: Despite being packed with sophisticated electronics, the Fly weighs only about five pounds.*

# PARKER P-44

SINCE THE LAUNCH OF THE FLY, Parker's range has expanded to include new models such as Niteflys (featuring bolt-on necks instead of the complex "multifingered neck joints" used on the original Flys), as well as basses and even acoustics; and in 2002, it introduced its less expensive P-Series—a welcome development for players unable to afford thousands of dollars for one of the firm's premium guitars. Among the most successful of the "Ps"—whose construction is contracted out by Parker, although the finished instruments are set up and checked at its headquarters just north of Chicago—is the P-44, which is shown in our photographs, and has recently been re-introduced after a period of absence from the company's catalog.

Like the Niteflys, the P-44 has a bolted neck; this is made from maple, and has a rosewood fingerboard. As usual with Parkers, there are dual pickup systems: a pair of humbuckers, plus a piezo transducer designed by Parker Guitars' co-founder, Larry Fishman. An on-board stereophonic preamp, incorporating low-distortion "voltage doubling" circuitry, allows their signals to be blended, while the humbuckers themselves can be coil-tapped.

A vibrato bridge is fitted, and the P-44 weighs in at 7 pounds—barely 2 pounds more than a Parker Fly. It currently sells for just under $1,000.

*Below: The P-44's body is mahogany.*

*This guitar retains the basic shape of the Parker Fly, although its construction is simpler.*

**Left:** *One of the humbucking pickups that create the P-44's distinctive sound. Immediately above it is the end of the instrument's truss-rod.*

**Top right:** *A rear view showing the guitar's neck bolts and back plates, as well as the contouring that contributes to its comfortable feel.*

393

# PEAVEY CROPPER CLASSIC

HARTLEY PEAVEY set up Peavey Electronics in his hometown, Meridian, Mississippi, soon after graduating from college in 1965. It is now one of the world's largest manufacturers of musical instruments and sound equipment, making a total of over 2,000 products that are sold in more than 130 countries. Among Peavey's extensive guitar range is the highly acclaimed Cropper Classic, inspired and endorsed by another notable Southerner: former Booker T. and the M.G.s stalwart Steve Cropper.

Much of Cropper's searing guitar work (which first came to prominence on the M.G.s' 1962 classic "Green Onions," and has since featured on decades of hits by a host of names from the Blues Brothers to Paul Simon) was performed on a Fender Telecaster, and the Cropper Classic, introduced in the late 1990s, is not dissimilar in its outline and overall construction. Its electronics, though, are radically different: in place of the Tele's single-coil pickups are two Peavey humbucking Blade units, whose name derives from the "radiused blade" pole-pieces clearly visible in our photographs. Used together or separately, these transducers can deliver the power and dynamism that a player of Steve Cropper's caliber demands; while the Cropper Classic's bridge pickup can also be coil-tapped for additional tonal variety.

*This model has a maple-topped mahogany body.*

# PEAVEY GRIND 5-STRING BASS

OVER THE LAST four decades, Peavey has won countless awards and accolades for its instruments and sound reinforcement gear, and its basses—which include student, mid-price and professional models—are perennial best-sellers. The 5-string Grind shown here was introduced in 2001; like the 4-string Grind that debuted at the same time, it has an alder body and two passive, humbucking pickups. The transducers fitted to the 5-string are Peavey "J-styles" (named in tribute to the Fender Jazz Bass), while the 4-stringer boasts both a J-style and a staggered-coil "P-style" unit inspired by those found on Fender's Precision Basses. Though the pickups themselves are passive, the Grind has an active, three-band EQ system, as well as treble boost, master volume and blend controls. Its maple neck is bolted on, and there is a 24-fret fingerboard with a 34-inch scale.

More recent Grind models boast a neck-through-body design, and carry the self-explanatory suffix NTB. The choice of woods has also changed—the center section is now mahogany and maple, with the body "wings" now being made from attractively striped Imbuya wood imported from Brazil—and the range has been augmented by a 6-string Grind.

This contouring makes the bass more comfortable to hold.

*Left:* The Grind's striking "Metallic Tangerine" finish will certainly stand out onstage!

*Right:* The Peavey Grind's headstock is slightly tilted back to optimize string pull.

# PEAVEY JD-AG1

*Below: This dreadnought-style acoustic boasts a rosewood fretboard with an "Old No. 7" inlay at its 12th fret.*

IN 2004, Peavey announced that it had obtained an exclusive license to produce musical instruments and related equipment bearing the trademark of one of America's most celebrated whiskey makers, Jack Daniel's of Lynchburg, Tennessee. It is not known whether Mr. Jack himself—who lived from 1850 to 1911, and took over the still that was produce his "smooth sippin'" liquor at the age of just 13—was especially partial to music. However, he would surely have been pleased to see his brand promoted so ingeniously, and the Peavey-manufactured, Daniel's-adorned guitars and amps that began appearing in Summer 2005 certainly have novelty value! Pictured here is the one of three currently available Peavey/Daniel's acoustics, the JD-AG1. It has a spruce top, mahogany back, neck and sides, and a built-in piezo pickup, and is intended, in Peavey's words, to appeal to "Jack Daniel's enthusiasts, avid music fans, serious collectors and dedicated musicians alike."

*Below: Guitar builder and whiskey maker share the credits on the JD-AG1's smart black headstock.*

*Note the Jack Daniel's filigree on the soundhole above.*

# PEAVEY JACK DANIEL'S ELECTRIC EXP

To COMPLEMENT THE THREE Jack Daniel's acoustic guitars referred to on the previous pages, Peavey has introduced no less than five electric models—the most expensive of which sport such striking extras as truss rod and switch covers made from pieces of the famous Tennessee distiller's wooden whiskey barrels! These are not present on the Jack Daniel's Electric EXP that appears in our photographs, but this slightly cheaper instrument has many other desirable features. It is fitted with Peavey's patented Dual-Compression tailpiece, which, in the

*Above right: All the hardware on the Electric EXP is chromed.*

*The EXP has a ebony fingerboard.*

PHOTOGRAPHS COURTESY OF NEVADA MUSIC, PORTSMOUTH

*Above: Even the guitar's control knobs display the Jack Daniel's symbol.*

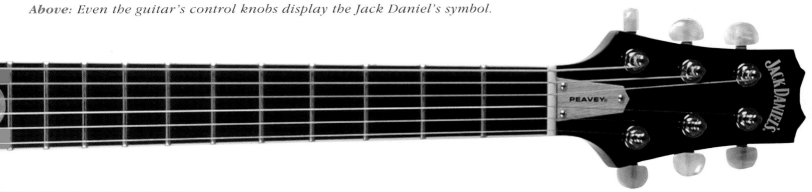

*Left: Other Peavey/Jack Daniel's products include a bass guitar, a combo amp, and a selection of picks and straps carrying the "Old No. 7" logo seen on this fretboard inlay.*

company's words, "creates a metal-to-metal connection for singing sustain and a stronger string presence," and also boasts two powerful humbucking pickups, as well as a quilted maple top to its mahogany body. Two finishes are available: "Transparent Whiskey" (as seen here), or—in honor of the substance that gives Mr. Jack's liquor its distinctive smoothness—"Transparent Charcoal."

**Right:** On "Artist Package" Custom 24s, Paua seashells (found only in New Zealand) are used to create the headstock and fingerboard inlays.

Gold hardware is fitted to this guitar.

The bridge pickup is a PRS HFS model; the initials stand for "hot, fat, and screams"!

# PRS CUSTOM 24

*Below: PRS Custom 24s and Custom 22s have carved maple tops and mahogany backs.*

THE CUSTOM 24 has a very special place in the history of Paul Reed Smith Guitars. Developed through lengthy trial and experimentation, during which Reed Smith, who had built his first guitar as a student, would craft instruments at his workshop in Annapolis, Maryland, "road-test" them at gigs, and then seek to sell them to musicians at local concert venues, it was this model that helped him obtain enough advance orders to launch the company bearing his initials in 1985.

Twenty years later, PRS, now acclaimed as one of America's most distinguished guitar makers, celebrated its two decades in the business at the NAMM (National Association of Music Merchants) trade show in Anaheim, California. Among the stars attending and performing there was Carlos Santana, one of Reed Smith's earliest clients, and the Custom 24 (described by the firm as "the core of our line") was prominently on display, alongside its 22-fret cousin, the Custom 22. Over their long lives, these classic solid-bodies has been produced with a variety of different finishes and options: the example in our pictures is an "Artist Package" model with special inlays and other luxury features.

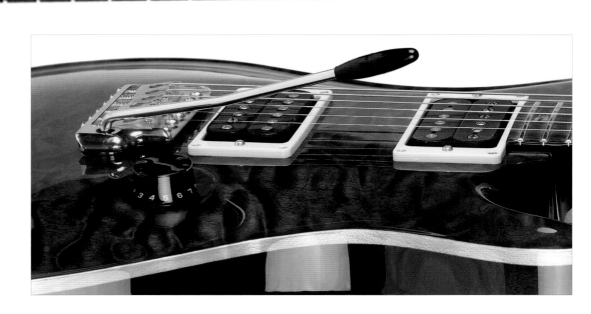

*This instrument,
finished in
"Opaque Black,"
was made
in 2000.*

*A non-vibrato
version of the
Swamp Ash
Special was
dropped from
the PRS catalog
in 2001.*

# PRS SWAMP ASH SPECIAL

SWAMP ASH—mostly grown in the southern states of the USA, as its Latin name *Fraxinus caroliniana* suggests—is appreciated by guitar makers for its relatively light weight, as well as its musical qualities. It is used to splendid effect on the Paul Reed Smith Swamp Ash Special, which has been in continuous production since 1996.

The model's pickups are also worthy of comment. Its neck and bridge humbuckers are "McCartys," named for former Gibson president Ted McCarty, the man behind the creation of the Les Paul and other famous designs. McCarty, who died in 2001, shared some of his lifetime's knowledge of lutherie and electronics with PRS in its early years, and the fine tone of "his" transducer is ascribed by PRS to the special way of assembling it he demonstrated to Paul Reed Smith

*Left: This plate conceals the bolts joining the PRS's neck to its body.*

and his colleagues, combined with the use of "a vintage alnico magnet and special nickel silver cover." Between the McCarty units is a Seymour Duncan Vintage Rails transducer, and there are comprehensive switching options, including a coil-tap activated by the guitar's tone control. A PRS vibrato is fitted.

*Below: The Swamp Ash Special has a 22-fret rock maple neck.*

*Note the locks on these PRS tuners.*

*Both the guitar's pickups are PRS "McCarty Archtop" units.*

# PRS McCARTY HOLLOWBODY II

IN 1998, PAUL REED SMITH introduced a series of guitars inspired by the classic, ES-335-style thinline/semi-solids (see separate entries) that had been developed by Gibson in the late 1950s during Ted McCarty's time as the company's president. The new instruments were named "McCarty Hollowbodies," and, as PRS publicity put it, their design "took the essential element of Ted's original idea—a guitar with a perfect blend of warm, acoustic jazz tones and the rich sustaining character of a solid body—and applied the PRS magic."

There were, of course, considerable differences between the Gibsons and the PRS electrics. Semi-solids such as the ES-335 contain a central wooden block that reduces feedback and increases sustain. PRS replaced it with a single "sound post," running beneath its guitars'

bridge/tailpiece units, which coupled the top and back sections of the instruments together but left their interiors truly hollow. This approach yielded exceptional tonal versatility, and Reed Smith himself has commented that "I can't think of a kind of music you would not be able to play on [these models]."

The three currently available PRS McCarty Hollowbodies use different combinations of woods, but have identical pickups. The Hollowbody Spruce has, as its name suggests, a spruce top, combined with carved solid mahogany back and sides. On the Hollowbody I, the spruce is replaced with maple, providing what PRS describe as "just a bit of extra high-end clarity," while the Hollowbody II, seen here, features maple on both its top and back, with mahogany rims.

*Left: The PRS's maximum body depth is 3 inches, narrowing to 1³/4 inches at its edges.*

*Above: A mahogany neck is fitted to this model.*

# PRS ELECTRIC BASS

PAUL REED SMITH'S INITIAL FORAY into electric bass production took place in 1986 with the Bass-4 and Bass-5. These 4- and 5-stringers shared the elegant looks and luxurious woods and inlays of the company's standard guitars, but were not very warmly received by critics or players, and were dropped in 1991. In 2000, a second generation model, named simply the PRS Electric Bass, was introduced: plainer and more functional than its predecessors, it had an alder body, a bolted on maple neck, and two passive pickups whose exposed blades were shaped to follow the radius of the instrument's fingerboard. The firm's publicity described their tone as "fat and clear," and ascribed their even string balance to the generous width of the

blades. A few months after the bass's launch, PRS began fitting a piezo transducer, designed in association with L.R. Baggs, as an optional extra.

One of these 2000-vintage PRS basses (without a piezo pickup) is seen here; reviewers praised the axe's

*Left: The PRS's neck is attached to its body via a 4-bolt plate.*

*Below: A three-piece alder body is used for this model.*

*Either rosewood (as here) or maple fingerboards could be supplied for the bass.*

These abalone dots
are less elaborate
than many
decorations found on
other PRS guitars.

**Below:** *This nut is made from Delrin, a
resinous substance developed by DuPont.*

versatility and exemplary finish, and Rick Batey, writing
in the UK's **Guitar** magazine, concluded a detailed
assessement by describing it as "a simple, righteous-
sounding bass that'll do just as good a job as you."
However, the model was discontinued in 2004.

# PRS SE SOAPBAR

PRS'S "SE" RANGE is designed at its headquarters in Stevensville, Maryland, but manufactured in Korea. SE instruments, some of them variants of the company's premium models, are exceptionally good value, and the Soapbar SE seen here is of particular interest because of the lengthy legal battle triggered by its "Singlecut" body shape.

The firm first used the Singlecut design, which boasts one cutaway instead of the two found on many other PRS instruments, in 2000. Its introduction led to a lawsuit from Gibson, centering on its alleged similarity to the latter company's classic Les Paul guitar body. In 2004, a federal district court ruled that the PRS's outline might, when viewed in certain circumstances (such as on a distant stage in a smoky bar), be confused with the Les Paul shape, and issued an injunction to PRS preventing it from making Singlecut bodies. As a result, several PRS instruments, including the recently launched Soapbar SE, were withdrawn. However, on appeal a year later, the theories of "consumer confusion" advanced by Gibson in the lower court were rejected, and PRS was able to resume Singlecut production, although the original single cutaway Soapbar SE has now been superseded by a double cutaway version.

Aside from their body shapes, the old and new Soapbar SEs are very similar. Both feature twin "soapbar" pickups (based on Gibson's vintage soap-shaped, and sometimes white-covered P-90 units), as well as 22-fret necks and solid mahogany bodies.

*Below: The SE Soapbar has a mahogany neck with a rosewood fingerboard.*

*A simple but effective "stop" tailpiece is fitted to the Soapbar SE.*

**Left:** *This model is finished in "Vintage Cherry."*

# RADIOTONE ARCHTOP, c.1935

THE INTRODUCTION of the Gibson L-5 archtop acoustic in 1922 opened up a new role for the guitar as a rhythm and solo instrument in jazz and swing ensembles—and European manufacturers, like Gibson's American competitors, were soon turning out archtops of their own that replicated some of its features. Germany, with its long tradition of lutherie, was a significant producer of such guitars, and the mid-1930s Radiotone seen in our photographs is likely to have been made there.

*Opposite page: The Radiotone has a spruce top, and back and sides of maple. Its fingerboard is ebony.*

Definite information about the provenance of the brand is hard to find; Radiotone ukuleles are known to have been in circulation in Britain before World War II, and our Radiotone, which was purchased in the UK, has a telltale "foreign make" marker, just visible on its headstock, that identifies it as an import. An elegantly finished, high quality guitar, it would have suited a busy professional who lacked the funds for a Gibson or an Epiphone. At least one "name" British performer, Jack McKechnie, used a Radiotone for a while in the 1930s, and instruments similar to the model shown here could be seen and heard throughout Europe during the post-war period.

*Left and right: Note the fancy tuners—and the "foreign make" stamp below the headstock logo.*

# B.C. RICH MOCKINGBIRD

Bernardo Chavez Rico (1941-1999) was a Los Angeles-based luthier who started out building high-end acoustics, but diversified into solid electric production in the late 1960s, shortly after he had anglicized his business name to B.C. Rich. Within a few years, his guitars were sporting increasingly sophisticated onboard electronics and neck-through-body designs; they were also beginning to assume the bold outlines that have since become one of Rich models' most immediately recognizable characteristics. The first of these shapes, the Seagull (with a protruding "beak" on its side that could cause problems for players!) debuted in

*Left: The Mockingbird is fitted with two B.C. Rich high output humbucking pickups.*

*Above: The guitar's basic shape has not changed since the 1970s, though its hardware (and finish!) are new.*

1972; the "Mockingbird" profile that appears on the recently made instrument in our pictures was introduced in 1976, and the same year saw the arrival of the Rich Bich—developed by Rico's colleague and collaborator Neal Moser (who was associated with the firm for ten years from 1974), and quickly taken up by top players such as Joe Perry of Aerosmith. The B.C. Rich story continues on the following pages.

The Rich Mockingbird featured here is one of the company's "Body Art" series of "graphically enhanced" guitars. This range was launched in 2003, but the design on our Mockingbird, "Forty Lashes" by Bruce Kroeber, dates from a year later.

# B.C. RICH VIRGO

DEMAND GREW for B.C. Rich guitars throughout the late 70s and 80s, and the emergence of the heavy metal movement, with its appetite for high quality, visually arresting instruments, was a particular boon to the company. Before long, however, Bernie Rico and his team were struggling to produce enough instruments to satisfy this increasingly voracious market, and were obliged to start outsourcing some of their manufacturing. According to Michael Wright's article on Rich published in **Vintage Guitar** magazine in 1995, bolt-on necks for budget versions of some models were already being made by the Charvel company by about 1976. The same period saw an unsuccessful attempt to import instruments from the

*Above right:* The Virgo has a single-coil neck pickup, and a humbucker at the bridge position.

The Virgo's "bitten-off" body matches its cutout headstock.

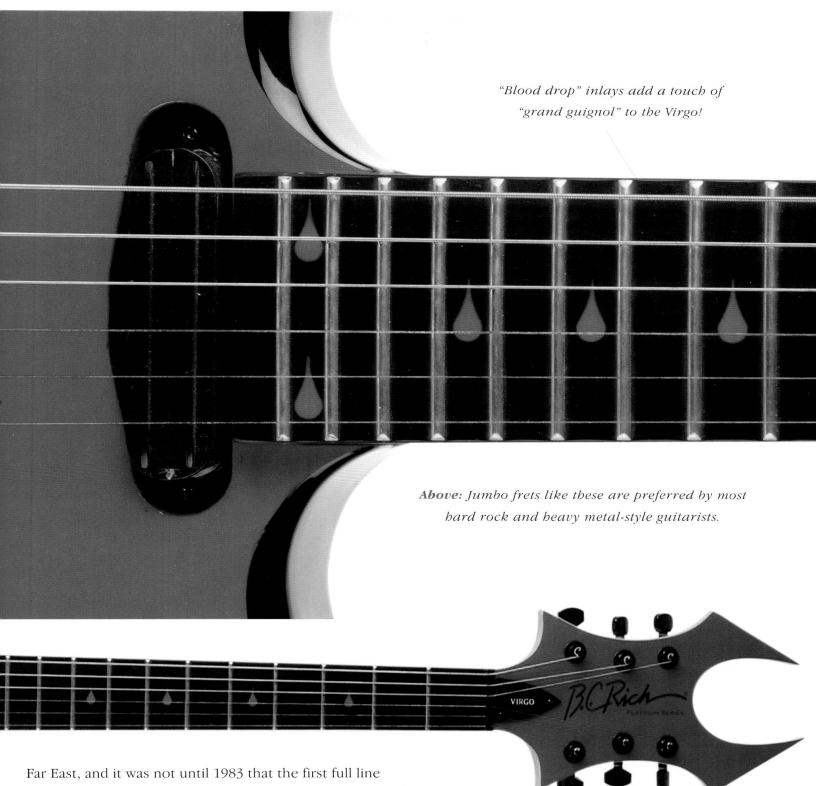

*"Blood drop" inlays add a touch of "grand guignol" to the Virgo!*

**Above:** *Jumbo frets like these are preferred by most hard rock and heavy metal-style guitarists.*

Far East, and it was not until 1983 that the first full line of Japanese-made Riches, named the "N.J. Series," made its debut. (These initials stand for "Nagoya, Japan," not New Jersey!) Production of N.J.s was moved to Korea later in the decade.

Among the axes available in overseas-made versions during the mid-1980s was the Rich "Virgin:" it remains in the catalog to this day, but the guitar seen here, the Virgo, represents a more recent take on the old design: the B.C. Rich website explains that it is "based on the Virgin body shape with a bite out of its bottom!"

# ELECTRO (RICKENBACKER) MODEL B LAP STEEL

THE ORIGINS of the modern Rickenbacker company lie in the oddly-named Ro-Pat-In Corporation, formed in Los Angeles in 1931 by a Swiss-born émigré, Adolph Rickenbacker (1892-1976), together with George Beauchamp (who was about to lose his job as General Manager for National String Instruments—see

*Left: Curiously, Electro's name plate mis-spells 'Rickenbacker.'*

*Right: Note the massive magnet on the picksup designed by Electro's George Beauchamp.*

separate entries) and another senior figure from National, Paul Barth. The trio collaborated on the development of an aluminum-bodied lap steel, nicknamed the "Frying Pan," which appeared in 1932 and was the world's first mass-made electric

*Adolph Rickenbacker, an engineer, had worked with Bakelite's inventor, L.H. Baekeland, before co-founding Ro-Pat-In.*

*The necks on Model Bs were bolted on.*

guitar. Ro-Pat-In, renamed Electro in 1934, went on to make some "Spanish"-style electrics, but focused most of its energy and resources on Hawaiian instruments such as the "Model B" seen here. The "B's" single pickup was designed by Beauchamp, and its body and neck are made from Bakelite, which was less

**Right:** *Leaving these hollow sections in the Model B's neck reduced its overall weight.*

affected by temperature changes that could affect tuning than the aluminium used on the "Frying Pan." Electro's output during the pre-war decade also included double-necked Hawaiian guitars.

# RICKENBACKER 330

GEORGE BEAUCHAMP resigned from Electro/Rickenbacker shortly before his death in 1940, but Adolph Rickenbacker remained at the firm until 1953, when it was sold to F.C. Hall, a man with an impressive music industry track record, who had previously been involved in the distribution of Fender guitars. Under his

*All Rickenbacker 300s share the same headstockshapes.*

leadership, Rickenbacker (as the business was now known) was soon introducing models that would attract an enthusiastic new generation of customers to the company. The most iconic of these designs were the "300" series of thinline hollowbodies launched in 1958; they were created by Roger Rossmeisl, who had qualified as a guitar maker in Germany and was a former Gibson staffer. A Rickenbacker 330 is shown here: more information about the 300s' specifications is provided overleaf.

*Left: This 330 has a "Mapleglow" finish.*

*Right: The "Treble" and "Bass" labels on these knobs refer to (respectively) the guitar's bridge and neck pickups.*

# RICKENBACKER 360

ALL THINLINE (as opposed to "thin full-body" and "thick body") Rickenbacker 300s, with the exception of a few special instruments, are made from maple, have rosewood fingerboards, and share the same body shapes and depth (standardized at 1½ inches in 1962). Their principal differences relate to quantities of frets (21 or 24), numbers of pickups (2 or 3), presence or absence of vibrato, and types of decoration, all of which are categorized by the numerical codes by which the guitars are known.

21-fret necks are restricted to models numbered 310 to 325; these, together with other lower-ranking 300s (up to 345) are "standard" thinlines, and have no bindings and only plain dot fret markers. However, instruments coded 360 and above are classified as "deluxe," and boast extra decorative touches—including Rickenbacker's famous triangular fretboard inlays. A Model 360 dating from 1976 is shown here.

**Below:** *A three-pickup version of this model, coded 370, is also available.*

*These pickups are high gain single-coil units.*

*Right:* Unlike the 330 on the last two pages, the Rickenbacker 360 has a contoured body.

Rickenbacker's stylized f-holes (with bindings on this deluxe model) add to its guitars' appeal.

# RICKENBACKER 360/12VP 12-STRING

RICKENBACKER ANNOUNCED its first electric 12-string guitars, including the 360/12, in 1963; they were introduced the following year, and early adopters included The Beatles' George Harrison, who used one on the Fab Four's 1964 movie *A Hard Day's Night*, and Jim (later Roger) McGuinn of The Byrds. By 1965, McGuinn and his colleagues were riding high in the charts with Bob Dylan's "Mr. Tambourine Man," which strongly featured the sweet, jangling timbre of McGuinn's 360/12, and Rickenbacker's ads were heralding its 12-strings as "a new dimension in sound."

The 360/12 shares the normal features of its 6-string Series 300 counterparts, including a 24-fret neck and $1\frac{1}{2}$-inch body depth. Perhaps its most striking innovation was the re-ordering of the string pairs that caused their lower-octave notes to be sounded first on a downstroke; other companies' 12-string groupings place the higher-pitched strings before the lower ones.

*Left and bottom left: On Rickenbacker 12-strings, the Schaller tuners are mounted from both the back and sides of the headstock— a ingenious space-saving feature.*

*Above: "Rick-O-Sound" allows pickup signals to be split between two amps. Normal output is provided by the lower jack socket*

# RICKENBACKER 4001 BASS

RICKENBACKER'S FIRST electric bass, the 4000, was a single-pickup model with a comparatively unadorned appearance. It was introduced in 1957, and was joined just four years later by the twin-pickup 4001, which boasted neck and body bindings, as well as triangular fingerboard markers (the 4000 had only dot inlays). From around 1963, the 4001 also featured the latest version of the company's distinctive string mute, whose dampers, located in the instrument's bridge/tailpiece assembly, could be raised and lowered by means of two thumbscrews (unfortunately the 4001 in our photographs has lost one of these).

The 4001, like Rickenbacker's 6-string guitars, benefited considerably from its association with The Beatles. Paul McCartney was given one of the basses by the firm's President, F.C. Hall, in 1964; he went on to feature it on several of the group's LPs, and remained faithful to Rickenbackers during his post-Beatles projects in the 1970s. Among the 4001's numerous US devotees was Rush's Geddy Lee, and in 1977 it appeared in a Playboy centerfold, when Star Stowe (the then-girlfriend of KISS frontman—and non-Rickenbacker user—Gene Simmons) posed with it as that year's "Miss February."

Though the first 4001s were offered only in "Fireglo," more options were eventually added;

*Below: The 4001 has a 33$\frac{1}{2}$-inch scale. Its neck is reinforced with two steel truss rods.*

*"Checkering" enhances the look of the 4001's body binding.*

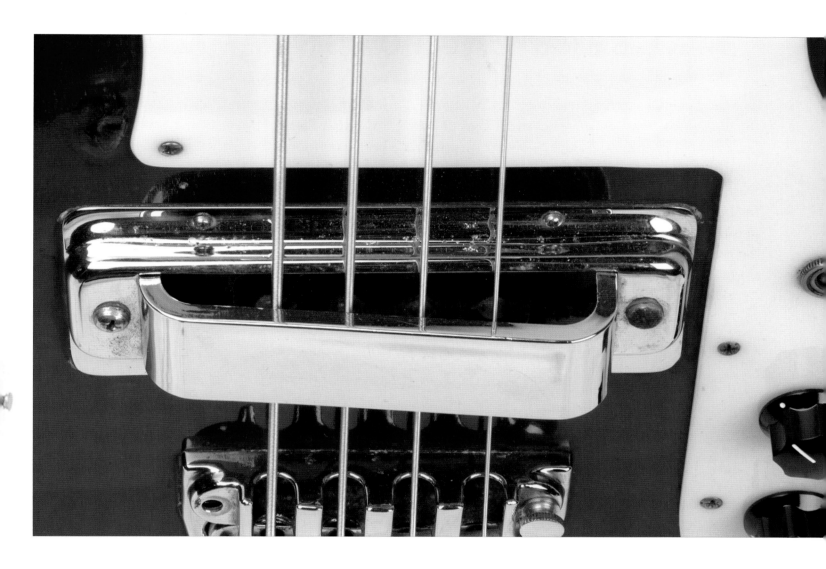

the example here, which dates from 1973, has an "Azureglo" finish. The model's "Rick-O-Sound" pseudo-stereo output (see previous pages) and the somewhat intrusively positioned cover over its back pickup divide opinion among players; however, the former is easy to ignore, and the latter can be removed without unduly affecting the character of this classic 1960s design.

*Right:* The "cresting wave" headstock shape, which imitates the shape of the guitar's body cutaways, is found on many Rickenbackers.

# SANDBERG CALIFORNIA PM 4 BASS

THE SANDBERG COMPANY is based southeast of the German city of Hannover, in the town of Braunschweig. It makes an extensive range of both guitars and basses, and high-profile users of its instruments include Richard Jones of The Stereophonics, as well as top session man Ken Taylor. In both 2004 and 2005, the firm received awards for its basses from the influential British magazine **Guitar & Bass**; its products are now readily available across the USA, thanks to a recent distribution deal.

The Sandberg California PM 4 bass shown in our pictures has a "Tobacco" body coloring ("Aged White" and "Voodoo" finishes can also be supplied), and may be used in active or passive modes. Its pickups are designed and built by another leading German manufacturer, Delano: the upper, spilt-coil unit is a PC 4, modeled on the classic Fender Precision bass transducer, with a sound graphically described by

Delano as combining "'oomph' and greasy swamp bottom," "grinding wire attitude," and "a slight Delano twist to enhance dynamics and articulation!" In the bridge position is a PowerHB humbucker.

The Sandberg's bolted-on neck, which has a 34-inch scale, is Canadian maple, with a rosewood (or, optionally, maple) fingerboard. Our PM 4 has an alder body, but ash is used on some examples. The California range also features JM models incorporating Fender Jazz Bass-type pickups, and both PMs and JMs are produced as 4- or 5-stringers.

*Left:* The PM 4's outline is reminiscent of Fender's Precision bass.

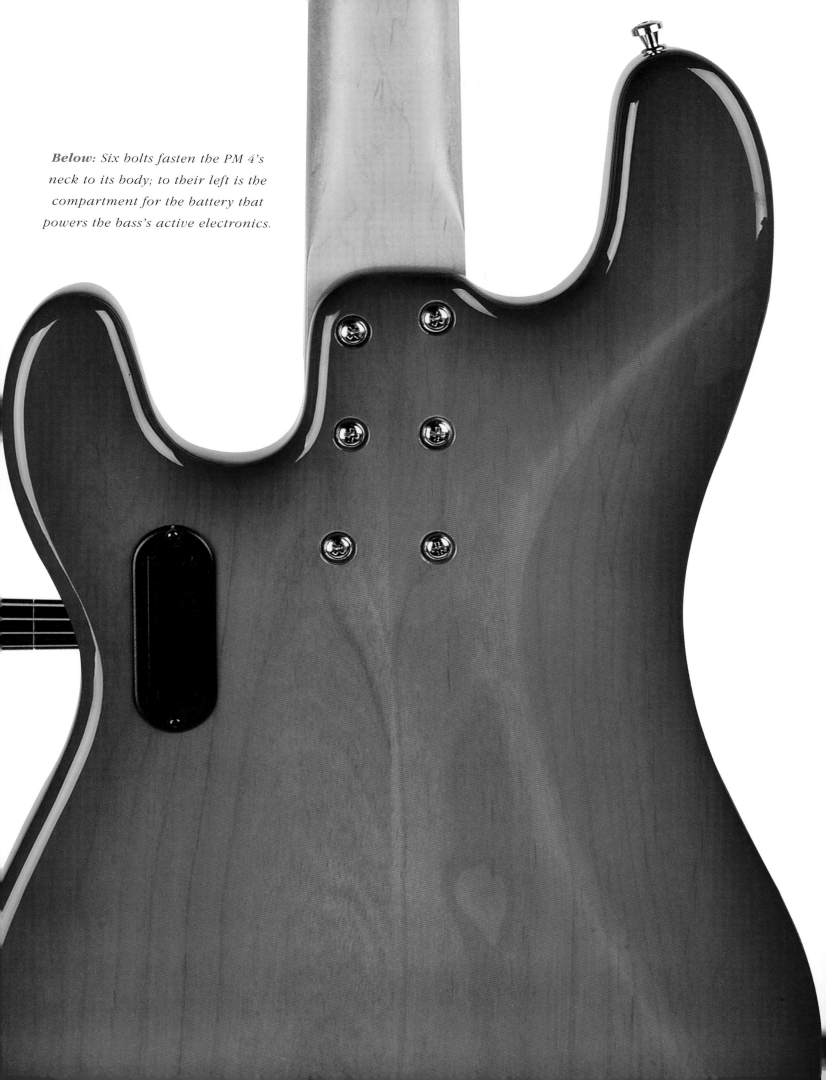

*Below: Six bolts fasten the PM 4's neck to its body; to their left is the compartment for the battery that powers the bass's active electronics.*

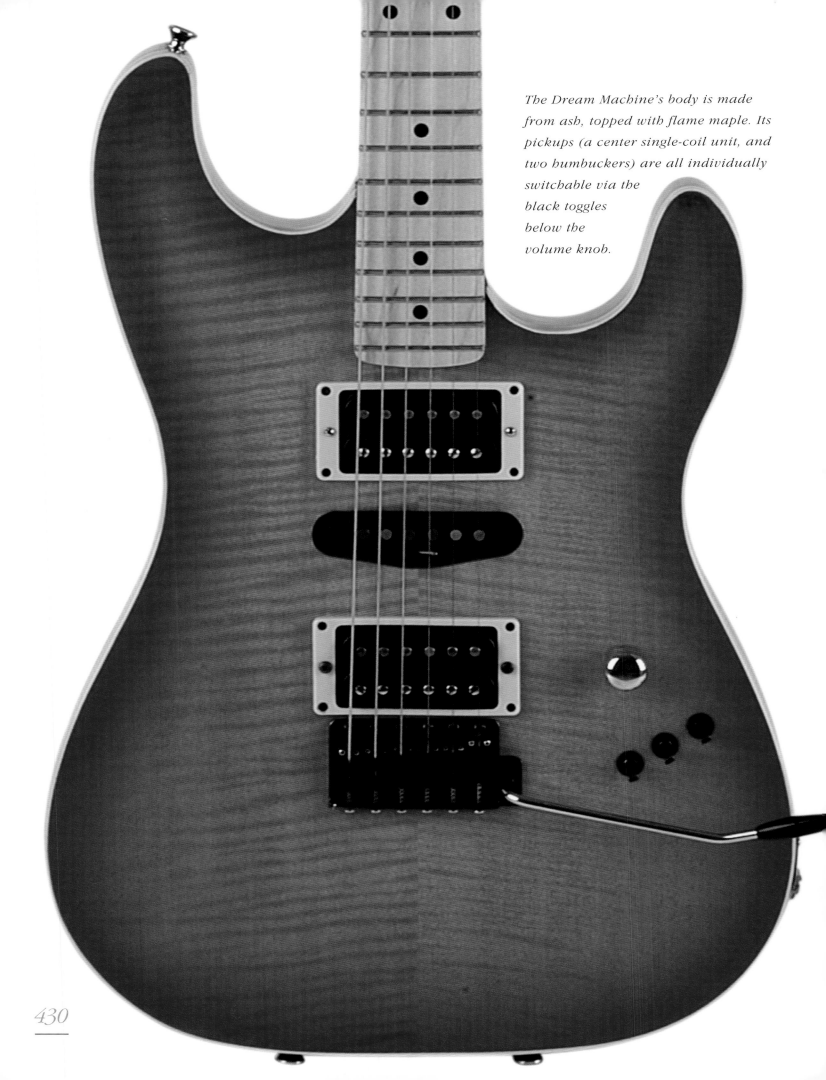

The Dream Machine's body is made from ash, topped with flame maple. Its pickups (a center single-coil unit, and two humbuckers) are all individually switchable via the black toggles below the volume knob.

430

# SCHECTER DREAM MACHINE

IN 1976, DAVID SCHECTER, a Southern California-based guitar customizer and repairer, set up Schecter Guitar Research in order to produce high performance replacement pickups and other components. The following year, his firm published a catalog showcasing an extensive range of substitute transducers, among which were ready-wired assemblies of coil-tapped pickups for Fender Telecasters and Stratocasters. The brochure also

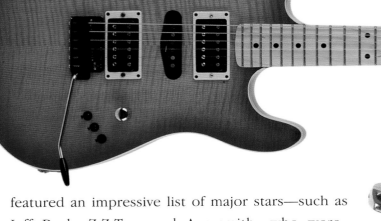

featured an impressive list of major stars—such as Jeff Beck, Z.Z.Top, and Aerosmith—who were already satisfied Schecter customers.

Before long, Schecter and his colleagues, including soon-to-be-famous luthier Tom Anderson (see pages 18-23), were making guitar bodies and necks as well as electronics—and it was only a matter of time before the company began using these and its other parts as the basis for complete Schecter instruments like the Dream Machine shown in our pictures. This model dates from before 1982, and may actually have been constructed by Tom Anderson himself: as Dave Crozier of the

Guitar Junction store where we photographed it comments, "There is an A signed in [its] neck pocket which just might be Tom's signature A!" The Dream Machine has a Strat-like outline, and its sophisticated pickup switching options and six-point vibrato are typical of Schecters from this period.

Though neither Tom Anderson nor David Schecter himself is now involved in Schecter Guitar Research, the firm continues to flourish. After a spell in Texas during the 1980s, it has now returned to the Los Angeles area; there, it builds custom models, and creates designs for the "Diamond" guitars which are manufactured to its specifications in South Korea.

*Left: The guitar's neck is maple, and its brightly painted headstock is fitted with chromed Schaller tuners.*

# SILVERTONE 1448 ELECTRIC

S EARS, ROEBUCK & COMPANY of Chicago first used its "Silvertone" brand name on a wind-up phonograph introduced in 1915; a few years later, the same logo began to appear on Sears radios. In the 1930s, the firm also applied it to musical instruments, which had previously carried the "Supertone" marque, and by the 1940s, Sears' catalogs had become a principal source of inexpensive guitars for budding American players.

Silvertones were supplied to Sears by a number of different manufacturers, known in the trade as "jobbers." These included the Chicago-based Harmony and Kay companies, and Teisco of Japan, but the first electric Silvertones came from Danelectro in New Jersey. Danelectro-made Silvertone guitars are immediately distinguishable from the work of other Sears jobbers thanks to the "lipstick-tube" pickup covers favored by their creator, Nathan Daniel. The instrument seen here dates from 1964, and incorporates other typical Daniel touches like the metal and rosewood bridge seen in closeup opposite. Bearing the Sears catalog number 1448 (1449 had two pickups), the guitar was supplied in a hardboard case featuring a built-in amplifier and 5-inch loudspeaker.

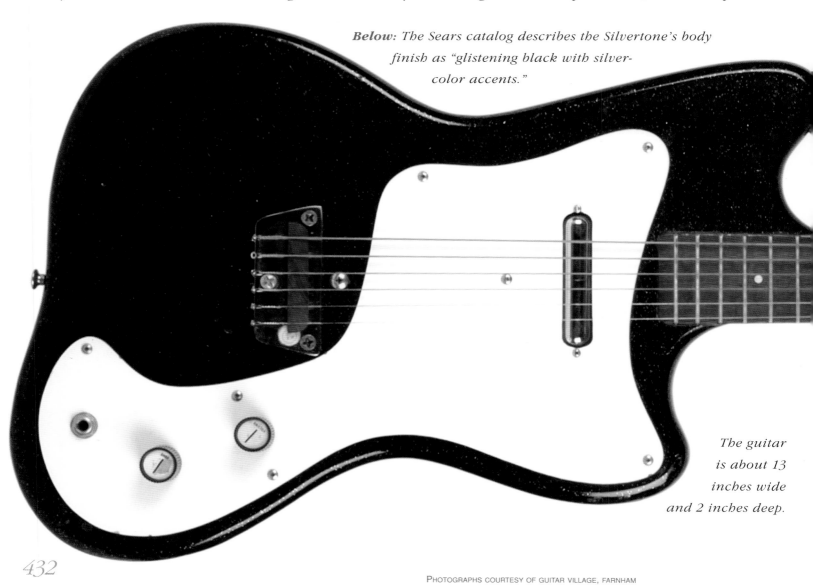

**Below**: *The Sears catalog describes the Silvertone's body finish as "glistening black with silver-color accents."*

*The guitar is about 13 inches wide and 2 inches deep.*

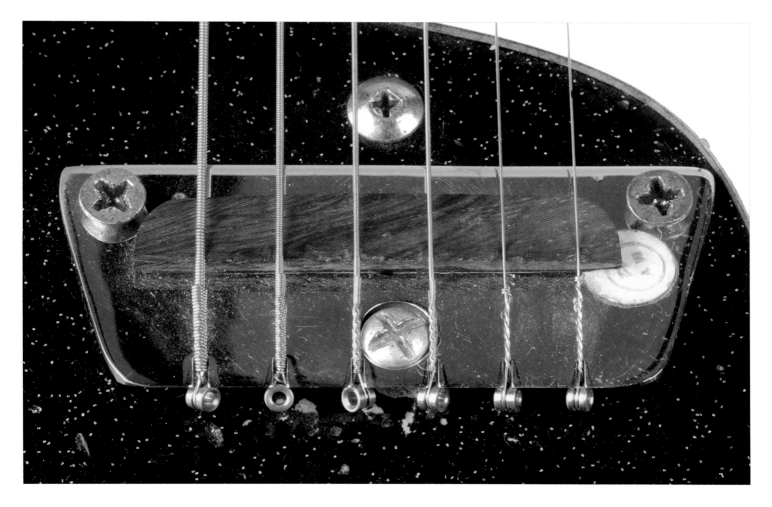

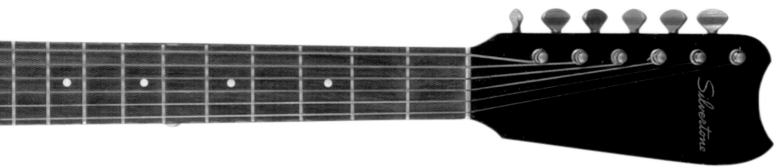

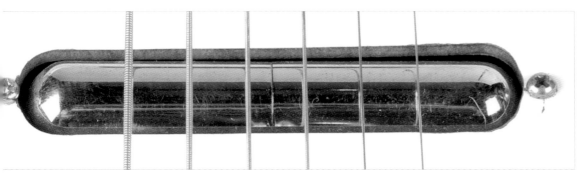

**Top:** The Silvertone's indented, "six-a-side" headstock only appeared on "amp in case" models like this one.
**Left:** The 1448's "lipstick-tube" pickup.

# KEN SMITH BT CUSTOM 6 BASS

KEN SMITH, who had previously enjoyed a successful career as a session musician, formed the bass building firm that carries his name in 1978. Located in Perkasie, Pennsylvania, it has gone on to establish an enviable reputation for producing high-end instruments, and is especially noted for the variety and quality of its woods, which are air-dried and acclimated for several years before being used. The company describes itself as "a marriage of Old World tradition and modern innovation;" its basses are hand-made, and Ken Smith himself is responsible for their final set-up. Among his famous customers are jazzman Marcus Miller, Mike Gordon of Phish, and Grateful Dead founder member Phil Lesh.

Smith's range of basses includes models with bolted-on necks as well as neck-through-body designs. The BT Custom 6 seen here is, of course, one of the latter: its center section is a five-layer "sandwich" of aged hardrock maple and bubinga , while its body "wings" are made with shedua, a very dense brown wood, grown in west and central Africa, which is reckoned to be some 130% harder than some species of oak.

The BT boasts a QSR (Quick String Release) brass bridge, and its pickups are twin Smith "soapbars": the firm makes both bridges and transducers to fit 4-string, 5-string, or 6-string models, and can supply them as components to be installed on other manufacturers' basses.

*Above:* This Smith BT bass is several years old, but its bridge shows comparatively few signs of wear and tear.

*Left and far left:* The instrument has a 24-fret neck with an ebony fingerboard.

*Thanks to the BT's neck-through-body design, there is no heel to get in the way of the player's fretting hand.*

*This back view clearly displays the various types of wood used to make the bass.*

435

# SQUIER "OBEY" TELECASTER

THE "SQUIER" TRADEMARK was acquired by Fender from the V. C. Squier string-making firm in 1965 and, since 1983, has been used as a brand name for budget-priced, mostly Far Eastern-manufactured versions of the great American guitar company's instruments. Squier models, though good value, are usually too derivative to be of interest to books such as this one; however, its "OBEY" range, launched in 2006 and featuring graphic finishes by American artist Shepard Fairey, are too striking and original to ignore.

Fairey (b.1970) made his name as the creator of posters and street art bearing Orwellian slogans such as "Obey," and "You Are Under Surveillance." He has now produced three "graphic schemes," intended (in his words) "to stimulate curiosity…[and] revitalize the viewer's perception and attention to detail," for a special series of Squier Telecasters and Stratocasters. The Fairey artwork seen here is named "Collage;" the Tele to which it is applied has an agathis body, and features unplated, "Rustic & Worn" hardware.

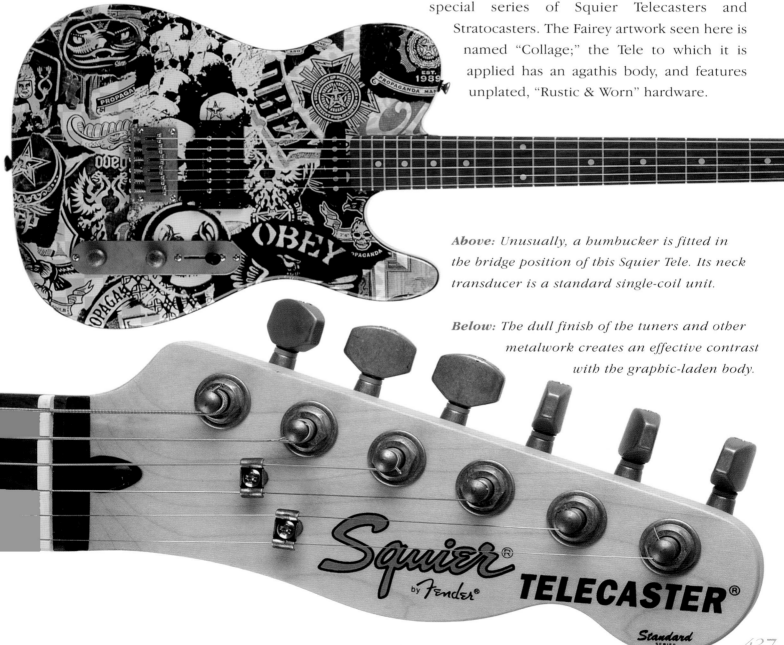

*Above:* Unusually, a humbucker is fitted in the bridge position of this Squier Tele. Its neck transducer is a standard single-coil unit.

*Below:* The dull finish of the tuners and other metalwork creates an effective contrast with the graphic-laden body.

# STATUS GRAPHITE SERIES 2000 BASS

IN 1981, Status Graphite, a British company headed by Rob Green, displayed its first bass guitars at one of the world's principal music trade shows, held in Frankfurt, Germany. Since then, the firm's instruments have gained a wide following: it produces both all-graphite basses, like the Series 2000 seen here, and models with graphite necks and hardwood bodies.

The Series 2000 dates from Status Graphite's early years, and was, at the time of its introduction, the only bass ever to have been made from a one-piece carbon graphite molding. Graphite, according to Status,

enhances an instrument's dynamics and sustain, and makes it more responsive over a wider range of frequencies. The material is also extremely rigid, and as a result, the Series 2000 has no need for a truss-rod, although later Status basses are fitted with them.

The 2000 has a phenolic (resin) fingerboard, two humbucking pickups, and active circuitry, and many of its users have praised its wide tonal range and exceptional tuning stability. Though it has now been discontinued, Status's currently available Stealth bass shares its 100% graphite construction.

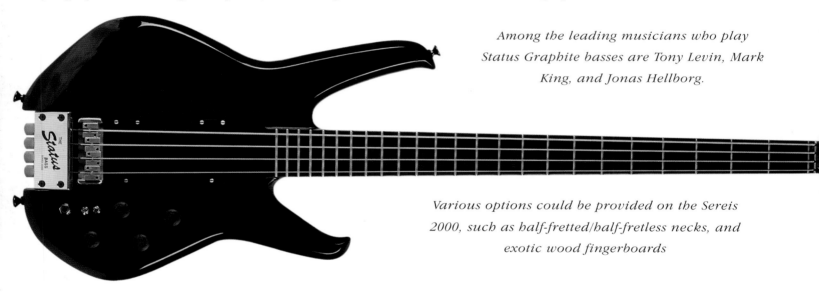

*Among the leading musicians who play Status Graphite basses are Tony Levin, Mark King, and Jonas Hellborg.*

*Various options could be provided on the Sereis 2000, such as half-fretted/half-fretless necks, and exotic wood fingerboards*

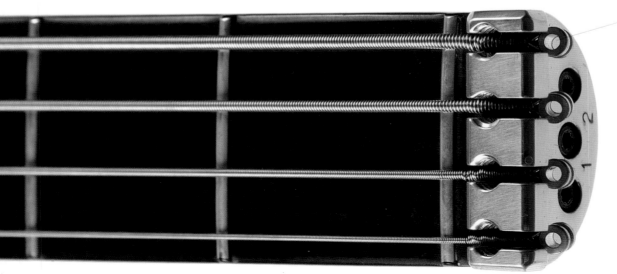

*All hardware on the Status 2000 is made from brass.*

**Right:** *On this headless instrument, the string ball-ends are attached at the neck end, and tuning takes place at the tailpiece.*

**STEINBERGER**

# STEINBERGER L2 BASS

I N THE LATE 1970s, New York-based furniture designer Ned Steinberger was renting space at a woodworkers' co-op in Brooklyn. One of the other craftsmen based there was luthier Stuart Spector: the two men quickly became friends, and Steinberger's fascination with guitar design led, in 1977, to his taking a key role in the development of Spector's NS-1 electric bass.

This experience inspired Steinberger to start building basses by himself, and also alerted him to the inherent tendency for the heavy headstocks on their necks to create an imbalance, and cause discomfort and strain to players. The NS-1 had a lead weight built into its tail to surmount this difficulty, but on his own models, Steinberger

*These are the relocated tuner knobs..*

adopted a more radical solution: the complete removal of the peghead, and the repositioning of the tuners at the instrument's bridge end. He was also dissatisfied with the sound produced by wooden basses, and was soon fabricating prototypes from graphite-reinforced epoxy resin.

The outcome of Steinberger's experiments was his "headless," single-pickup L1 bass, unveiled at the NAMM (National Association of Music Merchants) trade show in 1979, and marketed the following year; the dual-pickup L2 seen here first appeared in 1981.

*Above: The Steinberger's nut is also a string anchor.*

*The L2's small, symmetrical body maximizes comfort and balance...but when the instrument debuted in the 1980s, it surprised and shocked players used to more conventional shapes.*

*Above: The Steinberger has no neck joint, as its neck and body are formed from a single piece of resin.*

# STEINBERGER L2 FRETLESS BASS

NED STEINBERGER'S bold L1 and L2 bass designs quickly attracted interest from prominent musicians: among the first players to purchase them were John Entwistle of The Who, and King Crimson star Tony Levin. Their enthusiastic advocacy, combined with widespread press and media attention (in 1981, the L2 was declared one of the "Five Best Designs" of the year by *Time* magazine), generated huge demand for Steinbergers; this was to grow even greater following the introduction of a number of new models, including a headless 6-string guitar, and a fretless bass similar to the one shown in our photos.

In 1980, Ned Steinberger and a small group of partners had set up the Steinberger Sound Corporation to produce the L1. Within three years, SSC had been obliged to move to larger premises in order

*Below: This fretless L2 is fitted with two EMG humbucking pickups.*

*These are position markers, not frets!*

**Above:** *A removable leg rest provides a comfortable support for seated Steinberger players*

to cope with its expanded product line, and as the decade progressed, managing the company became an increasingly onerous task for its founder. As he explained to Jim Reilly on the nedsteinberger.com website, "We weren't really making money....we were just breaking even and having all kinds of capital problems." Ned decided to turn to Henry Juszkiewicz, who had recently taken charge at Gibson, for some business advice; their discussions led, in 1987, to the purchase of Steinberger by the Nashville-based guitar giant, which continues to supervise the production of both US-made and imported Steinberger models.

# TACOMA PAPOOSE

TACOMA GUITARS, now the third largest US acoustic guitar manufacturer (after Martin and Taylor), had its origins in a Japanese-owned wood processing firm, the Sound Mill, set up in the early 1990s in Tacoma, Washington State, to produce soundboards for pianos. It also supplied woods to luthiers throughout America, and, in 1997, launched its own Tacoma brand guitars. The first of these was the model shown here, the Papoose—an unusual, small-bodied instrument that sounds a perfect fourth (five half-steps) higher than a standard guitar; from bottom to top, its open strings are tuned to ADGCEA.

It is not only the Papoose's raised pitch (playing it provides a similar effect to using a regular acoustic with a capo at its fifth fret) that sets it apart. Like nearly all Tacomas, it boasts an offset, "paisley"-shaped

*Above: Tacoma's distinctive bridge plate is also found on the normal-size guitars in the company's range.*

soundhole and a characteristically contoured bridge, and is built using a combination of traditional craftsmanship and state-of-the-art computer numeric control (CNC) technology that guarantees both high productivity and maximum consistency.

Tacoma's instruments (including mandolins and acoustic basses as well as guitars) have gone on to find favor with amateur and professional players; among the leading performers who have used them onstage and in the studio are Bob Dylan, the Dixie Chicks, Bonnie Raitt, and Jackson Browne. In 2003 the firm, which had gained independence from its Japanese parent four years previously, won the Marco Polo award: this, in the words of its sponsors, the Russell Investment Group, is given to small and medium-sized businesses "for first-time success and accomplish-ments in international trade."

By now, Tacoma was selling no less than 60 different

*Right: Despite its small size, the Papoose presents no problems for players used to standard-pitched guitars. It has a 19$^{1}$/$_{10}$-inch scale length, and 15 frets clear of its body.*

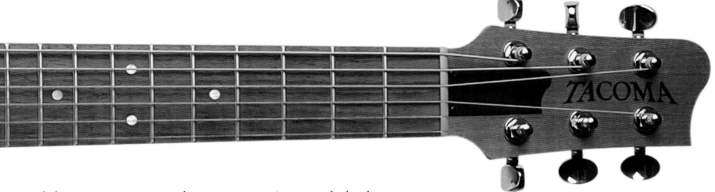

models in over two dozen countries, and had established a network of 450 dealers throughout the USA. In 2004, the company was bought by Fender, but it still operates from its own factory in the Pacific North-West, and seems set to continue delivering high-quality guitars to a growing number of customers at home and abroad.

*Above: Standard Papooses like this one have cedar tops, a mahogany neck, back and sides, and a rosewood fingerboard; more exotic woods are also available.*

*The Papoose is produced in both 6-string and 12-string configurations.*

# TACOMA CHIEF

THE PAPOOSE'S distinctive soundhole, and the special top construction that goes with it, are shared by the other members of Tacoma's "Wing" range of acoustic instruments. The company's reason for placing its characteristically shaped vents on the upper bass bouts of these models is that this unusual location is an area of low inherent tension (unlike the high torque middle section of the top), where the soundhole can be "naturally supported by the sides and neck block." With no central cutout to be reinforced, the top itself can, therefore, be less rigidly braced and more flexible at its edges—and the result, according to Tacoma, is a "significant improvement in its…tonal response and volume."

These theories, already tested and proved on the Papoose, are borne out further by the impressive performance of the guitar that appears in our photos, the Chief. A single cutaway "mini-jumbo" with a solid Western cedar top, plus a back and sides of solid mahogany, it delivers a powerful sound that belies its

*Below: The Tacoma Chief's natural coloring is enhanced by what the company terms a "light satin finish."*

*Above: Thanks to the Chief's unconventional soundhole shape and location, its label has had to be resited!*

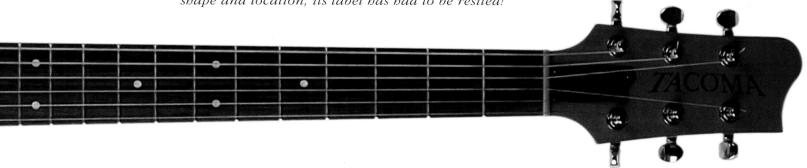

relatively small size. Its bridge and 22-fret fingerboard are rosewood, its tuning machines chrome, and its bolted-on neck mahogany. The standard version, seen here, has a natural finish and no on-board electronics; other colors are available as optional extras, and the Chief can be supplied with three different pickup systems (by, respectively, L.R. Baggs, Fishman and B-Band), at an additional cost of between $150 and $250.

The Tacoma "Wing" series also includes larger-bodied regular and baritone guitars and basses, as well as two mandolins. The company describes them collectively as "highly unique instruments featuring innovative designs and…technology, for players who want their voice to be just a little different." Examples of Tacoma guitars with conventional soundholes can be found on the next four pages.

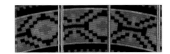

# TAKAMINE EC132SCX NYLON-STRUNG

**M**ASS HIRADE'S original inspiration for the nylon-strung guitars that he and his team of Takamine craftsmen began producing in 1968 was the great Spanish luthier Antonio de Torres (see separate entry). Torres' instruments, built in Seville and later in his hometown of Almería in the mid- and late nineteenth century, had an immense influence both on his contemporaries and on almost all subsequent luthiers and classical players, and Hirade's blueprints, still used for a number of Takamine classics, contain many elements derived from his great predecessor.

However, musical styles and conditions of performance have changed radically since Torres' day, and Takamine's guitars have moved with the times. Consequently, the firm's more "purist," "concert classic" models co-exist in its catalog with ones offering features borrowed from other branches of lutherie, such as cutaways and built-in transducers and preamplifiers. The cedar-topped EC132SCX belongs in this latter category: it has a six-element pickup embedded in its bridge, plus a "SoundChoice" CT-4B preamp with with three-band equalization and a tuner.

*Below: The EC132SCX has a rosewood back and sides; the same wood is used for its fingerboard.*

**Above:** *This elegant soundhole rosette is produced using marquetry techniques.*

**Bottom of page:** *The invisible pickup beneath the bridge has no effect on the guitar's acoustic performance.*

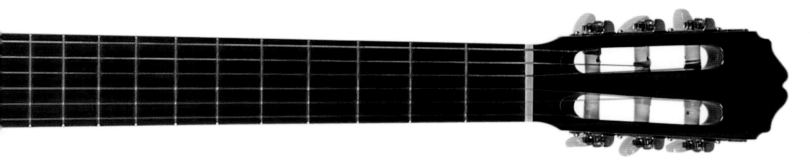

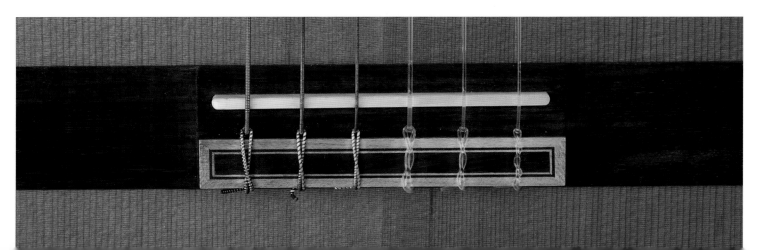

# TAYLOR XXV-GA

THE TAYLOR COMPANY WAS FOUNDED in 1974 by two friends, Bob Taylor and Kurt Listug, who, since the previous year, had been working side by side at the American Dream guitar-making shop in Lemon Grove, near San Diego, California. When American Dream's proprietor, Sam Redding, sold his business, Taylor, Listug and a third partner, Steve Schemmer, took it over and changed its name—first to the Westland Music Company, and then to Taylor Guitars.

Times were hard during the firm's early years, but Taylor gradually gained a well-deserved reputation for the excellence of its acoustics, and major names such as John Prine and 12-string virtuoso Leo Kottke began using them. Following a period of steady growth from the mid-1980s onwards, the company (minus Schemmer, who left in 1983) relocated to larger premises in Santee, a few miles northeast of Lemon Grove, and in 1992, it established its current headquarters in nearby El Cajon. Here, Taylor has installed state-of-the-art Computer Numeric Control (CNC) technology, which streamlines production, ensures precision and consistency in the manufacturing process, and reduces costs, allowing staff to, as Bob Taylor himself puts it, "deliver more guitars to people at reasonable prices that really give them what they're hoping to have."

Taylor is now recognized as one of the world's premier guitar makers, and the instruments featured on the following pages demonstrate the range and quality of its designs. The model shown here is one of the limited edition XXV-GA Grand Auditorium models issued to mark the firm's 25th anniversary in 1999.

**Below:** *The XXV-GA has a sitka spruce top, and back and sides of sapele. Only 500 of these instruments were ever made.*

*18-carat gold is used for this "XXV" inlay.*

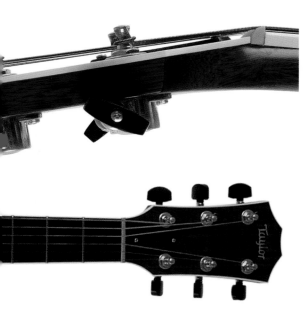

*Right: The XXV-GA's soundhole rosette is embellished with koa and tropical padouk woods.*

# TAYLOR 110

TAYLOR CATEGORIZES its guitars by "series." In company parlance, a series is a group of instruments made from the same tonewoods, and sharing identical inlays and hardware; it is usually identified by the first digit of an individual model's three-figure catalog number. The simplest and least expensive full-size Taylors belong to the 100 series: these have solid sitka spruce tops, as well as backs and sides made from laminated sapele (most commonly sourced from the rain forests of West Africa, though it also grows as far east as Uganda and Tanzania), and comparatively plain decorative features such as wood fiber soundhole rosettes and pearloid fingerboard dots. The second digit in the model number indicates whether the guitar is a 6-string (1) or a 12-string (5), while the final figure refers to the body shape, with 0 representing a dreadnought, 2 a Grand Concert, 4 a Grand Auditorium, and 5 a Jumbo.

*Below: Like all Taylor dreadnoughts, the 110 is 16 inches wide, with a body depth of 4⁵/₈ inches.*

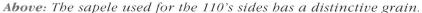

*Above: The sapele used for the 110's sides has a distinctive grain.*

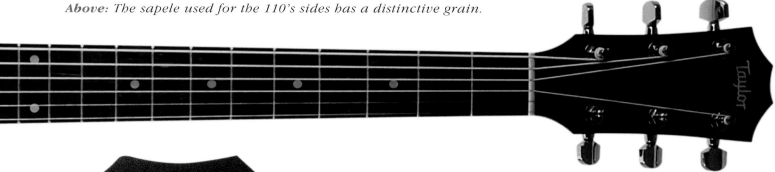

This key reveals that the Taylor 110 in our photos is a Series 1 6-string dreadnought—a modest looking, but highly durable instrument that provides outstanding performance and playability at a surprisingly low cost.

*Left: This headstock is faced with black Lexan thermoplastic.*

# TAYLOR 310

WHILE THE TAYLOR 100 and 200 series offer only a restricted choice of instruments, the 300 category includes a full range of body types, as well as both 6- and 12-string guitars. All 300s have solid sitka spruce tops; until a few years ago, their backs and sides were made from solid sapele, but Taylor now uses a more exotic timber, African mahogany (*khaya ivorensis*), for them. Its sound, characterized by the company as "warm and open," combines with the "bright and snappy" qualities of spruce to deliver the highly distinctive tone quality for which the 300 series has been very widely praised.

310 dreadnoughts like the one shown here are full-fledged professional models; in Summer 2002, Taylor's own quarterly journal *Wood & Steel* carried a profile of San Diego-based musician Dennis Caplinger, who bought a 310 for his studio work because he liked the timbre provided by its mahogany (as he told interviewer Andy Robinson, "all my banjos are mahogany too"), and used it "on every acoustic guitar

*Below: The Taylor 310 has a gloss finish to its top. Black fiber provides its body binding.*

*Above:* *Both the 310's fingerboard and bridge are made from ebony.*

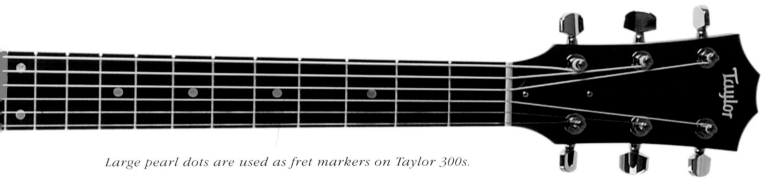

*Large pearl dots are used as fret markers on Taylor 300s.*

session [I did] for five or six years." After it was stolen, Caplinger immediately replaced it with another one, which continues to give him good service, and has been heard on several episodes of ***The Simpsons***, as well as on numerous other TV and ad soundtracks.

Taylor also produces a cutaway version of the 310 with built-in electronics, the 310CE.

# TAYLOR 414-CE-L7

THE ELEGANT TAYLOR FLAT-TOP shown here is part of the company's 400 series, and the "-14" in its name signifies a "Grand Auditorium" size instrument with a 15¾-inch wide body. The "C" and "E" suffixes reveal that it has a cutaway and onboard electronics, while the concluding "L7" identifies it as a limited edition model issued in Fall 2004.

Like all Taylor 400s, the 414-CE-L7 boasts a sitka spruce top; however, the West African-grown hardwood ovangkol normally used for the backs and sides of 400 series guitars has here been replaced by Indian rosewood, though the instrument's ebony fingerboard and tropical mahogany neck are identical to those on standard 400s. The 414's nut and bridge saddle are carved from "Tusq," a synthetic material now being substituted for bone by Taylor and other leading luthiers such as Gibson, Larrivée and Breedlove. It is also equipped with Taylor's highly acclaimed

*Below: The 414-CE-L7's cutaway is in the so-called "Venetian" style; this is more shallow and rounded than a "Florentine"-type cutaway.*

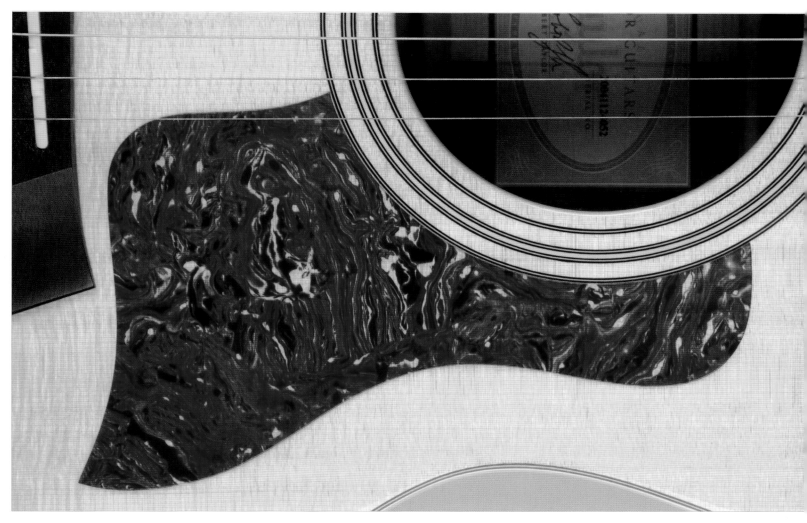

*Above: The guitar's binding and its soundhole decorations are made from wood fiber.*

*Left: The built-in Taylor Expression System pickup can be adjusted by these three miniature knobs, controlling (from left to right) bass, treble and volume.*

Expression System pickup-cum-preamp, which features no less than three magnetic transducers—one for string output, the others to (as the company's publicity puts it) "capture the actual vibrations of the guitar top."

Grand Auditorium-type instruments are Taylor's most popular acoustics, and this model, offered at a list price of $2,618, was quickly sold out.

*White plastic is used for the 614CE's binding.*

*The inlay on the soundhole rosette is abalone.*

# TAYLOR 614CE

*Below:* *The 614CE is 16 inches wide, and just over 4¹/2 inches deep.*

THE TAYLOR "600" SERIES of acoustics currently comprises six regular models: all of them have sitka spruce tops, distinctive "pearl leaf" inlays, and backs and sides of big leaf maple—a wood that the company considers rather less prone to feedback when instruments are used in noisy onstage situations. Built-in "Expression system" pickups and preamps also help to make these guitars ideal for live use.

This Grand Auditorium 614CE offers, in Taylor's words, "the width and depth of a Dreadnought with a narrower waist." It delivers a rich, crisp tone whether fingerpicked or strummed, and is available in an extensive range of finishes, including "Red" (as seen here), "Natural," "Black," and various shades of sunburst.

# TAYLOR 710CE

TAYLOR CURRENTLY OFFERS four instrument types in its 700 series: a dreadnought, a Grand Concert, a Grand Auditorium and a 12-string Jumbo, all available with or without the company's "Expression System" electronics. Their tops are made from Engelmann spruce (*picea engelmannii*), which is grown in high-lying areas of Canada (chiefly Alberta and British Columbia), and also in Nevada, Utah and several other

for the Brazilian rosewood that was widely favored by luthiers until import restrictions limited its supply.

Like the other members of this high-end Taylor range, the 710CE acoustic/electric dreadnought shown on these pages has a number of luxury features, including gold-plated machine heads, a soundhole rosette inlaid with Hawaiian koa wood, and a gloss, ultra-violet cured finish.

*Below: This Taylor dreadnought sports a rounded (Venetian) cutaway.*

*The 710CE's neck is made from tropical American mahogany, and has an ebony fretboard.*

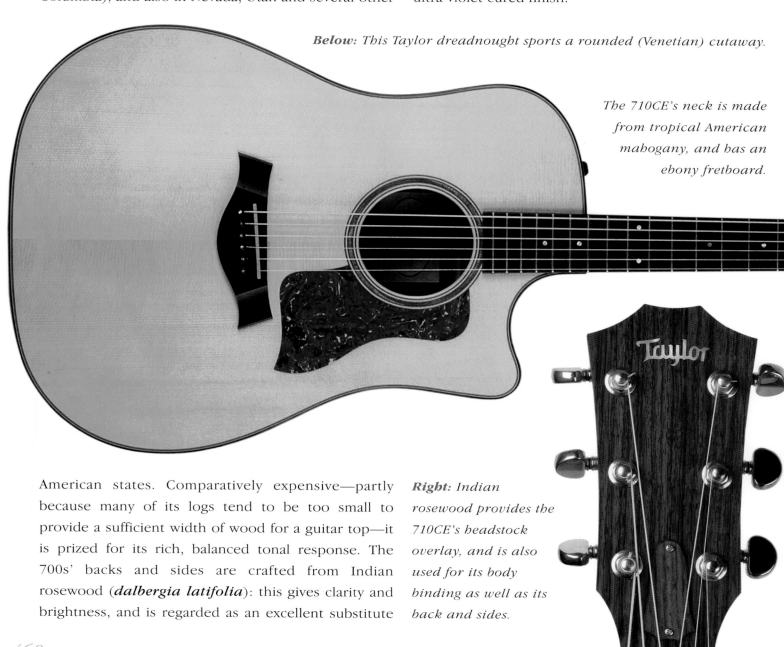

American states. Comparatively expensive—partly because many of its logs tend to be too small to provide a sufficient width of wood for a guitar top—it is prized for its rich, balanced tonal response. The 700s' backs and sides are crafted from Indian rosewood (*dalbergia latifolia*): this gives clarity and brightness, and is regarded as an excellent substitute

*Right: Indian rosewood provides the 710CE's headstock overlay, and is also used for its body binding as well as its back and sides.*

PHOTOGRAPHS COURTESY OF THE HOUSE OF GUITARS, LONDON

# Taylor

# TAYLOR K65 12-STRING

THE TAYLOR COMPANY'S Koa series, unlike its "regular" guitar categories, is identified simply with a "K," and individual models within it are given a two-digit suffix, plus (where applicable) a "CE" to indicate the presence of a cutaway and electronics. As supplies of the Hawaiian Koa wood that makes these instruments so visually and tonally outstanding can be uncertain production levels vary, and the limited edition K65 12-string jumbo in our photos is not currently being built—making it something of a collectors' item for players seeking the unique sound that only this timber can impart.

*Below:* The K65 is a jumbo, with a 17-inch body width.

*Right:* Solid koa wood is used for this guitar's top, back and sides.

These abalone inlays are found on all Taylor's "K" series models.

*Below:* The ebony-faced headstock is embellished with abalone, like the fingerboard.

PHOTOGRAPHS COURTESY OF THE HOUSE OF GUITARS, LONDON

# TAYLOR T-5 STANDARD

THE T-5, which made its debut in 2005, is Taylor's first-ever electric guitar. Aimed at players seeking to obtain both clear, acoustic-sounding tones and "hotter," overdriven timbres from a single instrument, it contains three transducers (only one of which—the humbucking pickup mounted near the bridge—is visible), plus an active pre-amp system that gives precise control over the sounds they provide.

Standard T5s, like the one here in our photographs, have chrome fittings and dot inlays, while "Artist" versions feature gold-plated hardware and more intricate fret-markers; both models are offered with sitka spruce, koa, or (as shown here) maple tops. Sapele wood is used for all the various versions' backs and sides, and their necks are made from tropical American mahogany.

*Below: This T5 has a "Cherry Sunburst" finish; "Tobacco" and "Honey" are also available. Its white-bound, 21-fret fingerboard is made from ebony.*

*Optional foam plugs are available to seal these f-holes, reducing the risk of feedback.*

PHOTOGRAPHS COURTESY OF GUITAR VILLAGE, FARNHAM

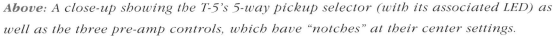

**Above:** *A close-up showing the T-5's 5-way pickup selector (with its associated LED) as well as the three pre-amp controls, which have "notches" at their center settings.*

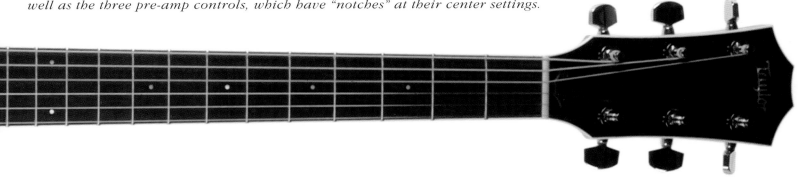

A magnetic pickup is concealed within the guitar's neck/body joint, and a "body sensor" (a Taylor-designed alternative to the piezo-type transducers typically used on electro-acoustics) lies behind and beneath its ebony bridge. Different permutations of these pickups, as well as the bridge humbucker mentioned earlier, are accessible via a five-way switch on the instrument's upper shoulder.

Position one (neck p/u + sensor) gives a warm, though authentically "acoustic" sound; position two (neck p/u only) renders the tone darker and "jazzier;" position three (bridge humbucker only) produces a more conventional "electric" feel, while the remaining settings combine the two magnetic pickups in series or parallel to create other variants. On the T5's top, adjacent to the pickup switch, are the volume, bass and treble controls associated with its 9-volt battery-powered pre-amp.

# TAYLOR BABY TAYLOR

THE BABY TAYLOR, designer Bob Taylor's 12½-inch wide miniature Dreadnought, is perhaps the best known "travel guitar" currently on the market. Sufficiently compact to qualify as airline carry-on baggage, and light enough to suit both children and adults, it also packs a surprising tonal punch, and, though principally intended to be used only at home and "on the move," has frequently found its way into recording sessions, and has even been seen and heard on stage.

Launched in 1996, the Baby is available with a sitka spruce or mahogany top (the instrument seen below has the latter), and its laminated back and sides are made from sapele, a durable, West African-grown

*Below: The Baby has an x-braced top, just like larger Taylors, and is fitted with an ebony bridge and fingerboard.*

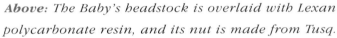

***Above:*** *The Baby's headstock is overlaid with Lexan polycarbonate resin, and its nut is made from Tusq.*

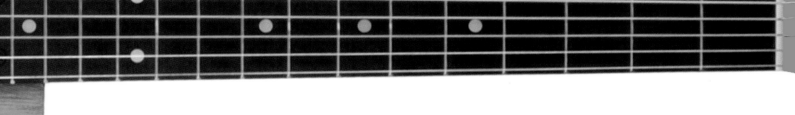

timber. Despite its short, 22³/₄-inch scale length, its neck is only ¹/₁₆-inch narrower at the nut than a standard Taylor flat-top; this gives the Baby a decidedly "grown-up" feel, and ensures that players accustomed to a full-size model can quickly adjust to it without needing to make any fundamental changes to their technique. However, anyone seeking a slightly larger travel guitar may prefer to opt instead for the recently introduced

Taylor's Big Baby, which features the same woods as its sibling, but has a 25¹/₂-inch scale length, a 15-inch wide body, and 20 frets (one more than the original Baby). Both instruments boast laser-etched soundhole decorations and a durable varnish designed to protect them from the rigors of the road.

In 2000, a dedicated Baby Taylor manufacturing facility, making an average of 120 guitars a day, was opened at Taylor's headquarters in El Cajon, California.

# ALAN TIMMINS F1 RESONATOR

ALAN TIMMINS, WHO LIVES and works in the English city of Nottingham, built his first metal-bodied guitar in 1989: a replica of a 1930s National Style 97 tricone, it was commissioned by a locally-based collector, Mark Makin. The model was much admired, and Timmins' skills were soon in demand from other customers; however, the difficulty of assembling so many metal parts led him to contemplate a radically different method of construction, in which his brass guitar bodies would be replaced by ones made from carbon fiber, formed in just two individual moldings—one for the front of each instrument, the other for its back and sides.

To Alan's delight, this new approach proved highly successful, resulting in a guitar that was not only easier to make, but superb-sounding, and relatively impervious to rough handling. His choice of material also brings greater visual clarity to the decorations on his instruments, which stand out vividly against the matt surface of their fronts, backs and sides.

Alan's resonators carry the F1 brand, and are currently used by a number of leading players thorough Britain and Europe; the guitar in our pictures dates from the late 1990s. He is also recognized as a skilled repairer of more conventional National and Dobro-type guitars.

*Below*: The guitar's neck is made from laminated maple and ebony.

*Right*: Sea and palm trees grace the back of this F1.

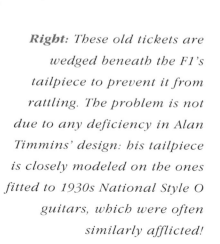

*Right*: These old tickets are wedged beneath the F1's tailpiece to prevent it from rattling. The problem is not due to any deficiency in Alan Timmins' design: his tailpiece is closely modeled on the ones fitted to 1930s National Style O guitars, which were often similarly afflicted!

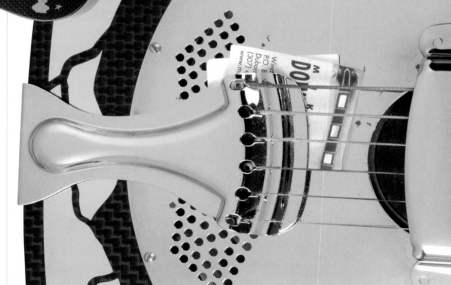

# TOKAI FV 40

THE TOKAI COMPANY was set up in Hamamatsu, Japan (also the hometown of Yamaha) in 1947 by businessman Tadayouki Adachi. Initially a harmonica manufacturer, it diversified into guitar building in the 1960s and, by the mid-70s, was producing a range of flat-tops and electrics whose designs closely resembled those of, respectively, Martins and Gibsons. Later in the decade, Tokai started to make replicas of 1950s-style Les Pauls (the originals were, by now, collectors' items, and there was a considerable demand for reasonably priced copies), and also turned out instruments modeled on Fender Stratocasters and Precision basses.

By the early 1980s, the international market was becoming deluged by Far Eastern imitations of classic US guitars, and Tokais, which had previously only been available in Japan, began to be sold in America in about 1983. They soon acquired a reputation for quality and value, although, for obvious reasons, Tokai and its fellow "copy" makers were regarded less warmly by the firms whose designs they had replicated, and the period saw a number of high profile legal disputes over trademark and copyright infringements. Unlike some other Far Eastern replica producers, Tokai also had an extensive line of original instruments; however, it undoubtedly owed its fame and most of its sales to its

*Below: The Tokai FV 40's body is made from alder; it has a maple neck and a rosewood fingerboard. It can be supplied in a choice of three finishes.*

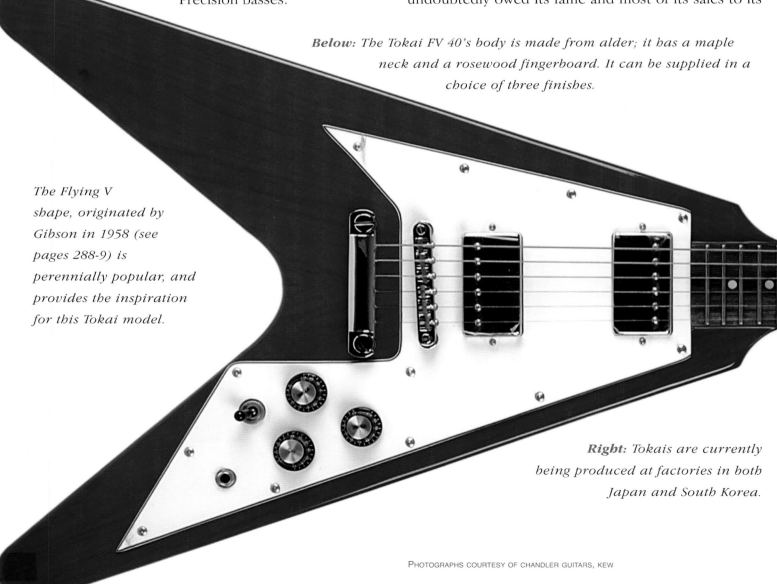

*The Flying V shape, originated by Gibson in 1958 (see pages 288-9) is perennially popular, and provides the inspiration for this Tokai model.*

*Right: Tokais are currently being produced at factories in both Japan and South Korea.*

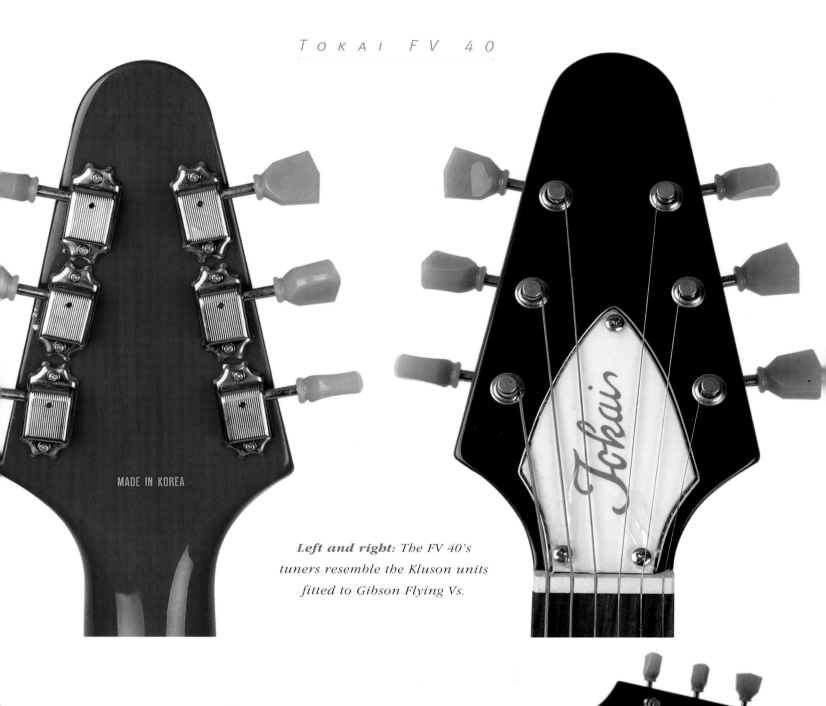

**Left and right:** *The FV 40's tuners resemble the Kluson units fitted to Gibson Flying Vs.*

MADE IN KOREA

copies, which were sometimes termed "traditional" or "classic reissues" in its catalogs.

After a period out of the limelight, Tokai is currently undergoing something of a renaissance, and the Flying V-like FV 40 in our photographs comes from an extensive batch of electrics and acoustics recently released by the company.

# VIGIER ARPÈGE

PATRICE VIGIER'S DECISION to set up the guitar- and bass-making company that bears his name in 1980 came after several years of experience as an instrument repairer—and as a result of growing dissatisfaction with the major-name models that were ending up on his workbench.

From the start, the designs produced by his firm in Grigny, France, were bold and challenging: they included the Surfreter fretless electric (Vigier himself had previously built a prototype nylon-strung fretless with a glass fingerboard, which quickly shattered!), and the Arpège bass, a more recent example of which is pictured here; versions of both remain in production to this day. Among the key features that make Vigier basses like the Arpège special are their pickups (highly responsive units designed by the late Michel

*Above: According to Vigier publicity, its Grigny HQ "builds as many guitars in a year [as] an industrial manufacturer does in a few days. [Hence], our guitars receive the attention that an expert musician looks for."*

*Left: Vigier Arpège basses are produced as 4-, 5-, or 6-stringers; all have a neck-through-body construction.*

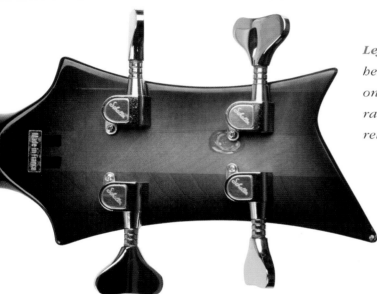

*Left: This distinctive headstock shape appears on both the Vigier Arpège range and the company's related Passion basses.*

*Above: The Arpège's twin pickups work in tandem with powerful active electronics that offer twelve preset tone settings.*

*Bottom left: Vigier necks are leveled to tolerances of one hundredth of a millimeter.*

Benedetti), and the composition of their necks, which are made from 90% wood and 10% carbon—the latter material taking the place of a conventional truss-rod.

High-profile Vigier players include Adam Clayton of U2 and Roger Glover of Deep Purple.

# VOX PHANTOM BASS

IN 1957, Tom Jennings and Dick Denney, the co-proprietors of a thriving music store in the southern English county of Kent, began manufacturing "Vox" branded guitar amplifiers. Their first model was the AC15 15-watt combo, and it was followed, two years later, by the 30-watt AC30, which became a favorite with countless pop groups.

Buoyed by this success, Jennings and Denney decided to diversify, and launched their first guitars in the early 1960s. Initially, these were made in England, but by 1962—the year Vox introduced its distinctively shaped Phantom solid electric—production of some instrument components had moved to Italy, and before long, all Vox guitars were being built overseas. The Phantom line expanded to include both guitars and basses: some (including the original 1962 6-string, and the mid-60s Phantom bass shown in our photographs) had five-sided bodies, while others, such as those used by Brian Jones and Bill Wyman of the Rolling Stones, were made in a lute-inspired "teardrop" shape.

Like many European electrics of the period, the Phantoms featured a proliferation of on-board electronics (see captions for details) that now makes them seem somewhat dated; Vox amps, in contrast, are

*Above: A distortion switch, plus an adjustable treble/bass boost, add to the Phantom's complexity.*

*Left: Another unusual feature on the Vox is a built-in tuner, giving out a "G" to which the bass's top string can be set.*

**Left:** *Unsealed tuners can suffer from the effects of wear and grime; however, these are in excellent condition, despite being some 40 years old.*

**Below:** *Vox models like this one were manufactured at the Eko guitar factory in Recanati, Italy.*

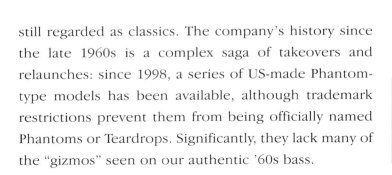

still regarded as classics. The company's history since the late 1960s is a complex saga of takeovers and relaunches: since 1998, a series of US-made Phantom-type models has been available, although trademark restrictions prevent them from being officially named Phantoms or Teardrops. Significantly, they lack many of the "gizmos" seen on our authentic '60s bass.

Made in Italy by Vox

# WARWICK INFINITY LTD 2000 BASS

HANS PETER WILFER, son of Framus founder Fred Wilfer (see Framus entry) formed Warwick in the German town of Erlangen, Bavaria, in 1982. Thirteen years later, the company moved northeast to Markneukirchen in Saxony, where it now produces Warwick-branded basses and amps, as well as guitars carrying the Framus trademark. The company's range of products is a most impressive and very extensive one, and the growing list of "name" players using its basses includes Hootie and the Blowfish's Dean Felber,

as well as Dan Roberts of the Crash Test Dummies.

Among Warwick's most highly-rated models is the Infinity 2000 LTD, introduced, as its name suggests, at the start of the 21st century, and pictured here. The Infinity's hollow body is made from ovankol wood (sometimes known as shedua) grown in West Africa, topped with a thin layer of maple. Its transducers and electronics, like those on all Warwick basses, are made by another German firm, MEC (Music Electronics Company), located in the town of Wernitzgrün near

*Below: The Infinity's body is shaped for maximum comfort and easy access to the top of the neck.*

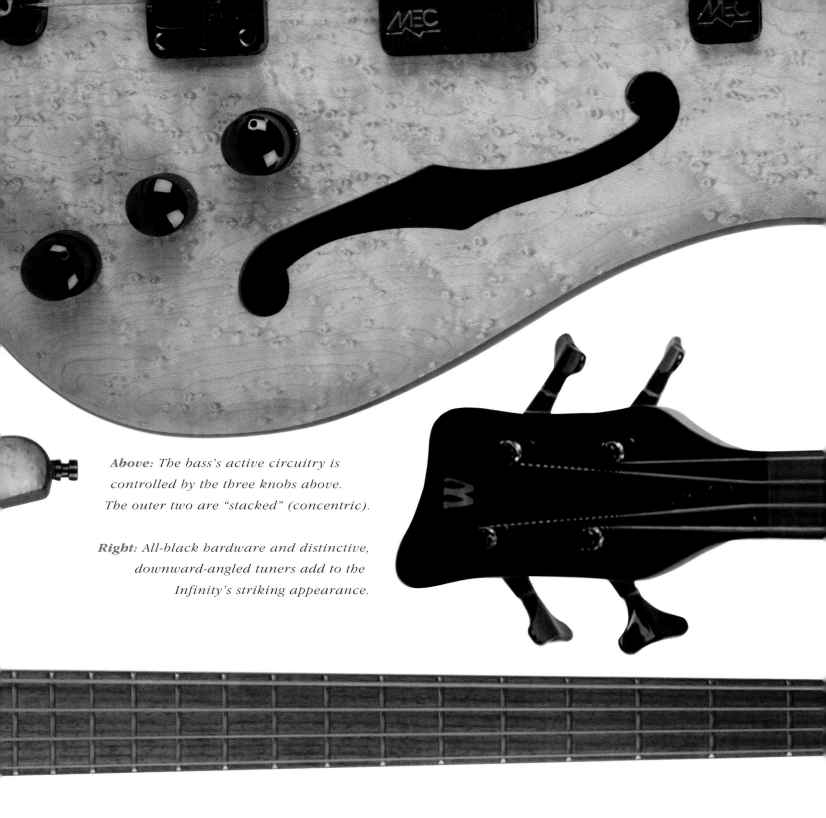

*Above:* The bass's active circuitry is controlled by the three knobs above. The outer two are "stacked" (concentric).

*Right:* All-black hardware and distinctive, downward-angled tuners add to the Infinity's striking appearance.

Markneukirchen. A single-coil MEC "J" pickup is mounted in the Infinity's neck position, with a humbucking "Twin J" at the bridge; the latter can be coil-tapped, and the bass's active preamp incorporates a powerful 3-band EQ. The instrument's neck-through-body design contributes considerably to its overall sound, which Warwick characterizes as offering "great attack, similar to an acoustic bass, [but] without loss of sustain…[plus] fantastic growling mids, which always cut through in a band setting."

Both 4- and 5-string Infinity LTD 2000s are available, and the company also produces a less expensive, set-neck version of the bass, the Infinity SN. This has identical pickups, but a 2-band onboard preamp, and a chambered body of zebrano (zebra wood) with an ovankol neck.

# WASHBURN MONTEREY 12 CUSTOM

THE WASHBURN TRADEMARK was derived from the middle name of George Washburn Lyon, a partner in the Chicago-based Lyon & Healy company, founded in 1864. Originally music publishers, Lyon & Healy began making instruments carrying the Washburn label in the 1880s; the brand was later used for a while, but then dropped, by another Chicago manufacturer, Tonk Brothers, which had acquired L&H in the 1920s. A new company with no direct connection to either L&H or Tonk revived Washburn in 1964, and now produces a comprehensive range of Far Eastern- and American-built guitars. The Washburn Monterey 12 Custom Studio model shown here dates from 1982, and was specially designed for ex-Free and Bad Company vocalist Paul Rodgers.

*Right:* This preamp enables signals from the guitar's neck and bridge pickups to be blended.
*Below:* The model has a rosewood top, back and sides, and white body and neck bindings.

*Paul Rodgers regularly used this model for live gigs in the 1980s and 90s.*

*These screws are part of the pickup unit built into the guitar's neck.*

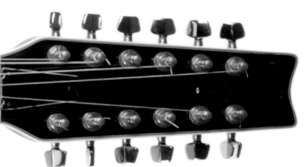

**Above top:** *The headstock's rosewood facing matches the rest of the instrument's body.*

**Left:** *This logo is slightly confusing, as it omits the surname of Washburn's co-founder, G.W. Lyon.*

# WATKINS CIRCUIT 4

LONDONER CHARLIE WATKINS is one of the largely unsung heroes of the British musical equipment scene. His engineering background, combined with his experience as a professional accordionist in the years following World War II, led him to develop a range of instrument amplifiers and P.A. systems, marketed under the WEM (Watkins Electric Music) marque, that were widely used by amateur and professional performers in the UK from the 1950s onwards; he was also responsible for creating the Copicat, one of the first-ever tape-based delay units.

By the end of the decade, Watkins' firm had diversified into electric guitar manufacturing. Its instruments were largely the work of Charlie's brother, Reg, and they carried the names Watkins, Wilson, WEM and España on their headstocks. While clearly influenced by the work of Leo Fender, they sometimes featured a bewildering proliferation of electronic gadgetry that would have never been found on the no-nonsense designs emanating from Fullerton; and the English firm's attempts, on models such as the Fifth Man and Project 4, to combine guitar, organ and effects in a single instrument proved commercially disastrous. However, many of their other products were competitively priced and highly successful, especially among "entry-level" and impecunious players.

The Watkins Circuit 4 shown here dates from about 1964, and was originally sold in Britain for 47 guineas (roughly equivalent to $86). Its plethora of knobs and switches cannot have been easy to manipulate in the heat of a live performance, but it is an attractive "period piece," whose good condition and comparative rarity make it highly collectable.

*Left: Watkins' mid-1960s catalog describes the Circuit 4 as "presenting the latest concept in modern sound."*

*Right: The knob on the right of the picture is a click-position pickup and preset tone selector; to its left is one of the Circuit 4's two volume controls.*

*Right:* The simple but effective "HiLo" vibrato also featured on several of the Watkins company's other instruments.

*Above:* These buttons provide further tonal variations, but are prone to damage..

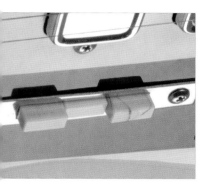

# WATKINS RAPIER BASS

WATKINS ELECTRIC MUSIC (see previous pages) was the second-ever UK firm to market a line of British-made electric guitars; its Rapier solid-bodies debuted in 1957, only a few weeks after the appearance of the London-based Dallas company's now largely forgotten Tuxedo line. Watkins was a family business, run by inventor and engineer Charlie Watkins, whose brothers Reg and, later, Sid were responsible for the Rapiers' design. The guitars' double cutaway shape was clearly influenced by Fender, and the three-pickup Watkins Rapier 33 was widely known among British musicians as "the poor man's Strat."

Another undoubted star of the Rapier range was the bass model shown here. It sported twin pickups and a heavy-duty, chromed steel bridge, and was intended to be used with WEM's own sturdy amplifiers and speaker cabinets. Its appearance remained unchanged for much of the 1960s—though the metallic tuner buttons fitted to the earliest examples were eventually replaced by the plastic ones seen on our Rapier—but underwent considerable later restyling. The bass was discontinued at the end of the 70s.

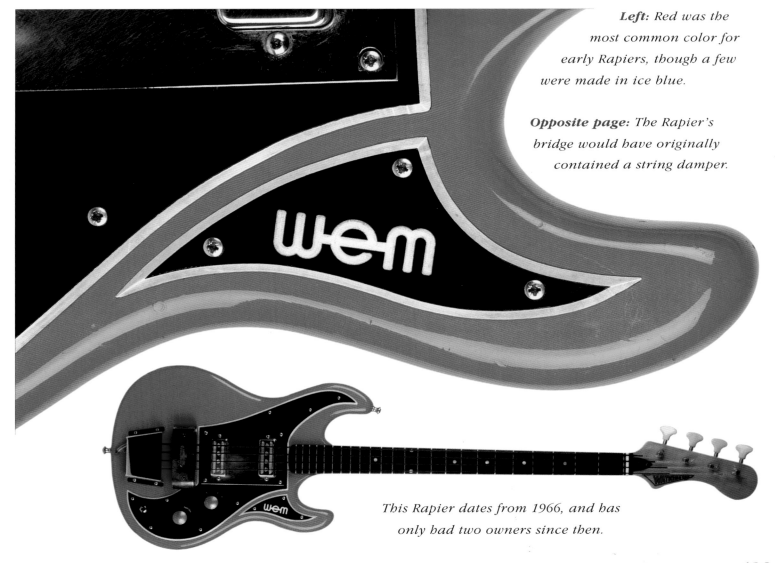

*Left: Red was the most common color for early Rapiers, though a few were made in ice blue.*

*Opposite page: The Rapier's bridge would have originally contained a string damper.*

*This Rapier dates from 1966, and has only had two owners since then.*

PHOTOGRAPHS COURTESY OF GUITAR JUNCTION, WORTHING

# WECHTER PATHMAKER

Abe Wechter first attracted widespread attention in the mid-70s, while he was working at Gibson, where he was involved in the creation of a special acoustic guitar for John McLaughlin. He established a lutherie business of his own in Paw Paw, Michigan, where he went on to build custom instruments for a number of top players, including John McLaughlin and top Swedish bassist Jonas Hellborg.

In 1994, Wechter completed the prototype of his distinctive "Pathmaker" double-cutaway flat-top, and, three years later, he set up a manufacturing facility to produce it in greater quantities. It is currently available in a variety of versions. "Elite" Pathmakers are custom crafted in Paw Paw.

# WURLITZER WILDCAT

The Holman-Woodell company, made this guitar in Neodesha, Kansas (around sixty miles due south from Topeka). The company also built their own brand, Holman, alongside the Wurlitzer models, and the famous "body-less" La Baye 2x4 guitars.

Three Wurlitzer models were produced, the Cougar, the Wildcat, and the Gemini. All were two-pickup offset double-cutaways with increasingly far-out styling, which included a six-in-line headstock. The Cougar was a Fender-style instrument, with a large, white pickguard. The Wildcat was a very similar guitar, except that its styling was even more exaggerated, and it had a narrower waist. Model 2520 was Taffy White, 2521 was Lollipop Red, and 2522 was Sunburst.

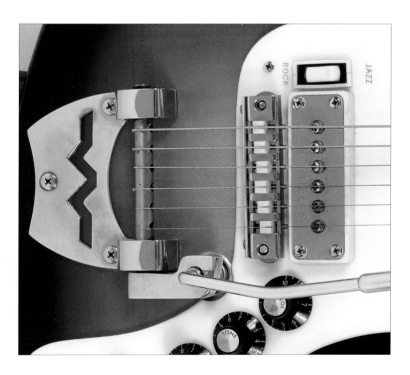

*Here is a close-up of the Wildcat's Sensi-tone pickups, Tunemaster adjustable bridge, and "Wurlitzer Vibraton" vibrato (Wurlitzer's version of a Bigsby) with its W cutout in the base.*

# WESSELBAUM CLASSIC

SURVEYS HAVE SHOWN that Australians purchase more guitars, per head of population, than residents of any other country, and that, on average, each of the nation's households buys a new guitar every eight years. It is thus scarcely surprising that the continent, although it possesses only one major, internationally known guitar manufacturer (see previous Maton entries), is blessed with numerous smaller-scale luthiers. One of the most original and accomplished of these is Holger Wesselbaum, who lives and works in the Gold Coast area of Southern Queensland. Wesselbaum combines his guitar making with work on motorcycles and electronics; he studied his craft in Spain, and now builds classical and flamenco models using the finest woods available to him. These include supplies of Bavarian spruce sourced from a secret Alpine location, rumored to be close to the spot from which the great Antonio Stradivari acquired his tonewoods in the 17th and 18th centuries. This timber is used for the top of the

*Wesselbaum guitars are slowly and painstakingly constructed; individual parts may take months to complete.*

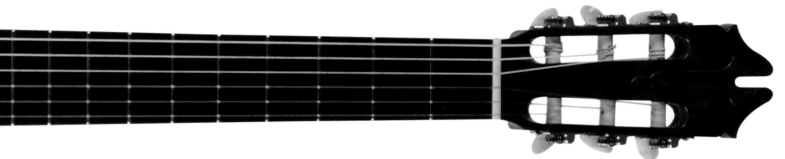

Wesselbaum guitar shown here, which also boasts a back and sides of Brazilian rosewood, and an African mahogany neck. Intriguingly, its distinctive soundhole rosette is crafted from sliced avocado nut!

*Right:* Paired bridge saddles give more scope for adjustment than a single one for all six strings.

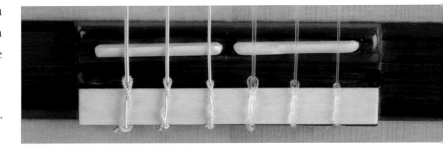

# K. YAIRI CY 118

ACOUSTIC GUITARS BY K. YAIRI are made at the company's headquarters in Kani, a town in the mountainous central Japanese area of Honshu. The firm's owner, Kazuo Yairi, himself a skilled luthier, learned his craft from his father, an internationally recognized guitar and violin builder, and its craftsmen pride themselves on making instruments that, while substantially handmade (Yairi's publicity describes its factory as "about as far from a modern mass production high-tech computerized guitar plant as you can get"), are also competitively priced. K. Yairi guitars should not be confused with those made by Kazuo's cousin Sadao Yairi, and sold under the S. Yairi name until the 1980s.

The first of the three K. Yairis featured in this book is a CY 118 classical model. It has a back and sides of South American jacaranda wood (Yairi's extensive timber stocks, drawn from many different countries, are sawn and seasoned in its own workshops), a cedar top, and a rosewood bridge.

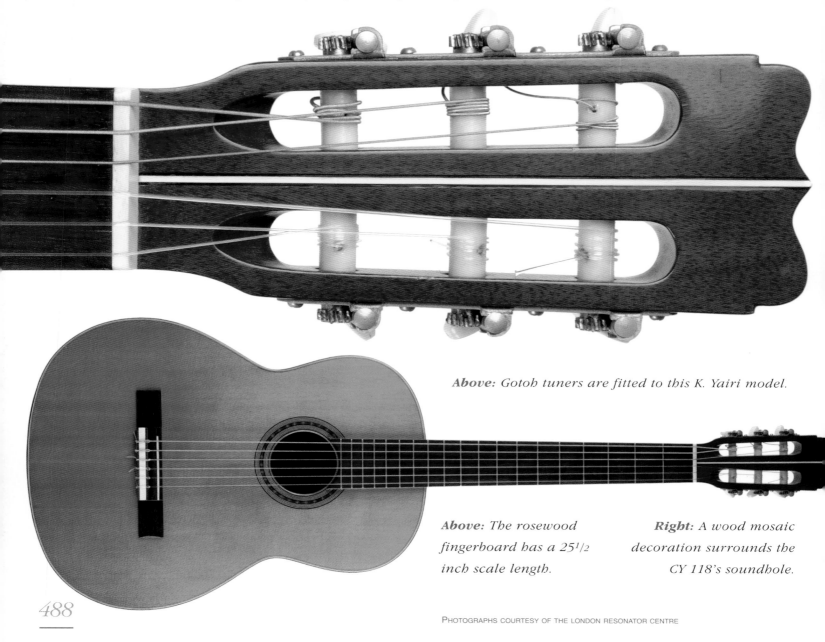

*Above: Gotoh tuners are fitted to this K. Yairi model.*

*Above: The rosewood fingerboard has a 25¹/₂ inch scale length.*

*Right: A wood mosaic decoration surrounds the CY 118's soundhole.*

# K. YAIRI DY 40

YAIRI FLAT-TOPS are endorsed by a host of major popular music names. Some of them, like Grateful Dead rhythm guitarist Bob Weir, have played Yairis for many years: the company released its first Weir "Signature" model back in 1991, and has recently produced the WY1BW, a replica of the instrument's original prototype. Other notable Yairi users include the singer-songwriter Ani DiFranco, whose ADY1G acoustic/electric cutaway has a specially widened scratchplate to protect the guitar's finish from her famously vigorous picking hand!

These steel-strung instruments come in various categories and sizes: the one seen here is a DY 40 dreadnought incorporating the firm's innovative "Direct Coupled Bridge" system, also fitted to much of the rest of its acoustic range. This patented design is intended to stop the problem of upward string pull encountered on conventional bridges (which can lead

*Below: The DY 40's woods are perennial favorites: spruce for the top, and mahogany for the back and sides.*

PHOTOGRAPHS COURTESY OF THE LONDON RESONATOR CENTRE

**Left:** *Ivory and pearl are used for the DY 40's body bindings and decorations.*

**Above:** *The strings are inserted into the top through this ebony "reinforcement" plate.*

to the bridge becoming unglued from the guitar's top) by anchoring the strings behind rather than within the bridge unit itself. It also has the effect of steepening the angle at which the strings meet the saddle, thereby, in Yairi's words, making for "a maximum transfer of string vibration energy" that improves the instrument's tone and sustain.

# K. YAIRI FY 94

IN ADDITION TO CLASSICAL ("CY"-prefixed) and dreadnought ("DY") instruments like the ones shown on the previous pages, K. Yairi, known as Alvarez Yairi in the USA, produces several other categories of guitar—such as WY acoustic-electrics (all fitted with piezo transducers and Yairi's own System 600T preamps), and a range of small-body models that, as the company's publicity puts it, "comes in all flavors." This group includes two cedar-topped "parlor" guitars, the RAG 6 and the cutaway FY 6C, as

*Below:* This flat-top, which has recently been discontinued, has a spruce top and mahogany back and sides.

*Below:* The Yairi's 20-fret fingerboard (with 14 frets clear of the body) is made from rosewood.

*Above:* The FY 94 boasts gold die-cast machine heads.

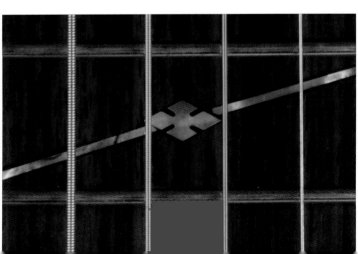

well as the slightly larger FY 94 featured in our photographs. Inspired by the OM-style flat-tops originally developed in the late 1920s by Martin, the FY 94 is especially designed for fingerpicking, and, like other similarly dimensioned Yairis, provides a rich yet delicate tone perfect for folk, blues or country-style playing; many musicians also find it ideal for recording.

*493*

*"Palm-tree" and "porpoise" decorations add to the CPX's "South Sea" feel!*

***Far right:*** *The CPX15SA's preamp allows outputs from its pickup and microphone to be combined.*

***Above:*** *The Compass has a spruce top, and white sycamore back and sides.*

# YAMAHA

# YAMAHA COMPASS CPX15SA

*CPXs are described by Yamaha as "mini-jumbos."*

THE YAMAHA CPX RANGE of acoustics includes four themed instruments inspired by the points of the compass: this "south" model, finished in "Miami Ocean Blue," is intended, in the manufacturer's words, to evoke "a tropical island paradise." Thanks to its "two-way" onboard electronics, boasting both a bridge saddle pickup and an internally mounted microphone, the guitar is sure to sound good in the often less than idyllic environment of a live gig—where any feedback can be eliminated by fitting a specially designed cover over its elegant soundhole. The other three Compasses are equally striking: the "north" CPX boasts an "Arctic" finish, while its "east" and "west" cousins feature (respectively) Egyptian and Wild West motifs!

**Right:** *Diecast gold tuners grace the instrument's mahogany neck.*

# YAMAHA

# YAMAHA FG730S

YAMAHA'S FOUNDER, Torakusu Yamaha (1851-1916), was a man of many skills: his first business, a watch-making firm, failed due to lack of funds, but by the 1880s, he had established himself as a surgical equipment engineer in the town of Hamamatsu, on Japan's Pacific coast. He went on to apply his expertise to the maintenance and manufacture of reed organs, and these were the first items to be exported by the Nippon Gakki company, which he set up in 1897. Nippon Gakki's corporate headquarters remains in

sellers, and the FG line has since become a benchmark against which many other entry-level flat-tops are judged. In 2002, FGs underwent a major upgrade, intended to ensure, as Yamaha executive Gary Cook explained at the time, that they "continue[d] to provide professional quality specs at attractive price points." Significant changes included the provision of solid spruce tops for all models, as well as improvements to internal construction. The FG730S shown here is a fine example of the current range.

*FGs are made at Yamaha's factory in Taiwan.*

*Right: This FG730S is finished in "Vintage Cherry Sunburst"; "Natural" and "Tobacco Brown Sunburst" colors are also available. Below and left: Rosewood is used for the guitar's attractively bound fingerboard, and also for its back, sides and bridge.*

Hamamatsu to this day, and the Yamaha brand is now associated with an extraordinary diversity of products, from musical instruments to fitted kitchens, electronics, and motorcycles. Yamaha's first classical guitars appeared in the mid-1960s, and its FG series of steel-strung acoustics followed in 1969; competitively priced (the cheapest sold for just $85), but offering clear, crisp tone and easy action, they became best-

PHOTOGRAPHS COURTESY OF NEVADA MUSIC, PORTSMOUTH

# YAMAHA PACIFICA 112

IN 1990, YAMAHA LAUNCHED its "Pacifica" range of solid-body electric guitars; according to a company catalog from that year, they were characterized by "power, style and innovation, [and] bred to perform in the most demanding musical situations, with features and playability far beyond the competition." The instruments, which included both single- and double-cutaway designs, and were fitted with DiMarzio pickups, were created by Rich Lasner, a highly

relatively inexpensive beginner's guitar: *Guitarist* magazine considers it "so expertly put together that [we'd] challenge any similarly priced instrument to fare any better against it." Unusually for a cheaper axe, one of its three pickups is a humbucker; it also boasts a robust vibrato (whose arm was removed when our photographs were taken), a comfortably contoured alder body, and a 22-fret maple neck; both rosewood and maple fingerboards are available.

*Below: The Pacifica 112 has a 25$^1$/$_2$ inch scale length.*

regarded music industry figure who had previously worked at Ibanez (where he was involved with the development of Steve Vai's "JEM" range—see separate entry), and has subsequently been associated with Peavey and Modulus. The Pacificas' bold styling and impressive specifications made them best sellers, and there have been many subsequent models.

The Pacifica 112 seen here has been widely recommended by reviewers and teachers as an ideal,

*Right:* Modern
manufacturing techniques
make it possible to produce
high quality guitars at far
lower cost than was once
possible, as the Pacifica 112
demonstrates.

*Though pleasingly
resonant, alder is
relatively light,
making it an ideal
wood for guitars like
the Pacifica.*

*Below left:* The use of the tuning
fork as a Yamaha company logo
dates back to the late 1890s.

# YAMAHA PACIFICA 912 (with MIDI)

LIKE THE PACIFICA 112 (see previous pages), Yamaha's more expensive, though now discontinued, Pacifica 912 is a highly versatile solid-body. It boasts three DiMarzio pickups: a PAF Pro at the bridge (this high-output device is inspired by Gibson's classic, 1950s "Patent Applied For" humbucker); and two Stratocaster-style HS-2s, featuring noise-canceling circuitry, in the middle and neck positions. These transducers provide an impressive range of sounds by themselves—but were not quite sufficient for the previous owner of the 912 in our pictures, who decided to take his axe's capabilities even further by adding a synthesizer interface to it!

The unit, a GK-2A made by the Japanese Roland Corporation (which has been an innovator in the complex and challenging area of guitar synthesis since the mid-1970s) enables signals from the Pacifica to be used to trigger sounds from external synths and samplers. This makes it possible for the guitar to

*Left: This socket handles the output from both the Roland sensor and the Pacifica's DiMarzio pickups.*

*This is the understring sensor for the synth interface device. It is mounted between the Pacifica's vibrato and its humbucking bridge pickup.*

*The guitar's body is of swamp ash.*

PHOTOGRAPHS COURTESY OF AMERICAN GUITAR & BASSWORLD, TONBRIDGE

*Left: A close-up of the control module for the MIDI interface. Note the connection between the "regular" pickup output (via the jack plug on the side of the guitar's body) and the box.*

*Above: Yamaha's Pacifica guitars all share the same distinctively shaped headstock.*

"become" a trumpet, a sax, or almost any other instrument, and also allows notes and chords to be recorded as MIDI (Musical Instrument Digital Interface) data. The GK-2A detects vibrations from the strings via a sensor mounted behind the bridge pickup and connected to a module fixed to the Pacifica's body.

The output of the guitar's regular pickups is also fed into the box, whose onboard switching allows the player to choose between or combine signals from the pickups and sensor; these are then routed, via a special 13-pin cable, to a controller placed on the floor, and onward to amplifiers and other equipment.

# YAMAHA

# YAMAHA SA500

YAMAHA'S "SA" (SEMI-ACOUSTIC) electric guitars were first introduced in the early 1980s; they incorporate feedback-reducing, sustain-enhancing internal center blocks of the kind pioneered by Gibson on its ES-335 (see separate entry), and have proved enduringly popular with a wide range of players.

The current "top of the line" SA is the SA2200, a maple-bodied model with an elegantly traditional look. It has recently been joined by the less expensive SA500, an example of which is shown in our photographs. The newer instrument shares many of the 2200's classic features, but has a more contemporary appearance, thanks to its reshaped f-holes, and the provision of an "AES"-style tailpiece system (named for Yamaha's AES range of electrics, where it originated) in place of the older guitar's more conventional "stud" unit. The SA500 is fitted with two humbucking pickups and, like a number of modern Yamahas, has a fingerboard made from sonokeling, a type of rosewood grown in Indonesia.

A second striking addition to the SA line is the SA503 TVL, endorsed by Queens of the Stone Age guitarist Troy Van Leeuwen, a former member of A Perfect Circle, whose other credits include session work with Korn and Depeche Mode. Van Leeuwen has previously been associated with Yamaha's cutaway AES1500, which he has praised in the company's **All Access** online magazine for its ability to "go from that pristine, hollowbodied clean sound to a fat, high-gain sound." His SA503 has the same modified f-holes as the 500, but sports a Bigsby vibrato, as well as a trio of single-coil "soapbar" pickups.

*Below: The SA500's body is made from laminated maple, and it has a glued-in mahogany neck.*

*Right: The chromed tailpiece hardware is both functional and elegant.*

*Right: This model lacks the more sophisticated pickup switching of the SA2200, which provides coil taps.*

# YAMAHA

# YAMAHA SG500B

THE "SG" LINE of solid-body electrics, launched in 1973-4 and discontinued in the late 1980s, played a crucial role in establishing Yamaha's international reputation among rock musicians—not least because Carlos Santana became a keen user of two SG guitars: the SG-175 (one of the very first batch of SGs to be released), and the later SG-2000. Initially, the range included a handful of models with single-cutaway bodies slightly reminiscent of a Gibson Les Paul, but these were soon dropped, leaving the more famous double-cutaway outline—as seen on Santana'a axes, as well as on the instrument shown here, the 500B—to establish itself as the classic Yamaha SG shape.

The SG-500B debuted in 1976 and remained in the catalog for about three years; our example dates from 1978, and is in almost mint condition.

***Opposite and bottom left:*** *The Yamaha SG500B has a maple-topped mahogany body, and a rosewood fingerboard. It was available in "Cherry" (as seen here) or "Black" finishes.*

# YAMAHA TRB 6 II 6-STRING BASS

YAMAHA'S BASS GUITARS are as highly regarded as its standard acoustics and electrics. It produces over 40 models, including basses aimed at beginners and musicians on a tight budget, as well as state-of-the-art instruments endorsed by some of the leading names in rock and jazz. Among these luminaries are Nathan East, Billy Sheehan, Dave Santos and John Myung, as well as John Patitucci—the respected bandleader, soloist, composer and teacher who first gained international fame in the mid-1980s as a member of Chick Corea's Elektric Band.

Patitucci is closely associated with the company's TRB range, which Yamaha recently characterized as "the highest level of professional basses available for discriminating players." He currently uses a six-string TRB JP2, a "signature" version of the standard TRB 6 II seen in our photographs. Both instruments boast twin Alnico V double-coil pickups, 24-fret necks, and on-board active EQ, though there are some differences in the two models' body woods and the configuration of their electronics, and the TRB 6's 35-inch scale length is slightly longer than that of the Patitucci bass.

6-string basses, whose BEADGC tuning provides extra low and high notes, are especially favored by jazz

*Opposite and below: The TRB 6 II has a bolted-on neck with a rosewood fingerboard. This model's ash body is finished in "Magenta Burst."*

*Below: The TRB 6 II's bridge, like the rest of its hardware, is crafted from solid brass.*

*Above: The three smaller knobs seen here control the TRB 6 II's treble, midrange and bass response. Above them is a master volume and a pan pot.*

*Left: The straight path of the TRB 6 II's strings from nut to machine head optimizes the instrument's tuning stability.*

PHOTOGRAPHS COURTESY OF AMERICAN GUITAR CENTRE & BASSWORLD, TONBRIDGE

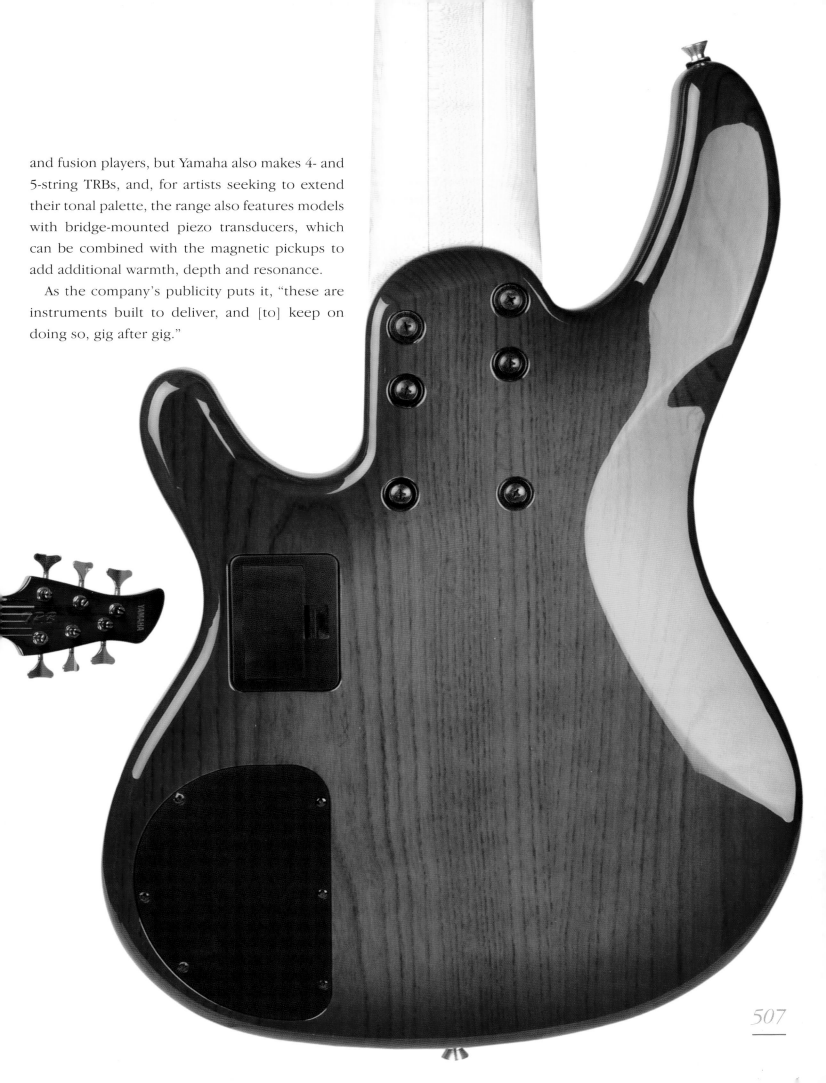

and fusion players, but Yamaha also makes 4- and 5-string TRBs, and, for artists seeking to extend their tonal palette, the range also features models with bridge-mounted piezo transducers, which can be combined with the magnetic pickups to add additional warmth, depth and resonance.

As the company's publicity puts it, "these are instruments built to deliver, and [to] keep on doing so, gig after gig."

# TONY ZEMAITIS

TONY ZEMAITIS was born in London in 1935. He acquired his basic woodworking skills during a five-year apprenticeship as a cabinetmaker, but was also a keen musician, and became increasingly involved with guitar repair and construction. By the early 1960s, his instruments were starting to attract buyers, and as the volume of commissions increased, he was eventually able to devote himself full-time to lutherie.

Both his acoustics and electrics (the latter often featuring elaborately engraved metalwork by his friend and colleague Danny O'Brien) were highly sought after by star performers throughout the 1970s and 80s. Beatle George Harrison was an important client, as were Ron Wood of The Faces (and later the Rolling Stones), Eric Clapton, and the late Marc Bolan of T.Rex, and the comparatively small number of his guitars in circulation—he produced no more than ten a year—added to their desirability and value. Sadly, this scarcity has led to some counterfeiting of Zemaitis instruments, though none of the fakes measure up to

*Below: This distinctive Zemaitis flat-top was made in 1968.*

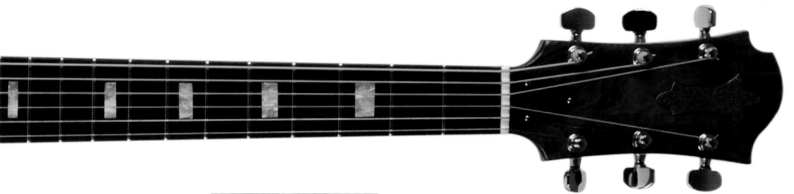

*Top: The soundhole shapes on Tony's guitars are many and varied, including moons and hearts as well as this "D."*
*Right: A close-up of the luthier's elegant headstock nameplate.*

the visual and sonic excellence of the originals.

Tony Zemaitis retired in 2000, and died two years later. An Owners' Club, set up some years previously, is a valuable repository of information on his life and work, and recently, the Zemaitis family has given its support to the production of a series of high-quality replicas of some of his designs.

509

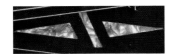

# ZENITH SUPER CUTAWAY

BOOSEY & HAWKES, a long-established British music publisher and retailer, was also, for many years, a manufacturer and supplier of instruments. In the early 1950s, it commissioned the German guitar maker Framus (see separate entries) to produce a line of archtop acoustics that would be branded with the "Zenith" name and distributed by Booseys throughout the United Kingdom.

To help promote the new models, B&H enlisted top British jazz guitarist Ivor Mairants (1908-1998), who was also well known as a teacher, composer, arranger and music magazine columnist. Most photographs of Mairants show him with Gibson and Epiphone archtops, but he provided a warm endorsement for the Zeniths, stating that they "had a tone superior to any other at twice the price." The Zenith guitar in our pictures was Ivor's own, and is on display, alongside other Mairants memorabilia, at the Ivor Mairants Musicentre in London, the store he founded in 1962 (see Acknowledgments).

Thanks to Mairants' approval and B&H's marketing skills, the Zeniths sold impressively: among the many players who purchased one was Paul McCartney, who acquired his at a department store in his home city of Liverpool in 1956, when he was just 14 years old.

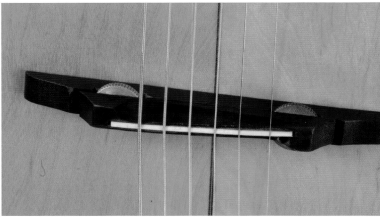

*Above: This basic bridge, like those on many other archtop acoustics, is held in place only by string pressure.*

*Left: No catalog details of the Zenith have been traced, but it is probably made from plywood maple.*

*Left:* Sadly, the Zenith logo on the instrument's headstock has almost completely worn away.

These inlays are very similar to those on the Framus archtop featured earlier in this book.

# ACKNOWLEDGEMENTS

This book could not have been produced without the kind and generous cooperation of the guitar store proprietors, collectors, musicians and luthiers who allowed their instruments to appear in it, and the author would like to express his sincere thanks to all of them. Some of those who assisted in this way have asked to remain anonymous; the others include:

Guitar Village, Farnham (www.guitarvillage.co.uk)

Guitar Junction, Worthing (www.guitarjunction.co.uk)

The American Guitar Centre & Bassworld (www.psst.co.uk/americanguitars/)

Peach, Blake End, Braintree (www.peachideas.co.uk)

Chandler Guitars, Kew (www.chandlerguitars.co.uk)

The House of Guitars, London
(www.acousticcentre.com and www.basscentre.co.uk)

Guitar Classics, London (www.guitar-classics.co.uk)

Tom Anfield (www.ukguitars.com)

The London Resonator Centre (www.resocentre.com)

Nevada Music, Portsmouth (www.nevadamusic.co.uk)

The Ivor Mairants Musicentre, London (www.ivormairants.co.uk)

James Westbrook, The Guitar Museum, Hove (www.theguitarmuseum.com)

Thanks also to Colin Gower, Marie Clayton, Charles Alexander, Gary Boner, Roger Hurrell, Andy Robinson, Taro Takeuchi and Ulrich Wedemeier, and to Neil Sutherland (who photographed all the guitars with his customary skill) and designer Phil Clucas.